S0-BBO-772

RABOTYAGI

PERESTROIKA AND AFTER
VIEWED FROM BELOW

RABOTYAGI

PERESTROIKA AND AFTER VIEWED FROM BELOW

Interviews with Workers
in the Former Soviet Union

David Mandel

Monthly Review Press
New York

HD
8526.5
M268
1994

Library of Congress Cataloging-in-Publication Data
Mandel, David, 1947–
  Rabotyagi : perestroika and after viewed from below : interviews
with workers in the former Soviet Union / by David Mandel
      p.   cm.
  ISBN 0-85345-879-0 : $34.00. — ISBN 0-85345-878-2 (pbk.) : $16.00
  1. Working class — Former Soviet republics — Interviews.
2. Trade -unions — Former Soviet republics. I. Title.
HD8526.5.M268 1993   93-26619
331.88'0947—dc20   CIP

Monthly Review Press
122 West 27th Street
New York NY 10001

Manufactured in the United States of America

10 9 8 7 6 5 4 3 2 1

CONTENTS

V: THE COUP AND AFTER   **199**

INTRODUCTION

This book offers a "view from below" on perestroika and its aftermath. It is a perspective from the ranks of the workers: those once heralded by the Soviet state as the heroic *rabochii*, more often referred to on the street by the informal *rabotyagi*, working stiffs. Idealized or disparaged, these are the people whose labor over the centuries has been used to create privileged lives for various ruling classes and elites, including the present "democrats."

Their point of view is rarely reflected in the body of academic and popular literature that has arisen about the changes in the Soviet Union and its successor states. Yet, workers form the vast majority of the population of that region and their view of things often conflicts with the simplistic image of "democrats versus hard-line communists" purveyed by our media. Moreover, these workers have no obvious vested interest in embellishing or otherwise distorting their reality.

The scope of the interviews has limitations which should be noted. Most of the workers interviewed here are from Russia, with two from Ukraine and one from Belarus. Most are activists, a rather thin stratum in the working class today, though they are all closely linked to the rank and file. Many key economic sectors are not represented.

There was nothing very "scientific" and much that was accidental in the selection of people I interviewed. These were mainly workers whom I had met in the course of my research on the labor movement, people who, in my opinion, had something of interest to say and were willing to say it into a tape-recorder. In this choice, I make no claims to neutrality (which, in any case, would be false). However, in translating and editing the interviews, I have remained to the best of my ability faithful to the speakers' words and intentions. I am convinced that, taken as a whole, this book offers a unique and in

7

many ways a more valid view of the period in question than can be obtained from most "scholarly" publications and certainly from our press.

Over the five years during which these interviews took place, 1988 to 1993, the social and political situations changed rapidly, to say the least. This is well-reflected in the interviews, which are presented here roughly in chronological order. I have also provided interjected notes to explain the more obscure references and terms.

The following brief overview of the evolution of the workers' situation and of the labor movement may provide the reader with some further help in situating the interviews.

Until the political liberalization initiated by Mikhail Gorbachev in 1985 gradually expanded under popular pressure, there was no labor movement in the Soviet Union. As early as the 1920s, the state and party bureaucracies had replaced the workers as the social basis of the ruling Communist Party. Soon after, the trade unions were completely subordinated to the political and economic administrative apparatuses. Their main functions for over half a century were to keep workers in line and producing, and to "allocate" various goods and social benefits to them. (Workers are only now realizing just how significant these benefits were.) Collective actions, when they occurred (after Stalin's death), were almost always spontaneous, of very limited scope and subject to various forms of repression. Only in very exceptional cases did even the lowest-level union shop committees lead or even support these actions.

In the final analysis that system rested upon repression and the threat of repression—this is clearly shown in the first interviewee's description of the Novocherkassk massacre in 1962. At the same time, the system was grounded in the state-owned and -managed economy, in the social rights and benefits it guaranteed, and in the ideology that accompanied it. Although deprived of political rights, workers did enjoy important social rights, some of which will always remain out of the reach of workers under capitalism. (This is not to deny that the quality of these rights was often wanting.) These included a guaranteed job, job security, a more-or-less guaranteed wage that rose significantly over the course of the post-Stalin period until the late 1970s, and an increasingly significant "social wage" that included free education, health care, virtually free housing, and heavily subsidized communal services, transportation, child daycare, leisure and cultural activities, and basic food products.

The combination of antagonism and corporatism or paternalism that characterized state-worker relations had its parallel in relations between management and workers in the (state-owned and -run) enterprises. Managers acted both as representatives of the central state in the enterprise—their job was to meet the plan targets set by the state—and as lobbyists for the enterprise before the central state.

Soviet managers did not have the same incentive as their capitalist counterparts to constantly reduce labor costs. Their main interest was to meet, at least formally, centrally established output targets. They had to do this under inherently unstable conditions, especially the unreliable material supply system. This required the maintenance of a relatively large and flexible work force. Faced with the chronic labor scarcity that such conditions fostered, managers tried to give workers relatively better wages and social benefits (many of which were linked to the enterprise) than were allowed by centrally set regulations.

The complex nature of these relationships helps to explain why, despite eventual political liberalization (paradoxically, the high point of this "democratization" was probably reached before the demise of the USSR and the "democrats'" final victory), a strong, independent labor movement has proven so difficult to build.

A central problem, as will become clear especially from the later interviews, is the widespread lack of faith among workers in their capacity to defend their interests through their own independent organizations and collective actions. Most workers, especially those who have not had the personal experience of independent collective actions, have a hard time seeing themselves as autonomous social and political actors. The temptation is still strong to look to management or to the state authorities (the "good tsar" syndrome).

However, this cannot be explained solely by the legacy of the past. Probably a more important factor is the insecurity created by the profound economic crisis, as well as the workers' difficulty in conceiving an alternative to the "transition to the market," in view of the discrediting of the formerly dominant Communist ideology.

The nascent labor movement has gone through several stages since Gorbachev came to power. (For a detailed analysis, see my

Perestroika and the Soviet People [Montreal: Black Rose Press, 1991].)
The initial reaction among workers to Gorbachev was positive, if
restrained, reflecting workers' sad experience with past reforms,
generally carried out at their expense. But the improved economic
results of 1986 did in part reflect the popular enthusiasm evoked by
the prospect of renewed dynamism and change, officially presented
by Gorbachev as a socialist renewal, a return to Leninist norms.

In 1987 Gorbachev announced his market reform, which included an overhauling of the wage system to enhance its incentive
role and the introduction of a "cost-accounting" regime in the
enterprises, which were to be given broad autonomy. The idea was
to link workers' income more closely with enterprise performance
and to measure this performance primarily by profits. In the
reformers' conception, this would create a common motivation
among managers and workers to uncover and release productive
reserves, to increase individual and enterprise efficiency, and to
produce quality goods that met consumer needs.

It was these reforms, coupled with the relaxing of repression, that
gave rise to the first wave of collective protest. The wage reform that
was supposed to be carried out in consultation with the workers was
in fact marked by widespread managerial arbitrariness, resulting in
the demotion of workers to lower skill-grades and even loss of wages.
At the same time, the new "cost-accounting" regime, to the degree
it was introduced, undermined the old paternalistic relations, which
in turn made workers less tolerant of abuses they had accepted in
the past: "black (working) Saturdays," the irregular rhythm of production with its frequent stoppages, bad work conditions, managerial corruption.

These protests invariably bypassed the unions, which often took
management's side. They were led by informal leaders and sometimes gave rise to elected strike or workers' committees. With the
end of the conflict, these new organs generally disappeared.

To some degree, Gorbachev had foreseen the problems these
reforms would provoke, and to soften them he put in place a State
Enterprise Law that went into effect at the start of 1988, providing
for the election of the enterprise directors by the entire work force.
It also called for the election of work-collective councils, or STKs,
that were given broad self-management rights, though the law was

vague and contradictory on these powers and their limits. Moreover, even the elected directors had to be confirmed from above.

Gorbachev explained these steps toward producers' democracy in the following terms: "The well-being of the worker will depend upon the abilities of the managers. The workers should, therefore, have real means of influencing the choice of director and controlling his activity" (*Pravda*, 28 January 1987).

In the great majority of cases, however, the STKs were subservient to management, which, until a special party directive, were often headed by enterprise directors. This was partly due to managerial resistance, and in part to the workers' inability or unwillingness to make use of this reform, which had been initiated from above. But this in turn was related to the widespread perception that the STKs had no control or that they were a trick to shift responsibility onto the workers for problems over which they had no real power. Moreover, until 1989, the ministerial apparatus was still largely intact, so that even in the rare cases where management was prepared to accept the independence of the STKs, the workers saw that real power lay outside the factory.

The general coal miners' strike of July 1989 marked the apogee of the strike movement unleashed by perestroika. This was the first strike to involve more than one enterprise and the first to give rise to new and continuing organizations: the strike committees, which transformed themselves into workers' committees and which were at the origins of the foundation of the Independent Miners' Union (IMU) in the fall of 1990.

The decision to create a new miners' union followed failed attempts to reform the old one. But those failures were due not only to the resistance of the old union bureaucracy. Even more, they reflected the lower level of mobilization and solidarity among the majority of workers in the "old" Union of Workers of the Coal Industry. The founders of the IMU hoped that their union would soon displace the old one and that their example would spread to other sectors of the economy. But that has not come about; even among underground coal workers themselves, IMU members are still only a minority, though the union's influence is much broader than its membership. So far, significant new unions have arisen only among small, strategically located groups of workers: pilots, locomotive engineers, longshoremen, air-traffic controllers.

Today, the great majority of workers remain within the old unions. The miners' strike and the collapse of the power of the party apparatus initiated a process of reform in these unions, but it has been painfully slow and remains, with a few significant exceptions, very far from complete. Paradoxically, while the new unions, at least in Russia, have asserted their independence from enterprise management, they tend to be very loyal to the government, to the extent that some have dubbed them the new state unions.

On the other hand, the old unions have adopted more independent, oppositional stands toward the government and its neoliberal policies but tend to remain subservient to management. This is not simply a matter of corruption. The cozy relationship with management has a certain objective basis in the fact that capitalist relations have only very partially been restored in the enterprises. For example, mass layoffs have not yet occurred, even though most plants, thanks to state economic policy, are working at a fraction of their capacity. Moreover, managers are often limited in their capacity to respond to workers' demands, since the government, through its tax policy, strictly controls wages and remains the only available source of funds for investment. In a collapsing economy, many unions—and workers—look to an alliance with management to lobby government and thus save their factories and jobs.

Around the same time as the IMU was founded, the self-management movement finally seemed to be taking off after years of false starts. Ironically, it arose at a time when Gorbachev was turning away from the original official conception of market reform as a renewal of socialism (in practice, it had always been far short of this), toward promoting the market reform as the restoration of capitalism. This meant privatization of the state enterprises and the abandonment of the self-management idea. This shift was reflected in a government directive to end election of management by workers and in the new 1990 Law on Enterprises, which essentially abolished the STKs.

Not unrelated to this attack on the STKs was a marked rise in the number of conflicts between workers and management in the enterprises over the issue of power. These centered around accusa-

tions of mismanagement on the part of the administration and of misappropriation of enterprise funds and resources through the creation of small private enterprises or "cooperatives" attached to the (state) enterprise.

It was in this context that the first All-Union Conference of Work-Collective Councils and Workers' Committees met at the end of August 1990. It condemned the new Enterprise Law and demanded the right of the work collectives to choose by themselves the form of property for the enterprise: collective workers' property or state property. In either case, the work collectives, through their elected STKs, would exercise broad self-management rights. In December 1990, a Congress of Work-Collective Councils formed the Union of Work Collectives.

But despite initial high hopes, the movement has failed to even approach its aims. In Russia, this was in no small part due to the liberal government's hostility to self-management and collective ownership and to the co-optation of the movement's top leadership. However, there is a more basic cause, one that also helps to explain the slowness of union reform: the deepening economic crisis and its demoralizing effect on workers. The high point in worker mobilization occurred in 1990, just before the economy went into its current nosedive. There were already marked shortages, but living standards and acquired social rights had not yet collapsed and very few yet felt the threat of unemployment.

Even a casual observer can see that today the labor movement in the former Soviet Union is very weak. The "democratic revolution," long awaited by many on the left in the capitalist world, has not taken the hoped-for form of a transition to a democratic socialism but rather of a transition to capitalism.

What is less obvious, however, is that the kind of people whose words fill this book can be found, even if in small numbers, in virtually every large and medium enterprise. And so where others have become despondent at the rightward turn of events—and I too experienced the disappointment of hopes for a swift return to socialist development in the Soviet Union—this knowledge has sustained my optimism.

I hope this book will have a similar effect on readers who remain committed to the cause of a more just and democratic world. If any conclusion emerges from this book, it is that the working class of the former Soviet Union has not yet spoken its last word, not by a long shot.

David Mandel
Montréal,
September 28, 1993

Acknowledgments

This book was a true labor of love. I feel it is a rare privilege that I can honestly say I deeply enjoyed virtually every minute I spent on it. For that I have to thank the people whose interviews appear in this book, many of whom are my friends.

I would also like to thank the following people, who, in one way or another, helped me in making contacts for these interviews: Dan Benedict, Sasha Buzgalin, Boris Ikhlov, Kolya Preobrazhenskii, Galina Rakitskaya, Galina Rogovina, Anna Temkina. Thanks also to Susan Lowes and Ethan Young of Monthly Review Press for their encouragement and help.

Finally, I especially want to express my gratitude to my wife Sonia for her understanding and long-suffering patience with my extended absences from home while I was doing this work.

The work that went into this book was funded by a Canada Fellowship from the Social Science and Humanities Research Council of Canada.

I

SURVIVAL AND RESISTANCE: A SOVIET FAMILY'S STORY

Petr Siuda
[Summer 1988]

In Moscow in the summer of 1988, I came across an unpublished article about the 1962 strike and ensuing massacre in the southern Russian town of Novocherkassk. The article was signed with the author's telephone number and address, something that struck me as very courageous at a time when the Novocherkassk events were still an officially taboo subject. I set out to find the author even though I knew I would have to travel without a visa (until the fall of 1991, foreigners required a visa for each town visited).

I found Petr Siuda, a small, wiry man with intense dark eyes and a goatee. We spent most of two days talking about the 1962 events and visiting the locations where they took place. You could still see the bullet holes in the back of Lenin's statue in the central square.

At the train station for my return to Moscow, I was arrested. Two and a half hours later, I was released to return on my own to Moscow, where I was eventually summoned to pay a small fine for traveling without a visa. Only later did I learn that my name had been put on a blacklist of people banned from entry into the Soviet Union.

In the spring of 1991 Petr was murdered in Novocherkassk, beaten and left to die in the street. In his briefcase were documents about the 1962 events. The murder remains unsolved, but the interview that follows makes clear that it was in all likelihood politically motivated. Petr was fifty-two.

From its very first to its last moments, Petr's life was tragically shaped by political repression. It was a concentrated expression of

15

the fate of the Soviet working class—to whose cause Petr, like his father before him, was dedicated to the end.

In a way, the story of my family is interwoven with the history of this country.

My father was born in a peasant family in Byelorussia, not far from the Polish border. Land hunger was acute, and peasants set off in search of wages to supplement the family income. So in 1898, at the age of twenty-two, my father left for the south of Russia, arriving in Novorossiisk where he got work in a cement factory. My father came to the defense of workers who were being dismissed, and they fired him. He finally came to Batumi in Georgia. There he joined a social-democratic circle and was chosen treasurer. It was a severely persecuted movement. The treasurer knew everything there was to know about the members and so he had to have their unconditional confidence. In 1903, he joined the Russian Social-Democratic Workers' Party [RSDWP] and was arrested the same year.

Soon after, my father was exiled under police supervision to the town of Rostov-on-Don. With the aid of the underground organization, he forged documents and escaped. In 1904 he was arrested again in Sevastopol but escaped. Traveling across the country through many cities he finally returned to Grozny, where he reorganized the underground organization of the RSDWP and led it in the 1905 revolution.

He describes an episode in which the authorities had arrested the local railroad workers' committee. The revolution was already on the decline, but had not yet been crushed. During the trial some 17,000 workers gathered in the square below and kept an orderly, silent vigil. The court was forced to exonerate all members of the committee, since the authorities feared unrest. When the workers saw the Petersburg defense lawyers off at the station, the lawyers said to them: "It was not we who won the committee's liberation. You did, through your solidarity and unity."

After a series of arrests he eventually returned to his birthplace where the word was out that he was a revolutionary who opposed the tsar. He soon left again for again for Baku, where he led the revolutionary movement in the Bibo-Eibatsk district. The class struggle in Baku was always intense, even in the dark years of reaction following the defeat of the 1905 revolution. It was a school for revolutionary cadres. [Bolshevik leaders] Krasin, Kalinin, Shaumyan, Dzhaparidze, Stalin, they all went through the Baku school. My father was active here from 1907 to 1918. When the February Revolution [1917] broke out, he was chairman of the oil industry party committee in the Bibo-Eibatsk district. He was elected on the Bolshevik list to the Baku Soviet, along with people like Shaumyan and Dzhaparidze.

After the October Revolution, when the specialists began to sabotage oil production, he tried to organize the work there, and oil output rose, surpassing even prewar levels. Of course, this was no thanks to him or even the Bolsheviks. It was the result of the high level of consciousness and skill of workers of many nationalities, who were working consciously for their revolution and no longer under the whip of capitalists or bureaucrats.

Then hunger set in. Before the war broke out, my father's mother had come to Baku. Besides her, he had to feed a wife—his first wife—and four children. The Bolsheviks insisted that he send his family to a region where food was more abundant. They gave him the task of analyzing the situation in the northern Caucasus and of reestablishing communications between Baku and the revolutionary center. But when he reached the Kuban with his family, he saw that the counterrevolution was consolidating itself there. He returned to Baku to report to Dzhaparidze. In May 1918, the Baku commune sent out a large detachment of Bolsheviks to the northern Caucasus and to Astrakhan to restore Soviet power there. This departure from Baku of so large a group of people with vast revolutionary experience weakened the commune and helped to seal its tragic fate.

Siuda himself was sent back to the Kuban. He arrived at the height of the counterrevolution and civil war and was at once coopted into the leadership of the Red forces. When they retreated from the northern Caucasus, it was decided to leave Siuda and two other comrades in Stavropol to continue underground work. My father was arrested several times but managed to save himself by posing as a Pole.

In 1920, with the White Army disintegrating, Buděnnyi's cavalry entered Maikop, which was in the hands of the red-green [pro-Soviet but independent peasant] forces. My father went out to the edge of the town to meet the Red cavalry. A short but smart-looking horseman rode up to him and asked for directions. He began to chat with my father and finally asked: "Petro, don't you recognize me? It's Volodya." It was Voroshilov, whom my father knew from their work in the revolutionary underground in Baku. [Voroshilov, a rather undistinguished military commander in the civil war and later in World War II, became a member of Stalin's Politburo.] The next day, Voroshilov asked my father to organize the funeral of the 3,000 people who had been shot or hanged by the White general Prizhevalskii. He described the event in his memoirs as something horrible.

After that, he was appointed commissar in charge of the nationalization and restoration of the Maikop oilfield. There were neither party nor trade-union organizations. Bands of white-greens [anti-Soviet peasants], 300 to 350 strong, roamed the area. Yet, with old equipment and no material support or subsidies, they managed to surpass prewar levels of output. On May 1, 1923, the Maikop oilfields were awarded the Red Banner of Labor, and my father received a personal award and an honorary rifle.

He describes that period with optimism. But even then, during the post-civil war reconstruction, one gets the sense from his memoirs that he saw the beginning of the process of decay of the revolution, when all sorts of careerist trash found its way into the party. He describes a confrontation with one of these elements, who said to him: "Siuda, you're old. Your time has passed." He wrote that the struggle with the external enemy was easier than with this internal, hidden enemy. He still believed in the revolutionary cause, but I sensed that by 1930, he was already broken politically and continued to work increasingly out of inertia.

But he remained a man of principle. In December 1937, he was expelled from the party "for direct support and defense of the enemy of the people, Korolev." In those days, betrayals were common. Voroshilov betrayed many comrades. Kalinin [a member of Stalin's Politburo] did nothing when his wife was arrested. But the Bolshevik Siuda remained true to his party comrade Korolev, who had been falsely accused and arrested, and he stubbornly defended him.

This was the start of the tragedy. My father was arrested himself on December 29, 1937. I was twenty-two days old.

Sometime after 1950, a man who had been his cellmate told us that when my father was taken out for interrogation, he walked on his own; but he had to be dragged back to the cell by guards—he was covered in blood. Yet he continued to believe and said: "The party will once again find the correct position." And he instilled this belief in his cellmates. He died in jail on January 7, 1938. Under torture.

What happened to your mother after his arrest?

She couldn't find work for several months, and when she did, it was always temporary. Almost every day she made the rounds of the offices and stood at the gates of the jail. Relatives of prisoners had an informal network and knew when the transit groups left for the camps. She came to the station every time a group was being sent out. Above the wagons stood wooden platforms with armed soldiers and dogs. My mother would run beside the wagons shouting: "Si-u-da, Petr Ilich!" And from inside the wagons: "Who? Who are you looking for, sister?" And she would repeat the name. My older bother, eleven years old, would run alongside her. My middle brother, six years old, held onto her skirt, and I was in her arms. The *okhranniki* [*okhrana* was the name of the tsarist political police] shouted back at her: "Get away from here with your degenerate brats, bitch, or we'll let loose the dogs!"

After she learned of my father's death, her son from her first marriage went to Moscow to try to inform Stalin of how his comrade-in-arms had perished. On Stalin's direct order, an investigation was made into the causes of the death in 1937. On August 2, 1939, my father was rehabilitated. Two investigators were blamed for the death and shot. There's an old saying: "Freedom for the dead; the living—under arrest!" This saying hasn't lost its relevance today. My father's party standing, however, was not restored. The party bureaucrats were frightened by the fate of the two investigators. But my mother was given a pension.

She began to work as director of the day-care center of the Don River Steamship Lines. She lived in Rostov, which was occupied twice during the war. During the second occupation, the children's families asked her to organize a nursery school. The occupation authorities gave her permission. It probably didn't hurt that she was the wife of a repressed person and also the daughter of a Don Cossack village chief. [Many Don Cossacks had sided with the Whites in the civil war.] Beyond a doubt, it played a key role in saving these children. When our forces liberated Rostov, the NKVD [the political police] thanked her. That was in the spring of 1943.

In August, she was arrested. The treasurer of the day-care center was a thief. After several warnings, my mother dismissed her. For revenge, the woman falsely denounced my mother for anti-Soviet agitation, accusing her of having conducted a religious service to mark the opening of the center. My mother got seven years, a relatively lenient sentence for those times.

We continued to receive my father's pension and rations, so the family seemed secure. Other families managed to stay together in much worse circumstances. But my eldest brother, yielding to the influence of our appointed guardian, handed us over after a few months to a children's shelter. And for three years after that he continued to receive the pension and rations for all three of us. He destroyed the family hearth, betrayed my father's memory and my mother.

When the policewoman carried me into the children's shelter, I went into hysterics, grabbed at her hair, sobbing and shouting, "Take me home! Take me home!" It was a terrible shock for me. If I recall the first six years of my life as a sunny period of family happiness, the period in the orphanages is all grayness.

What did they tell you at the orphanage about your mother?

They didn't say anything. We were taught one thing: the homeland is our mother, Stalin is our father. The children even competed with each other: "For one hour of Stalin's life, I'd give five of my own." Another would be more generous: "I'd give ten." Afterward, my mother told us that she had written to us. But she soon received a letter from the director of the orphanage asking her to stop writing because each letter had a very painful effect on the two brothers, especially on me. You can imagine what it means for a mother in the camps to lose contact with her children. But for our sakes she was forced to agree, and we were lost to her.

The times were very hard. The hunger was terrible. They couldn't feed us enough, though they did their best. Each spring they took us "out to pasture," that is, they showed us what plants were edible: for example, wild onions and garlic. We ate everything, including spruce buds. We caught sparrows, porcupines, anything to survive.

In all, I was in three orphanages and constantly running away. My brother Volodya, after running away from his orphanage, was working at a defense plant. But the foreman, a petty tyrant, used to take away the kids' wages, so my brother left. He changed his name because he feared the authorities would be looking for him, and enrolled in the technical school near where we used to live. [Under Stalin, it was a criminal offense to leave one's job.] He studied and waited for my mother's return. He was drawn to the family, even though it no longer existed. When she was released in 1950, my mother went to our old home, and the neighbors told her where to find Volodya. But she had already found out which orphanage I was in and came for me first, since I was the youngest.

She got work as a laborer at a construction site in Gornyatsk. We had little money. In 1950 a political ex-convict was a leper, someone carrying the plague, like the untouchables in India. Even in school, I felt that I was the "son of a political." One day they collected five kopecks from everyone in class so we could buy soap. I couldn't bear the insult and simply stopped coming. Our family was surrounded by an atmosphere of estrangement.

There were no cranes at construction sites in those days. My mother carried bricks, eight and ten at a time. She was faint with hunger; her nose and ears bled. She drove herself to exhaustion and kept her family half-hungry in order to save up a little money to travel to Moscow. You see, my eldest brother had been sentenced in 1947 to twenty years for armed robbery in Novocherkassk. She was trying to get to Voroshilov to ask his help.

One day she sat me down and said, "We have a chance to buy a sewing machine for 500 rubles. If we buy it, then we'll have to go hungry for a time. But I'll be able to sew and earn good money." Of course, I agreed. She was a first-class seamstress, a skill she had acquired as part of her education.

Whenever she managed to get a small sum together, she would leave for Moscow. In 1953, she finally got to Voroshilov. He remembered my father, and so he sent a telegram and my brother was released after serving fewer than six years. He told horrible stories about camp life in Kolyma, where a convict's life hung on the whim of sadistic guards. My mother knew the camps first-hand, and that's why she had done everything in her power to free her eldest son.

What was your mother's background?
She was a Cossack. Her father was a village chief, roughly equal to the chairman of a rural soviet today. Obviously, they weren't poor. She graduated from the women's high school. She was very well educated, and went on to study at teachers' college—much more cultured than my father, who had little formal education. During the civil war, my mother served as a nurse with the Whites, and her first love was a White officer, who was later killed. But I have the impression she served with the Whites more out of solidarity with her parents. In fact, she was always closer to the people.

Did your father forgive her for being a White?
Their union was based on love. My mother had many suitors but she always loved my father. When her brother Andrei learned that she had married a Bolshevik, he gave her a whipping. He didn't like the Soviet regime and later spent fourteen years in the camps, under Article Fifty-eight [anti-soviet propaganda]. But when he was released, my mother rushed to him. He had no family, no one except her.

The following incident from camp life can give you an idea of my mother's character. The camp was in Siberia. She worked as the camp's shipping agent and traveled with horses to bring food. Well, she had learned that the driver with whom she traveled was a *seksot*, an informer. One day, when they were returning to the camp in winter with a full sled, my mother stopped the horses and told the driver to get down. She took the whip and thrashed the driver, then rode off leaving her alone on the road five kilometers from the camp. When the guards asked about the driver, she just said, "Back there. Go for her, if you like." My mother knew the risk she was running, but she was decisive and unflinching when confronted with something she considered dirty.

When did your mother tell you about your father?
After she took me out of the orphanage. I wasn't shaken as much by her tragedy as by my father's. You see, I was proud of the Bolsheviks, and my mother now told me that my father had been

one of them, a close friend of Dzhaparidze and Fioletov, two of the Baku commissars. But the orphanage had also taught me to believe in Stalin, in our social justice, and this news about my father broke my faith. My idols were smashed.

It was also a difficult time for me because we weren't able to recreate a true sense of family. I felt a lack of concern on my mother's part. Of course, now I can understand her situation. She had gathered her youngest under her wing. She was also reassured about her second. But she lived in horror at the thought of her eldest's fate. It was a terrible tragedy. And her entire soul, all her thoughts, were filled with that concern. After the orphanage, I couldn't accept her distance. She didn't understand that a mother is more than a physical presence; it's a mother's soul and caress, her closeness.

That's why I repeatedly ran away from home. I never spent more than two or three months in a row there. I wandered. For a time, I worked for a former kulak [rich peasant] who had run away from the Kuban and doing plastering work on a private basis in rural areas. There was a lot of construction, and he made good money. He didn't pay me a wage—only food and shelter. My job was to mix and carry the plaster.

I traveled the length and breadth of the Soviet Union. My favorite place on the train was the roof of the cars. You could sleep well, and the inspectors bothered you less. I was a vagabond, but I didn't steal. My aversion to theft was probably the only good thing the orphanage taught me.

Still a minor, I enrolled in a technical mining school in Tula region. After graduation, they sent us to a new mine. It was damp, with an inclined shaft. Living conditions were nightmarish. We lived in corrugated-iron buildings, covering ourselves with mattresses in the winter. The pipes froze over. But we couldn't leave, since graduates were obliged to work a certain length of time. They even educated us. An instructor would bring newspapers and lecture us. Well, it was freezing—who was going to read those papers? The instructor picked them up the next day and checked it off in his report.

One day, we were sitting around the table in our padded cotton jackets. The instructor was spouting some propaganda, while I absentmindedly doodled on the newspapers lying in front of us. The next day, the instructor came for the newspapers, which were lying frozen on the windowsill. He picked them up and asked, "Who did this?" "What?" I asked. It turned out that I had scribbled "crap" on an article about Khrushchev and Bulganin's trip to Burma.

Soon after, plainclothes policemen came to see me and to search the room. It was the same article of the criminal code that had put my mother away. They worked me over: "You people steal; you conduct anti-Soviet agitation." In brief, they wanted to recruit me as an informer. I flew into a terrible rage, "My father died in jail, my mother did time too, and now you're coming to me with this?!" That was the last time they tried. But I became aware of the vast network of informants that exists in the USSR, in every work and student collective, small or large.

I succeeded in getting myself transferred to Novoshakhtinsk in Rostov region. Despite everything, I was drawn to my family. But my eldest brother had returned from the camp, and I couldn't live in the same house with him. So when the campaign to open the virgin lands began, I volunteered for Kazakhstan.

I worked on the construction of a cement elevator, the heart of the entire construction site. We worked like madmen, but we made good money, more than the other workers. The director was sympathetic, but the chief engineer couldn't stomach our high earnings. When the director was away and the chief engineer filled in, his first act was to cut our wages. The cement section immediately downed tools. Of course, I participated too, though it was largely an unconscious act on my part; I just followed everyone else. I was the youngest, but I had a big mouth. In one of the arguments between the workers and the administration, I shot out: "An idiot has piss in his head instead of brains, and everybody else has to choke on it." Everyone burst out laughing to hear such words from a young boy. But I had made an enemy of the chief engineer.

Here too, I ran into informing. Although it was a basic tool of Stalinism, the people had the deepest contempt for informers. I didn't really know much about the KGB, but I did notice curious people dressed in civilian clothes walking about. And the authorities seemed to know everything that was said. I soon found out how.

The construction site was not exactly a temperance zone, but alcohol was officially delivered only on November 7, the anniversary of the October Revolution. On that day, the whole place got plastered. Everybody had accumulated lots of money, and they spent it on vodka and wine. The police picked up drunks on the street, confiscated their knives and documents, and then tossed them back into the street. We were living in a tent city, sixty people to a tent, grown-ups and young kids like us, men and women. It was bedlam, a real Noah's ark. There was nothing that we didn't see there.

I was walking from the tent city with one of the workers when a comrade, who was drunk but already sobering up, came toward us. The police had confiscated his money and documents. We decided to try to get them back. But all we got at the station was a lecture. Suddenly the door to another room opened, and out came a recently demobilized soldier, a worker in our brigade. He hadn't seen our faces and began talking with the officer in a familiar tone: "Listen, Serezha, I just brought a bum in here...." When he saw us, his eyes nearly popped out of their sockets. He started to stammer, and we took advantage of the confusion to make our getaway. He caught up with us and offered to buy us drinks. We refused.

The two of us returned to the tent and recounted our adventure. The tent began to buzz like a hornets' nest. But the women said: "You men, don't touch him. Leave him to us." At about three o'clock in the morning I awoke to a terrible din. The informer had quietly slipped in and gone to bed. But the women weren't sleeping. They beat him with pokers and sticks. He howled and howled and finally fell silent. I had seen fights among men. And later in the prison camps there was little I didn't witness, but I don't think I've every seen anything as wild and cruel as those women. But the informer survived.

The next morning, the tent was transformed into a factory for forging passports. They erased the entries, the residence permits, forged new ones, and then fled the construction site. I returned to Novoshakhtinsk. It was there that I received my call-up to military service.

I was assigned to a course for middle- and long-range radio technicians and operators in Zaporozhe. The course was difficult because I didn't even have five years of school. But I graduated. My military service was stormy because I couldn't stand the petty soldiering that violated your individuality. We would stand at roll call, and I'd be chatting with a neighbor. When my name came up, I would absent-mindedly answer "uh-huh." One winter night, we were sent on a forced march in the mud with full pack. I refused to run, but the others carried me. The other soldiers always supported me. Our company consisted of Muscovites and natives of Novoshakhtinsk. It became very independent and protected its members' dignity.

In 1957, during the campaign against the "anti-party group"— Molotov, Malenkov, Kaganovich, Voroshilov and Shepilov—they assembled us in the big hall to add our voices to the chorus. [This campaign followed an abortive attempt by a majority in the Politburo to oust Khrushchev.] All this was of the greatest concern to me, that is, Stalinism and the repressions of the 1930s. I also knew that Voroshilov's telegram had freed my brother. Whatever the truth was, I could clearly see that Stalinism was still alive in the methods that were being used. So I spoke up at that meeting: "What moral right do we have to act as judge? We have only heard the accusers' version. Where are the voices of the accused? Every person has the right to a defense." The overwhelming majority of those present took no part in the vote. Only a few people voted, officers and sergeants seated in the front, and they naturally voted for condemnation. I was the only one to vote against.

After that, I was repeatedly called in by the Political and the Special departments. They used the carrot-and-stick approach: the Special department scared me to tears, and the Political department was kind, making all sorts of promises. They wanted one thing—that I sign the meeting's resolution. It was difficult psychologically, but I refused. Though I had already participated in the strike in the virgin lands, it was really from that moment that I adopted a stance of active resistance to Stalinism. I understood that it was not only the last leader who was bad, but the entire party that had nothing in common with Marxism-Leninism or with the ideals of the revolution.

Nowadays, scholars are discussing whether there were alternatives. Yes, it's important to study the underlying reasons for the revolution's degeneration so that it will become clear that there was indeed an alternative. Of course, they left a few red rags and feathers on the regime's facade. They didn't completely abandon the ideology of October that embodied the aspirations of the workers. But the regime's essence, its practice, is Stalinism, which fully expresses the interests of the party-state bureaucracy.

I took the final exam of the radio course at ten a.m., and at noon they called me to division headquarters, handed me papers, a train ticket and travel orders, and sent me off to Crimea. My pals were so envious. Crimea! A resort area! But my unit in Crimea turned out to be an airport construction battalion. When I arrived, a lieutenant asked me privately, "What did you do to get sent here?" I asked, "What do you mean? Is this a punitive battalion?" He answered, "Well, no, but we received some documents about you." I revealed nothing, of course. I worked on the battalion switchboard and did guard duty. When the battalion was sent out to build reserve airports, I was left behind, since they didn't trust me. I was already labeled a dissenter.

We had a Baptist there who refused to carry arms. The soldiers made fun of him, hung a rifle on him against his will. There are always some bastards in a flock of sheep, and that includes soldiers. I let the officer know what I thought in no uncertain terms. After that, he was left alone. He too was a dissenter, and I felt solidary with him.

I kept pressing for permission to study. I had missed my chance for an education because of my wandering, and now I wanted to make up for it. One day, some officers came from headquarters. They called me, then the Baptist. They asked me if I had any requests. I said I wanted to study. "Okay, we'll look into it." Somewhat later, the acting commander summoned me and asked, "How can we let you study, when we don't even allow that to Komsomol [Communist Youth League] members?" I was forced to offer a deal: "I'll join if you let me study." That's how I finished high school.

During my absence, my family had moved from Novoshakhtinsk to Novocherkassk, where my father had lived at the beginning of the 1930s. After demobilization I came home, but, again, the family was not a family. I signed on to work in Yakutsk, in the far north. We were sent off to the taiga to cut wood and photograph soil maps. This was hellish work in the most difficult conditions. We lived in tents and the temperature was minus fifty degrees celsius.

I well remember April 12, 1961. We were working at a mica mine and heard over the short-wave radio that a man had been shot into space. This made a tremendous impression on us, all the more so because we were so isolated.

I wanted to run off somewhere. But we had signed up with the labor recruiters. This is the lowest, most degraded category of wage labor. You sign a contract with the Organized Recruitment Agency for a specific period. But you never know what conditions really await you. They can trick you. They give you an advance of 600 or 700 rubles, part of which you get before you leave, part upon arriving. Then you see that the conditions aren't at all what they had promised. But you can't leave since you have no way of returning the money that would allow you to break the contract. In fact, you've sold yourself into slavery for a fixed period. But I had experience and ran away. And I wasn't the only one.

I arrived in Novocherkassk and enrolled as a correspondence student in the technical institute. I got a job at the Novocherkassk Electric Locomotive Factory (NELF) in the assembly shop where they fit the pneumatic system. I also got married for the first time. I was foolish—we had known each other only a day. My life lacked direction. We rented an apartment in the private sector. Rent was very high, thirty rubles. My pay was about 120 rubles a month. And my wife was pregnant.

On June 1, 1962, when the strike broke out, I was on the first day of my study leave to prepare for the annual exams. The landlord's wife came over and said, "Petro, the factory is in an uproar. Something must have happened."

Your essay gives the impression that the strikers were proud that they were workers. They marched into town carrying Lenin's portrait and red banners, singing revolutionary songs. They summoned the other factories to join them, and they made efforts to contact other cities. How did they come to do those things? Was there any sort of tradition there?

No, none. There was no industry in Novocherkassk before the revolution. The factories really first appeared during the Stalin five-year plans.

Novocherkassk was once a center of the Don Cossacks, although not since even before the revolution. There are probably few Cossacks left who can trace their families back to prerevolutionary times.

The Polytechnic Institute already existed at the time of the revolution. Afterward, they built the Land Reclamation Institute and many other technical institutes. So historically, the town evolved from an administrative center, a Cossack capital, to a student center, a town of institutes of higher education. In 1962, the town was still classified as "student" for purposes of food supply, even though it had dozens of factories, including one of the largest locomotive factories in the world, with some 12,000 workers. And, of course, the authorities considered that students don't have to eat so well.

The food situation was terrible. In Novocherkassk, workers had no choice but to buy much of their food at the peasant market. [Prices at the peasant markets were much higher than the fixed prices in the state shops.] Moreover, in earlier years many people had their own cows and gardens, but Khrushchev had put an end to that; as a result, the market itself grew poorer, and prices rose correspondingly. In 1962, there was nothing in the stores. People had to travel all the way to Rostov and Shakhty to buy food. It was only after the events that the town was given a higher classification. There is a story of an old women who said, "May God grant good health to all the victims. Now we have everything in the stores." Although the situation is very bad now again, the city is supplied at the same level as others.

The housing shortage was also acute. The worker town was made up of buildings of prewar vintage, barracks that probably dated from the construction of the locomotive factory. Several more buildings had been put up by 1962, but generally the housing sector was very neglected. People had to rent in the private sector. That meant twenty-five to fifty rubles a month. After the events, housing construction was immediately accelerated. Today, few people rent in the private sector. Of course, you can see what these buildings are like: you freeze in the winter, and in the summer it's like a steambath. You can't breathe.

How much were you personally hurt by the cut in wages?

I was hit very hard both by inflation and the wage cuts. This was one in a series of blanket wage cuts carried out in a purely arbitrary manner. Any reduction of piece-rates should be based upon productivity gains resulting from improved technology, mechanization, or automation. No such measures had been introduced. But there was the plan, and it included targets for raising productivity. And to top it all off, there had just been a currency reform in 1961 that had seriously hurt the workers. It was one attack after another on the workers' interests.

How did the workers react?

Well, they grumbled, but that's about all. You see, they didn't cut everyone's wages at once. On February 15, they cut wages in the assembly shop. The next month, it was the steel foundry, and so forth. People had begun to get used to the new rates. But one also shouldn't forget that Stalinism had for many years taught workers that you risked a two-year prison sentence for arriving twenty minutes late. A cousin of mine got five years for taking five kilos of apples. True, things relaxed somewhat after Stalin, but the psychological legacy was still strong; the workers had been forced to their knees. At that time, as today, there was no organization that represented the workers' interests. Therefore, although they were mad, no one thought of taking action.

That was the time of de-Stalinization. Did that have any impact on the workers?

Whatever you can say about de-Stalinization, the regime had its own self-interest at heart. They debunked the personality cult and left the cult of the party, as if the party was not complicit in the crimes of Stalinism and had managed to remain Bolshevik, the party of Lenin.

Who needed this cult of the party? Why, the new leaders, of course. Stalin was gone, but Stalinism, which expressed the interests of the party-state bureaucracy, was still with us. The bureaucrats allowed democratization up to the point where the workers tried to put it to use, where they mounted a real offensive against the essence of Stalinism.

Did the workers themselves understand that?

Not at once, although as time passed, disillusionment with the proclaimed de-Stalinization grew. But as I wrote in my essay, the workers at first really believed in these processes. They saw in them a sincere attempt to humanize Soviet socialism. Even on the eve of the events, this faith was to some degree still intact.

And then they announced the price increase.

Yes, early in the morning, on the radio: the prices of meat and milk and dairy products, as well as the price of eggs, had been raised.

These were announced as temporary measures, weren't they?

We have a saying: "Nothing is more permanent than the temporary." Prices have been rising for the last twenty years. Everything is temporary.

The workers were indignant. But there still might not have been a strike had the factory authorities been able to find the correct approach. They could at least have said, "Listen, we can't control food prices but we will restore the old piece-rates. We'll pay more attention to housing construction, the food supply, and so forth." But that's one of the traits of Stalinism: no one so much as dares to squeak in face of his superior, be it a worker before a petty official or a petty official before a higher boss. In other words, neither the officials nor the workers are prepared for independent thought.

But the workers, in contrast to the functionaries, were educated on the ideology of the revolution and had absorbed it. While the workers were arguing with the director in the yard, a woman walked past with liver pies. The director remarked cynically, "If you can't afford meat, then eat liver pies." This remark was a catalyst to the strike. When they came up against the reality, their proletarian instinct began to work. Yet, it was characteristic that the director was not harmed.

The movement was completely spontaneous. But the workers knew what to do. Some went to the dormitories, others to the compressor room, and another group went through the shops. Everyone had been storing up pain and anger. It was enough to toss out the word "Strike!" for it all to come pouring out. They downed tools at once. Of course, there were individuals, especially among the older workers, who had known the terror of the 1930s and refused to join. But the overwhelming majority joined without the slightest hesitation. They knew just what to do. They had seen it in movies and read it in books about the revolutionary movement. They got some sticks and attached a red cloth on which they had written, "We need apartments, meat, and butter," and they stopped the train. On the side of the train, they wrote, "Cut up Khrushchev for meat!" It was a joke, of course.

Despite all the efforts on the part of the authorities, the workers refused to reopen the line and let the train pass. They sent off delegations to the other factories to ask their solidarity and tried to contact the rest of the country. But all the roads were closed by police and military cordons. By noon the city was shut tight. A delegation left for Shakhty but was stopped on the road and sent back.

The workers understood at once that they needed support?

Yes, and first of all, of course, the support of the other workers of Novocherkassk. And what unity! As soon as the workers of the other factories learned of our action, they wanted to join. That's why the authorities got so frightened. They feared a mass movement. Mikoyan said that the government had learned of the Novocherkassk events twenty minutes after the train had been stopped. They understood that the Novocherkassk workers could be supported by other masses. This is where the main danger to the bureaucracy, to Stalinism, arises. And their reaction was immediately set in motion.

It was Lenin who explained how people have been divided into those who are managed and those who are specialists in managing. The specialists in management appropriate for themselves all sorts of privileges. To defend them, they create organs of repression, an army that is kept locked up for years in barracks and taught to shoot at the people. As soon as the workers threatened the bureaucrats' privileges and rejected their dictatorship, the bureaucracy got scared and threw against them the full force it had created to defend its privileges—not to defend socialism, not in the interests of the people, but to defend their own privileges against the people.

This helps me to see that today there is no real democracy, only a trend to pseudo-democracy, only the possibility to talk. They let you talk and even open the palaces to you. "Take your time. Blab to your heart's content. Enjoy yourselves!" They open a small valve. But try to create a force that would represent the workers' interests!

You were saying that despite the movement's spontaneity, there was no violence.

Not on the workers' part, only on the part of the authorities. After the events, they mobilized enormous forces—not only local forces, but KGB agents from Kiev, Moscow, and Leningrad. They kept digging and digging but couldn't find a single case of a worker using a knife or a club, not to mention machine guns. But I have a copy of the death sentence of seven people. They were accused of hooliganism, banditry, and mass disorder. Yet there isn't one bit of proof to support that. Take the incident with chief engineer Elkin, the only party member principled enough to come out and talk to the workers, though he had no mandate. His inability to answer their questions provoked the workers' anger. But when a few of them pulled him into the cab of the truck and were about to beat him, I was among the workers who formed a cordon to protect him. And he wasn't harmed.

In brief, the accusations are barefaced lies. It's interesting that the authorities circulated the rumor that it was a Cossack revolt. I heard this later on the trains. But if it had been Cossacks they would have "raised their sabers," as the expression goes. The workers behaved according to the methods of the revolutionary movement: they appealed to their comrades in the other factories and towns to join their movement.

Even before that, a group of shop managers and party and trade union activists had come outside. This, incidentally, is a measure of those unions that side with management instead of with the workers. They put on armbands and tried to convince the workers to let the train through. The workers wouldn't hear of it. We knew that to let one train through would reopen the line. It was a fundamental question. However, the heat was unbearable, and it was a passenger train with innocent people, children that needed water. So we decided to let it leave by a roundabout route, and it eventually got to the station.

Then there was the lemonade episode. We were dying of thirst, and along comes a truck with lemonade from the direction of town. They wanted us to seize the truck as an unorganized mob. Despite some calls to do that, we formed a corridor through the huge mass of people and sent it on its way. Less than one minute passed when people began to shout, "The cops are here!" So it was all staged. The police formed a double line on the soccer field, over 200 of them. Meanwhile, the trucks they had come in were turning around to head back to town.

I had an initial moment of panic, but then felt a rush. "So, the bastards want a fight!" What took place next was straight out of the movies. A mass of people seized by revolutionary enthusiasm set off in a human wave. When the police got a glimpse of this seething wall of humanity closing in on them, their ranks simply dissolved. The trucks were pulling out, and they ran after them for all they were worth. It was an incredible scene of cowardice. Only two elderly sergeants got left behind. Their hearts were too weak. But we didn't harm them. We just told them in plain Russian, "Keep your noses out of here!" And they left in peace.

The workers were burning mad now. Someone shouted, "They have a short-wave radio, and they're taking pictures from the car!" By the time I reached the car, it was already overturned. The one with the camera escaped. The second one was let go, though they mussed him up a bit. Then they righted the car.

Toward evening, we saw the first military units. These were soldiers from the local garrison. The workers ran to them, hugged them, exchanged kisses. The authorities barely managed to pull them away. After that, they sent officers in armored transport vehicles. After shaking them from side to side, the workers let them go. At this point, a mass meeting started, with the arch of the tunnel as our tribune.

I should make something clear: there were no calls to seize power in town. That would have required the seizure of the buildings of the city party committee, the soviet executive committee, the headquarters of the organs of repression, the jails. There were no such calls. There were, however, calls to seize certain state institutions, especially the post office and telegraph building, in order to contact other towns, to tell the whole Soviet Union what was happening in Novocherkassk and to appeal for support. When I heard some speakers proposing this, I got up and warned that that was just what the authorities wanted—extremism and violence on the part of the workers. I explained that our strength was our solidarity, and I proposed that we return to the factory the next morning, not to work but to assemble and march to the party committee, where we could present our demands to the authorities. Whereas the calls to seize the post and telegraph office had not found much response, my proposal was met with an ovation.

During this rally, some lads climbed the facade of the administration building—it was quite a feat with only their hands and feet—in order to remove a large painted quotation from Khrushchev. But as it was made out of metal, they only managed to cut out the letters "N.S. Khrushchev." At that point, it was decided to collect all of Khrushchev's portraits, and the crowd moved toward the building. But the doors were locked, with guards standing behind them. Some started to push. Their names are listed in the court's sentence. The doors gave way, and one of the guards received a couple of blows. A group of workers went through the offices collecting only Khrushchev's portraits and tossing them out the windows. Half of the managerial personnel were still there, but no one was touched. Down below, the portraits were gathered into a pile and set on fire.

After agreeing to return the next morning, people began to leave. My wife came and begged me to come home. We arrived around midnight.

Where were the factory director and party committee secretary all this time?

The director was probably somewhere off in the bushes. Or maybe he was already being dragged through party and government offices. There was no sign of the party secretary either. True, the first secretary of the provincial party committee, Basov, came to speak to us, but from the third story of the administration building. That was taken as a sign of contempt. The workers now felt themselves free and refused to be spoken to from on high, so the bottles flew.

What was the workers' mood like?

This will sound blasphemous, but it was a joyous time, a time of liberation. The mood was militant. There was freedom, independence. Yes, it was short-lived, but it was. You have to understand the slavish feeling, the constant wondering with every move you made about what the boss would think. There was none of that here. That's why if you were to ask any of the participants to recount the events in chronological order, they'd be at a loss. The workers didn't look at the clock. You'd have to consult the information collected by the organs of repression. The taste of freedom was heady; we were breathing the air of liberty.

Having breathed that air, I was no longer able to remain on my knees, and that's how I am to this day. But never again did I feel myself so free. And that goes for the present too, because I see the reality for what it is.

Many experienced a spiritual awakening, had their eyes opened. The mask was torn from the regime that claimed it was a popular government and that the enterprises belonged to the people. The events showed that our society is, in fact, antagonistic, that the state stands above the people. It's not the people's state. It exists to protect a class of exploiters—the party-state bureaucrats, whose platform is Stalinism. The class of the exploited stands facing them, left with nothing but the ideals of the revolution as a sort of pacifier.

When the workers came to the factory on the morning of June 2, they found tanks, soldiers armed with machine guns, and shops full of KGB agents. But the process was already irreversible. The mood was, "If they don't want to talk to us and to take us seriously, we'll go to the end." And if the massacre had not occurred, the movement would have continued, maybe for a long time, but the workers would not have retreated.

[On the second day, after Siuda's arrest, thousands of workers marched to the city center where they held a mass meeting in front of party headquarters, which they eventually seized. A part of the crowd went down the street to police headquarters to free workers arrested the previous night. The troops then opened fire simultaneously on the central square and at police headquarters.]

How were you arrested?
The tanks had come at night, before one a.m. Young workers who had remained there tried to block them with barricades made out of benches and other objects, but they got through easily. I was woken at five a.m. by explosions caused by a tank that had run into a pylon. I ran to the factory and saw soldiers, members of Caucasian nationalities. This is not by way of a reproach to these peoples. The authorities brought them when they saw that the local garrison was undependable. Shortly after, I was arrested and taken to the director's office, where KGB agents greeted me. "Siuda! Glad to see you! We've been waiting!"

They drove me to the police station. All the way, I heard nothing but insults and threats of violence. We weren't kept long there, though the crowd that came to free us later that day couldn't have known that. I was driven to Bataisk, about eighty kilometers away, and left alone in a large cell. They didn't even take my name and address. About a week later, I was taken with another comrade to Rostov in a convoy of three cars filled with a whole gang of KGB agents. I'm constantly amazed at the abundance of those parasites. The highway had been cleared for us.

I was put in a KGB interrogation cell. As I already mentioned, I had never eaten so well. But what struck me most was the absolute isolation from the outside world. Not even the tiniest bit of information reached me. We had just come from the events in Novocherkassk and had no idea what had followed them. It was as silent as a tomb. The corridors had soft runners, and the window in the door made no noise when opened.

The KGB guards were very polite, always addressing me very formally. For example, I have a habit of sleeping with the pillow over my head. Besides, the light never went out. The guard came in and carefully removed the pillow, saying, "It's against regulations." I fell asleep with the pillow under my head, but as I slept it found its way on top. He came in again. The third time I awoke shouting. In the morning, the captain came and said, "Please forgive us. I know it's inconvenient, but such are the regulations."

My mother didn't know that I had been arrested. I had dropped out of sight, and she feared I was among the victims of the massacre. She was searching for me. Then she was told that I was under arrest. Immediately, she wrote to Mikoyan [a member of Khrushchev's Politburo], reminding him that my father had been a comrade-in-arms, and asked him to help her son.

At that time, my eldest brother was working as a senior foreman or possibly assistant manager in the factory. He was moving up. How did he manage that? In 1947, he was part of a gang of eight men. They would enter a cafeteria with a revolver and shout, "Hands up! Everyone on the ground!" and make off with the cash box and a few bottles of vodka. The day after one of their holdups, they were sleeping off the vodka in their dormitory when the police broke down the door and arrested seven of them. The eighth had gone off to a rendezvous with his girlfriend. Six were sentenced to twenty years each, and one, the son of the prosecutor, who was already serving a six-year probationary sentence, got twenty-five years. But they protected the eighth. Loyalty among thieves: if you're caught, take the rap and protect the others. While my brother was in the camps, the eighth robber was making a career for himself. He had already become assistant department head. And under his benevolent wing, my brother also began to rise, when he got out of prison.

My brother refused to testify against me, but he didn't stop his friends and subordinates. But the most telling thing is that my brother, with his criminal record, was accepted at this time into the party. The KGB agents told me they had recommended his admission. After the massacre, he and his wife were getting ready to visit friends and they had a luxurious bouquet of flowers with them. My mother came to ask my brother's help. He said he was busy. She began to shame him. He hit her, and she fell, losing consciousness. He said, "She's faking, the bitch!" and then threw a pail of water on her and left. My mother told me this afterward.

The eighth gangster, a certain Vladimir Semyonovich Shevtsov, has made himself a grand career today. But during the 1962 events, he was only chairman of the factory trade union committee. After that, he became district party committee secretary and then first party secretary of the city committee. [The party secretary was the real boss of the city.] Today he is none other than chairman of the regional committee of People's Control [a semiofficial organization charged with investigating corruption, particularly in the service and trade spheres]. That says it all about official values.

On my second day in Rostov, I was taken out and shown my father's file. My muscles tensed and my eyes nearly popped out of my head. I asked, "What was the central point of the accusation against him?" The officer just replied, "Yes, it was too trivial for those times," but he would not tell me what it was. I asked, "Can I have something from the file?" And he answered, "No, there is nothing there." I got angry, but he said politely, "Excuse me, but I have done my duty. I am obliged to inform you that you can make a request for monetary compensation."

Somewhat later, a note came from Mikoyan. The KGB tried to help me, but I had already learned from my cellmates about the massacre, and I wouldn't accept their offer. Then they started to work me over psychologically, though always with extreme politeness. They made it seem that everyone else had repented and would soon be released, that I was the only holdout. But I just couldn't bring myself to step over that threshold. It wasn't as if I was debating whether it was worth the sacrifice. That question never even arose in my mind. I didn't need that kind of freedom. It seemed easier at the time to commit suicide. I don't know if you can understand that. You probably have to live through it yourself.

Did you blame the others for giving in?
No. I asked them to pass on greetings to people outside. Anyway, I met them all later in jail and in the camp.

The KGB decided to give me a rest. They sent me to jail, to a cell about one by three meters with a dozen prisoners in it. We slept on wooden bunks, full of bedbugs. Next door was a cell with deranged prisoners, criminals pretending to be crazy in order to avoid trial. We tossed them some smokes and whatever else we could. They didn't have to pretend for us. One day, the door opened and in flew a sergeant major. He was said to have another job as an instructor in the wing for "shut-ins" [solitary confinement] and on death row. [The "shut-ins" were prisoners who were completely closed off except for a twenty-minute daily walk. This was usually a short jail sentence, maybe two years, followed by thirty years of labor camp.] You see, they even tried to educate people condemned to death. Everyone stood up, like sardines in a can, as he shouted, "Name, name, name!" We answered, and he yelled, "You bastards, sons of bitches, scum, they should beat you like they did in Ivanovo-Voznesensk." [He was referring to the tsarist police treatment of the textile workers in this very militant region of central Russia.] I exploded, "Who gave you the right to shout at us?" "Who are you?!" he roared back. "I already told you my name," I said. "Get out of the cell!" As I walked out, he waved his band of keys in front of my face. We shouted back and forth, and gradually his voice grew softer. When supper came, I refused to eat. I demanded to see the prosecutor. He came a couple of hours later, and I signed a declaration of intent to press charges against the sergeant. After that, the guards were never rude again to the Novocherkassk prisoners.

Seven of us were tried together. Others were tried in groups of three, five, ten, twelve. At the time, we counted at least 105 people, but I am sure there were many more.

I experienced the trial itself in a sort of stupor. I was indifferent.

But I was glad to see my comrades and to chat with them. There was a certain worker in our group—he's still at the factory—who wasn't normal, and even from the point of view of our laws shouldn't have been tried. We joked with him: "Gen, listen. You get up now and tell the judge: 'Comrade Judge, my grandmother and grandfather and my mother and father love me and want to share my sentence with me. Please take into consideration that all five of us will serve together.'" That gives you some idea how the trial went. We sat there and laughed. The judge threatened to remove me, and the *okhranniki* promised to fix my wagon.

Even the twenty-year sentence made no impression on me. I had probably crossed that line when they had worked me over psychologically in jail. Of course, it was a terrible shock for my mother. I was condemned for active participation in mass disorders.

In your essay, you write that your mother came to live near the camp.

Yes. She rented an apartment in Sinder, where she spent several months at a time. She worked as a seamstress to earn additional money. And she bought off all the *okhranniki.* They sell themselves cheap. She would also travel to Moscow and make the rounds of the prosecutors. In one of those visits, she was told, "Marya Petrovna, look at what your son writes: he alone is a Leninist, and we are not. Now tell me, how can we release him?" He was referring to my letters in which I denounced the massacre as a crime before the revolution. I still refused to recant, and they promised that after everyone else was released, I would remain, even after my sentence was up.

They began to release the Novocherkassians in the winter of 1965. [Khrushchev was ousted in September 1964.] But they still wanted me to condemn the workers' actions, and I continued to refuse. I was released in July 1966, one of the last. And that was only thanks to my mother, who managed to buy me a favorable conduct report by bribing the camp authorities. I had a very strong mother.

How did your life turn out after the camp?

I returned to Novocherkassk, to the NELF. The KGB never called me into their offices. Instead, they would come to chat with me in the factory's administration building. They said that if ever I had any trouble with people who reproached me for my role in the 1962 events, I should turn to them and they would take measures. In reality, no matter where I worked, I was told the same thing, sometimes with hostility and sometimes with sympathy: "They called to ask how you were doing. They want a conduct report." I felt I was living under a bell jar. I had no intention of partaking in any kind of political or public activity, but I bore the mark of a political convict, condemned for Novocherkassk.

During the first years, I didn't think about politics because things weren't working out between my first wife and myself. After all, we had been married twelve years, most of which had been a nightmare, all the more so as we had married on a lark. So she really wasn't waiting for me. I tried for two years to make things work. We even moved to a rural area, away from my mother, my mother-in-law, everyone. It didn't help.

Did the others also come back to Novocherkassk?

Many did. But a lot of them were unable to rebuild a normal life. In fact, almost none of them succeeded. There was a lot of alcoholism, and some were sent back again and even a third time for criminal acts. Others just lay low out of fear.

How did you come to be politically active?

My initiation as an *antisovietchik*—as they called it—began with the following incident. I eventually graduated from the technical institute as a specialist in the cold processing of metal. I got a job at the NEFTEMASH [oil-drilling machinery] factory as a designer. Those two and a half years were the happiest years of my life. My work was very productive. In the course of a single year, my proposals saved the factory 120,000 rubles.

One of my proposals was so good that they suggested I formally request it be recognized as an invention. I was happy, until I saw that they wanted to make the party organizer co-author. He had absolutely no connection with it. More than that, he was a lazy, worthless person who constantly violated sanitary discipline in the shop. Yet, as party organizer, he lectured us on morality. Sometimes, while he slept on the job, workers would sneak up and draw obscenities on his back. And he wanted to be co-author! I wasn't going to let that one pass! It may be a good trait or bad, but I don't usually like compromise. I demanded categorically that he remove his name.

He wouldn't. We had a heated argument, during which he said, "What are you doing here anyway? You were condemned for 1962." I repaid him in kind.

That was when I wrote my first open letter, and the persecution began immediately. No sooner did I take my vacation when I noticed an entire brigade of KGB agents on my heels. You couldn't call this being shadowed. It was simply blackmail. They kept only fifty or even twenty meters from me. They followed in cars too. At first my wife wouldn't believe it. So she took a few days off and accompanied me as I photographed them while they were photographing me with a camera concealed in a briefcase.

That apparently really angered them, and they stepped up their hounding. Once, on a trip to Moscow, I lured them into the Fili district where there's a large hill. I turned down what seemed like a steep lane but was actually steps. They were five in a car and came bumping down after me. At the bottom, they jumped out, grabbed me, and threatened to unscrew my head unless I beat it out of town.

I had come to give my open letter to the party Central Committee and to the KGB. The conversation with the KGB was very harsh. I told them that theirs was a criminal, murderous organization, covered in blood, that it had destroyed the revolution. They replied, "Petr Petrovich, perhaps we can help you get treatment." After that, I wrote my "Notes of a Dissident." That was already in the mid-1970s.

Did you have any connection with the dissident movement?

No, I was on my own. I wrote letters and protests to *Pravda*, *Literaturnaya Gazeta*, and so forth. I didn't listen to the "voices" either [the Voice of America and other Western Russian-language stations directed at the Soviet Union]. I didn't have the patience. They were jammed. But I didn't need them anyway. I could see that they were basically just advertising their own system, so I didn't seek the truth from that source. People who listened to the "voices" needed information for rethinking things. I could already see the reality as it was. Some people suggested that it was better for people like me to leave the country, as many of the dissidents did. But I had no interest in going elsewhere. No one needed me there. Here the struggle was really interesting.

Were you still working at NEFTEMASH?

No. I quit when the KGB began to hound me. My situation there had become impossible. Then they tried to crush me by blocking all my attempts to find work. I would come to a factory, and they would say, "No openings." Yet there was a sign on the gate: "We invite you to work here...." I tried dozens of enterprises and even went to Shakhty. Finally I was hired by a rundown dump of an enterprise. It was a repair shop for the town's sanitary equipment. There weren't any rules here. As soon as I showed up, they took my documents and told me to start the next day. It was too late for the KGB to do anything about it: I was already hired, and it would have been a public issue to have me fired. They didn't want that. This method of persecution is still used today, though on a more modest scale.

The second time I was out of work was after my operation. They removed two-thirds of my stomach and the remaining third was supposed to distend after the operation but never did. I was told that that is extremely rare. As a result, food goes directly into my intestines, and I remained an invalid with a whole bouquet of associated problems. When I regained my strength, I again found that no one would hire me. After much effort, when I had already given up hope, I was hired as an engineer-designer by the Scientific Research Institute of Electric Locomotive Engineering. Since they knew my political status, I felt free.

For example, I could refuse to vote. I didn't want to give legitimacy to a system that gave you no choice. In 1980, the elections came around again. As before, I refused to take part and forbade my wife to vote for me. Around midnight, an assistant secretary of the party committee, accompanied by a KGB agent in civilian clothes, came around to ask why I had not voted. Somehow, we began talking about Afghanistan, which I characterized as a crime. Since then, under perestroika, that agent became chairman of the city soviet executive.

That year, I was the victim of a new provocation. As chairman of our association of truck gardeners, I was trying to improve the situation of these garden plot holders, who lacked all rights. One day, I went with one of the members, a pensioner, to buy beer at the kiosk. I had a three-liter jar. When we arrived, we saw that it was closed. But a cop got out from a police car parked nearby, walked over to the kiosk, and it opened. There were about six or seven people in the line. I also got in line, and about eight more came in behind us. I bought two mugs of beer for each of us and filled the jar. Almost immediately after I was served, the kiosk closed again.

We have a category of criminals or semicriminals who constantly break the law but enjoy protection of the police, who use them as informers and thugs. In retrospect, it's clear that they were just waiting for me to be served. I put the jar on the table, as we drank from the mugs. Meanwhile, this guy swaggers up, notices that the kiosk is closed, then points to my jar and says, "Ah, there's beer. The kiosk is open!" I put my hand over the jar and said: "No, it's closed." As he walked passed me, he hit me hard in my side. I immediately grabbed the jar and brought it down on his head. It broke into smithereens. Sensing what was brewing, I told the old man to walk away quickly but calmly to where there were more people.

At least six people took part in the beating. Some kids told my wife that I was lying unconscious, and she came running. The police arrived and took me to the hospital. But I was not attended to. No one even asked where I was injured. They just left me on a bed in the ward. After a day of that, I told my wife to take me home. She hired an ambulance, and somehow I managed to get up the four flights of stairs into the apartment. Afterward, some people came from the city health department to ask what had happened. A doctor visited me, and I was finally taken to the hospital again.

That year, 1980, was really the start of what was perhaps the most difficult period of my life. On October 18, I was summoned to the Rostov provincial party archives and told that a request had come from the Central Party Archives of the Institute of Marxism-Leninism in connection with the rehabilitation of my father's party status. I was astounded, since I thought he had already been rehabilitated by the party in 1938. They told me that in the 1950s party rehabilitations had not been automatic, only upon request. Following their instructions, I wrote out a request and took it over to the provincial party committee. But since I knew what the regional party authorities thought of me, I sent an identical request to the Central Committee.

On January 10, 1981, I received an unusually polite call from the city party committee asking me to come by at my convenience. They showed me the resolution of the Control Commission of the party Central Committee rehabilitating my father. But a formal rehabilitation is one thing, and the restoration of his name to history is quite another. That requires gathering archival data on my father's revolutionary and Soviet years. This was really the task of the party's archivists and historians, but I knew they wouldn't do that. So I started on it myself.

For six years, wherever I turned in search of material, I was met at first with a friendly, positive reception which soon turned into an attitude of total noncooperation. You see, the various higher and regional party authorities to whom I made requests would ask the Rostov provincial committee about me. The provincial committee, of course, piled filth on me. I wrote over 700 letters. And I became more and more depressed. After all, it wasn't about me, but about a Bolshevik. Yet at every step I encountered the meanest sort of antibolshevism. Only my wife knows the depth of my despair. On May 24, 1983, I attempted suicide by taking all the narcotic-bearing medicines we had in the apartment. My wife found me unconscious and got me to the hospital in time to save me.

After that, my requests related to my father went unanswered. I understood that they were exploiting the suicide attempt to label me as crazy. As in 1962, when I tried to kill myself in jail, a terrible indifference came over me. I shed no more tears and pulled no punches. I went to Azerbaidzhan, and in the end managed to collect over 100 documents. Now there is a street named after my father in Neftegorsk and a memorial plaque. A series of articles were published too. Those few things cost me dearly. Antibolshevism remains antibolshevism.

In the course of that struggle, I had forgotten about the Novocherkassk tragedy. But a certain professor, whose name I probably shouldn't mention, was working on the material in Moscow, and in the fall of last year [1987] he said to me, "Petr Petrovich, it's time for you to raise the issue of your mother's and your own rehabilitation." [As a result of Siuda's efforts, his mother was rehabilitated in 1989.] It was only when I returned home, that his words "...and your own" really sunk in. In December, I sent requests to the Central Committee, to the Presidium of the Supreme Soviet of the USSR, and to the Supreme Court. I was after the rehabilitation of the events themselves, of the Novocherkassk workers' protest.

The law stipulates a three-month maximum period within which there must be a reply. That was in December 1987. Three months went by without a reply. I left my work in March in order to devote my energies to this cause.

And how do you manage?
Well, we are poor.

Aren't you afraid of being arrested for parasitism? [The Soviet law required that every able-bodied citizen not studying or taking care of dependents be employed by the state or the cooperative sector.]
This is how I explained it to the local party bureaucrats: How are Gorbachev, Ligachev, and the first secretary of the provincial party committee, Volodin, employed? They are engaged in public activity. The only difference between them and me is that they are very well paid for it in cash and privileges. So why should I have fewer rights than them?

What support have you received from other victims of the repression or their relatives?
Although I have found people who agree with my position, none want to be active. For example, the local Komsomol paper published an article in response to my essay. Of course, it gave a terribly distorted account, but I thought that at least a few of those who had been condemned would get in touch with me. Only one came to me. He approves of what I am doing, but he's too frightened to join me. He has a family, and so forth. Why stir up old matters? Why draw attention to oneself again? One day I received a call from the wife of one of the thirteen who were sentenced with me: "The children didn't know why he was in the camp, and now, thanks to you, they found out!" That's the atmosphere. In general, the Novocherkassk events of 1962 served as a weight upon people's conscience everywhere. And, of course, it was heaviest in Novocherkassk.

But what of the relatives of those who were killed? Surely they tried to find out where they are buried?
They haven't, and to this day we don't know where they are buried. [Over 100 victims were immediately buried in unmarked mass graves and the soldiers who buried them were forced to take an oath of silence under pain of death. The graves were revealed in

1990 by an officer who had supervised the burial.] But even if people are still afraid to become active, there is a lot of interest. That issue of the Komsomol paper became an instant best-seller. People began to remember and talk among themselves. Public opinion is beginning to budge. One comrade recounted a meeting of party activists with Artemov, the local delegate to the Nineteenth Party Congress. Someone asked him how he felt about breaking down the walls of silence that surround the Novocherkassk tragedy. He tried to give the official line, but people shouted, "Give us your own opinion. What do you intend to do?" The hall erupted in shouts. Finally a resolution was voted unanimously "to create a commission to investigate and evaluate the events objectively."

Why is it important that workers know about the events, and what lessons should they draw from them?

First of all, I want the tragedy to be a part of the public record so that—and I won't mince words—if blood is shed again, it won't be only workers' blood. But I hope that the lessons of Novocherkassk will help to avoid such tragedies. Today, I see much that is analogous to that period. A process of democratization is occurring. Yes, we have gone further this time. In those days, there were revelations about the crimes of Stalin, Khrushchev's predecessor. Today, there are also revelations about Stalin's crimes, but they go deeper and further back than the period from 1934 to 1953. That's all good. They're telling us that it will never happen again, that they are giving us democracy. Moreover, there is even a kind of self-revelation about corruption at the highest levels, though this too is presented as a thing of the past.

But despite everything, the initiative in this perestroika and the main levers of power remain in the hands of the party-state bureaucracy. The Novocherkassk events revealed the truth about the Soviet state: it's a state of the bureaucracy standing on the platform of Stalinism and oppressing the workers behind a false facade of revolutionary ideology—that has not changed. At the beginning of this year, during a visit to Shakhty, Central Committee Secretary Lukyanov said that if the party had not spoken out in time—that is, if it had not introduced glasnost and perestroika—then the people would have taken to the streets.

So you see, glasnost and perestroika are not gifts from the

authorities but a small sacrifice that they were forced to make in order to save what is fundamental to them. They wanted to make the state more efficient. They knew that anger in society was mounting. They had to let out some of the steam to reduce the pressure.

What do you think about Yeltsin?
I'm not a fan of functionaries. Our party has been formed in such a way that to make one's career in the bureaucracy, you have to pass through a school of baseness and filth. The higher your office, the more seriously you have been tested. What do I mean by test? I mean that a bureaucrat will not betray the interests of the bureaucracy. That's why I didn't expect much from the proclamation of glasnost and perestroika.

The party-state elite are making small sacrifices; they are giving up the privileges and the prerogatives of the middle managers. And these mid-level bureaucrats are burning mad at Gorbachev and the others who brought in glasnost and the right to criticize them. But as soon as a real threat arises—not to the middle level, because the elite is ready to sacrifice it—but to the elite itself, or to part of it, then they will take the offensive.

A lot depends on leadership and organization. That's why I'm active in the social movement. But I was recently at a conference at one of Moscow's economics institutes. Speakers there argued that the fate of perestroika depends upon the intelligentsia, and not the workers. In fact, they denied any role for the workers. I told them they were speaking nonsense, that when the real test of forces comes, when people take to the streets and blood is shed, they will bear the moral responsibility, because they won't be able to offer any leadership. The intelligentsia is, and will remain, helpless without the workers.

The socialist intelligentsia must unite and go to the workers. It should stop its idle chattering in the corridors. The workers need an analysis of the fate of the workers' movement in Poland, of the Novocherkassk events, of the relationship between the workers' and national movements. But this process of unification of socialist forces is proceeding with great difficulty, and, of course, the regime is doing its utmost to prevent it.

Most of the intelligentsia is far from socialist. If its socialist minority

doesn't succeed in forging organic links with the workers, what are the chances that the liberal or nationalist intelligentsia will win them over?

I don't think that the workers will follow the "Westerners," who, after all, really want to restore capitalism. That goes double for groups like the Democratic Union [a militant liberal organization], which looks nostalgically to the prerevolutionary period, as well as for *Pamyat* [an ultranationalist movement], which claims the revolution was a Zionist plot.

But we have to recognize that at the start of the 1920s, even during Lenin's lifetime, a shift occurred and the revolution went off course. We should not dream of a return to the NEP [New Economic Policy] period [1921 to 1927, when there was a partial restoration of capitalism], and least of all to the prerevolutionary period. We should fight for the full control over the state by society, for genuine democracy, the kind that existed at the start of the revolution, when the popular masses took the fate of the country into their collective hands, and for the eventual withering away of the state apparatus. For that to happen, the workers must form independent organizations opposed to the apparatus, loyal to the interests of the workers, and controlled by the workers.

Despite everything, the workers somehow still believe in Bolshevism. I'm not saying that because I'm the son of an old Bolshevik. They intuitively understand that the healthy development of the country must occur on a socialist basis. That's their class instinct.

II

WORK IN THE PERESTROIKA PERIOD

Kolya Naumov: Autoworker
[July 1988]

I met Kolya, a foreman at a large Moscow auto plant, at a meeting of the "informal" movement. He did not hide his skepticism about this meeting, which had been called to formulate a common position on the official theses for the forthcoming party conference. It was little more than a parade of speakers, each insisting on the particular views of his or her own group. Yet these views seemed practically indistinguishable one from the other, particularly in their preoccupation with abstract principle at the expense of the concerns of ordinary people.

We agreed to meet at the *dacha*-museum of a children's writer and literary critic. For the last several years, Kolya had been spending much of his free time there as a guard and guide to the visitors. He was actively involved in the drawn-out battle to obtain official museum status for the *dacha* against the corrupt Writers' Union, which was trying to reclaim it from the deceased writer's family.

In the still, late summer afternoon, we sat on the veranda drinking tea, surrounded by pine trees and luxuriant flowers, an idyllic setting that seemed worlds away from the subject of our conversation.

I grew up in a provincial town. I liked to build things, read drafts, and buy technical journals. My grades were very good and I wanted to be an engineer. But when I went to the polyclinic to get a medical certificate to apply for admission to the institute, the eye doctor, a very nasty woman, saw that I couldn't read a single letter on the chart. She yelled, "You want to study at the institute?! With those eyes they won't accept you anywhere!" I didn't know any better, so I decided to enroll in *tekhnikum* [professional-technical school]. They were surprised to see someone with my grades, but they accepted me. I graduated with top marks in all subjects, except for a B in military training. I studied to be a mechanic specializing in machine repair.

After a year of classes, they sent us for practical training to a factory. Then one day, out of the blue, they said to us, "How about going to Moscow? There are great jobs waiting for you, and you'll see the capital." We went without the slightest clue about what we'd be doing. As it turned out, they had brought us to work on the assembly line. It was 1970, and there was a general shortage of workers. Of course, it wasn't at all what we'd been trained for.

I was eighteen. Some of us were seventeen. Those under eighteen were supposed to be on a reduced workday, but there was nothing of the sort. The day I arrived, they handed me a pair of overalls and put me on the night shift. Being a conscientious kid, I tried to do everything I was told. I kept up at first, but at a certain point I began to fall behind. I was running, running. Sometimes the line stopped, and I'd try to catch up but I just couldn't. My back ached. I had to put a gasket on the pipe of the gas tank, attach some wires, smear black glue on the tank, and stick on a piece of cardboard. Finally, I realized that I was totally exhausted. I felt like shouting, "When will you finally stop?" The assembly line is a cruel, horrible thing.

Eventually I got used to it. But later, I saw that healthy guys who had just finished their military service refused to do that work. They insisted on starting at something lighter and demanded a training period. I didn't known enough to do that.

Were there breaks?
Well, there is one official break, but it's usually ignored, since we often run out of parts and can't work anyway. The idle periods become our breaks. We live from day to day, because every day, in every shop, in every factory in the entire country people are running, running and they still don't meet schedules. Something isn't shipped on time, something doesn't arrive, some yell, others make excuses. It's crazy—always running in place with everyone yelling, "Faster! Faster!" and the country is still in a constant mess. The parts

that should have arrived at the start of the month are only shipped out at the end.

I've been working for many years now, but I still haven't developed the strength or the nerves for it, because you can't plan anything. You want to buy a ticket to go home to visit your mother on Saturday, but you never know—they might decide it's a workday. Of course, you could decide not to show up, but they'll remember that and pay you back for it.

What happened to your studies at technical school?

We worked half a year at the factory in Moscow, and it came time to write the final paper on machine repair for school. Of course, we didn't know a thing. So we got a textbook, copied from it, and sent the papers home. We were made fourth-grade repair mechanics [with sixth the highest grade]. Our teacher, who was quite a character, told us, "If you parasites return home and I catch you, I'll thrash the daylights out of you. I've managed to get you fourth grade, but you don't know a damn thing about equipment repair. You'd better stay in Moscow, because you'll disgrace me here." In Moscow they didn't object to our staying. They promised us permanent residence permits and apartments after three years, so we stayed. [Residence permits were required to move to a big city. Enterprises were allotted "limits" or quotas for immigrant workers, called *limitchiki*, who were given temporary permits.]

We lived in a dormitory for temporary workers, sixteen in a room, working in three different shifts. We came from all over. The foreman would come in the morning and wake up the ones on the morning shift. But the last shift had come in at midnight and was still sleeping and they would shout for us to be quiet. Of course, we weren't. And so every shift took its revenge on the next. We never got into real fights, but there was plenty of cursing and pillow throwing. The pillow fights were actually a lot of fun.

We ate in the factory cafeteria—coffee, a piece of salami. Sometimes we'd load up on loaves of white bread and cartons of milk. That was our food. No vitamins at all. That was probably when my gums began to go bad. Generally, I lived for many years without vitamins. Milk, a piece of cheese, salami, and bread. At the factory, you could get meat patties, sickening sour-cabbage soup, or milk soup. Most of the kids were from the countryside. Their bodies had developed under more normal conditions, and their health was better than mine.

The majority were Russians, Ukrainians, Armenians. More Armenians than Georgians. Also Azerbaidzhanis. There were few Uzbeks then, but now there are many more because they don't have enough jobs at home. They're recruited for three years and then they return. This is especially true since the *limita* was ended. [Though formally closed in 1986, there remained many exceptions, legal and illegal.] Before that, you worked for three years as a *limitchik* and then got a permanent residence permit. [These workers were, in effect, "guest workers" inside the Soviet Union.] Now after three years, you are told goodbye. It's convenient for the factory, since it doesn't have to supply these people with apartments and child care.

So you lived three years in the dormitory?

What three years! I lived there fourteen years. Of course, I spent only the first six months in a room with fifteen others. We were young, and it was a good time. On Sunday, we would rest. We'd send messengers for wine, milk, loaves of white bread. We'd lie on our beds and a mountain of empty packages would rise up in the corner of the room. In the evening we went to dances at one of the factory clubs.

After six months, most of my school friends went to the army for two years. I was exempt because of my eyes. I was moved to a different dorm. I was lucky to get a one-room apartment with four others. It had a kitchen, bathroom, and hot water, unlike the old dorm. In our department, there's a large changing room for 500 people with lockers and a small shower room with about fourteen stalls. But not everyone uses the showers. Some just wash at the sink.

Do you get work clothes?

Yes, that's free. At some factories they wash them for you, but not ours. When we first arrived, we would build up a layer of dirt that you could scrape off with a knife. I've noticed that young people don't take care of their work clothes. But people with a certain amount of work experience acquire the pride and dignity of a skilled worker. They keep their clothes and workplace clean and neat and take care of their instruments. Young workers don't give a damn.

They come just to kill time until the dances begin and don't care what really happens.

The relations between workers on the line are sometimes very interesting. For example, we were installing the front seats, me the left and him the right. The car is at waist level. We're yakking all the time. He'd fall behind and I'm already on the next car. Then he appears again, and you take up where you left off. We even developed our own language, variations on anecdotes that I won't repeat here, or just interesting ideas. We'd think them up at home and come to the factory not so much to work as to socialize with each other. Sometimes we'd laugh until our sides ached. This happens to everyone, especially when you find an interesting friend you get along with well.

Of course, even with experience it isn't easy. Sometimes a worker will be absent, and the foreman asks you to do two jobs. For example, installing the track for the seat as well as the seat itself. It's possible, but very hard. After a while, you fall behind. Everything is swimming before your eyes, and you feel nauseated. I remember one day I was given a new job that involved using an automatic screwdriver. I tried to work conscientiously, but the thread on the screws was bad. Everything is garbage here, the screws, the thread. The screws wouldn't go in, and I had to use force as if it were an ordinary screwdriver. I strained all my muscles and the next day I couldn't move my hand. But they made me work anyway. I was crying, but no one believed me. It happens that people cry on the assembly line. They fall and faint too. All kinds of things happen.

There's no air-conditioning, of course. In the winter, it's pretty well-heated but there are drafts, since there are no heat curtains. But it's cold in the spring and especially in the fall when there is an unexpected cold spell and the heating hasn't been turned on yet. We have a plan, after all. If it says the heat goes on on November 15, they won't violate the plan—even if snow has already fallen on October 15. So we steal pieces of the foam material they use for the seats, cut out holes for the neck and arms, and make jackets. The air's bad around the paint shop. It's supposed to be enclosed in glass, but the glass is often broken. Around the acid baths, it's really sickening.

Does the speed of the assembly line vary? Has it changed over the years?

The speed really isn't that important. What matters is what you're doing, how many operations. If management sees someone can leave to take a smoke or is earning too good a wage, they give him an extra operation. The intensity has actually changed. When I came in 1970, piece rates were reduced every year until Andropov came to power [1982]. After Andropov, there were some attempts to introduce innovations. We couldn't make any sense of them.

When they increased the intensity, it was presented officially as a productivity gain. But that's supposed to happen on the basis of new machinery, right? Every year the ministry ordered us to cut the number of workers. But what innovations can you think up on the assembly line? They just cut and increase the intensity. The director would order the department head to cut twenty workers out of 200, without any change in the technology. They'd eliminate a job, divide up the operations, and add them to other jobs. But they didn't increase the wages of the people who got the extra operations. In that way, piece rates fell, though take-home pay might have risen somewhat because every year the plan target rose. They would tell you that you have to do 150 every day; next year, 154; next, 160; and so forth. And we're running faster and faster.

This was under Brezhnev?

Yes. Maybe under Stalin too, for all I know. And come to think of it, it happened under Andropov too. I remember now that they reduced the number of workers by something like 12 percent. Anyway, by a lot. But they increased the wages of the rest. Starting from 1984, our new director raised the wages.

We have two shifts now and two lines, the body assembly and final assembly. The foreman distributes the jobs. The workers really know only that some operations are harder than others. But, yes, they do try to get jobs that pay a bit more. No one ever came by with a chronometer.

It happens like this. You're working on a somewhat easier job. Then another job is cut and its operations are distributed, and you get some of them added to your job. At first you say, "No way! I won't do it!" They answer, "You will or you can leave. We don't need you." Everyone resists at first, and either "sliding" workers [those not permanently assigned to any job who take over when line workers are absent] or the foreman himself will do it. But in the end, some worker will do it.

In order to meet plan targets, we have to make more cars toward the end of the month. The bosses quietly speed up the line. The workers finally notice that they can't keep up even though they are running. They get mad and begin to yell, "They've increased the speed again!" The bosses deny it. This occurs at the level of department heads. The director, on the face of it, opposes such practices. When the workers complain at a meeting, he says, "Tell me who increased the speed and I'll punish him." And this happens all the way down the line, even though the administration at all levels is in on the speedup. They all lie to the workers, who have difficulty seeing through this complicated mechanism.

When a norm-setter comes up to you and says, "We've been watching you, and we have to add some operations to your job," you have to yell for all your worth, "You can't! I'm already overloaded!" That's the only way a worker struggles. You have to know how to shout, turn red, go nuts, so that they'll be afraid of you.

The norm-setter, of course, is himself under tremendous pressure from his superiors. He is told to discover hidden productivity reserves, to cut back on the work force. If you are a quiet, conscientious person, you might object a bit: "It's too hard, I can't." But you'll end up doing it, and they'll pour it on until you die or leave. I finally left.

Is there a lot of absenteeism?

Not really. Basically they'll tell the foreman, "My television is on the blink, and I called the repairman. He said he'd come sometime during the day." Or else the mother-in-law has come, or he has to drive his wife to see her mother or has to get his children at the station. The foreman will say, "Okay, go and I'll put down that you worked today." Such are the relations. The foreman lets you go, and when there is work at night or a day off to be worked, you help him out. A worker understands it isn't the foreman's fault—the administration is forcing him.

If the foreman doesn't succeed in convincing the worker, the senior foreman comes, then the party organizer, then the department head. One guy, Serezha, told me how he had refused and then the head of the personnel department came down and even climbed into the body and embraced him, trying to get him to come out to work.

Do they get time and a half for that?
More. In the 1970s, they paid ten rubles for the extra shift. Later, it was raised to fifteen and then twenty, because workers wouldn't stay. Some get twenty-five. It varies depending on how hard the work is, like in our department.

Do workers use this as a way of putting pressure on the administration?
Yes. It's illegal to force someone to work overtime. The workers really don't threaten directly, but the foreman knows that if he pushes certain workers too far, they won't come out. He has to calculate all this when he's deciding whether to punish someone for a violation of discipline.

So this is the hardest part of the foreman's job. But sometimes he can't take it anymore, and he asks the senior foreman or department head to help. So there you are working on a car, and these three bozos are following you, "Come on, help us out. You know how difficult the situation is." Their arguments aren't rational. They're just pestering you until you can't take it anymore. And the longer you hold out, the more you force them to pester, the more they boil inside, and you know they're storing up the anger and someday they'll take it out on you. So at some point, you decide that if you continue to refuse, you'll completely ruin the relationship, and you give in.

I was telling you about Serezha. He finally agreed to work the night. The next day his "good buddy" the department head passed by and didn't even say hello.

That's why I didn't decide to become a foreman when I finished the *tekhnikum* and worked another year on the assembly line. I knew all the operations. It was hard, and I'm not so healthy. But I kept seeing strong young guys refuse hard jobs, which the foreman turned around and gave to me, so I finally left.

The worst is the psychological stress. If your health is normal, you get enjoyment out of the physical work. You don't get tired, you move without rushing, you joke. The movements have been mastered, and your muscles are developed. But the worst thing is when you know that there are only a half-hour's worth of parts left but three hours until the end of the shift. As you pick up each nut, you feel your heart dripping blood. When they're all gone, the assembly line will, nevertheless, keep on going. You keep telling the foreman that there soon won't be any nuts left, but he tells you to wait, something else is more urgent.

The foreman is constantly running. They aren't allowed to try to organize production. They are like loaders, constantly carrying something. When you've tightened the last bolt, you shout, "All gone!" and the foreman knows it's time for him to run for some more. Meanwhile, the car is moving, and when the nuts arrive, you have to catch up. The end of the shift is approaching, and you're thinking of grabbing a shower stall. Otherwise you have to wait in line in your underpants. They keep you going, and you yell, "No, I won't! Stop the line!"

So you left at the end of your fourth year.

I had a very good friend who had studied with me at the *tekhnikum* and was working as a repair mechanic in the section that repairs tools. He also didn't rise up into the administration but stayed a mechanic. He suggested I join him. The pay was less, but the work was easier. My eyes had begun to hurt a lot. The assembly line had changed: the cars were lower. I had to stoop over more, and that was bad for my eyes.

Do workers get any compensation for work on the assembly line? Is it in the "harmful" category? [Workers doing jobs officially classified as "harmful" received monetary compensation, discouraging demands for safety improvements which would be more costly to the administration.]

No. But about seven years ago, they introduced a bonus for work on the line. After three years, they pay you thirty or forty rubles extra a month. But if there is defective work, you lose both your regular and your assembly-line bonuses. My basic wage is 170 rubles a month, and my bonus is forty. Sometimes there is an extra bonus for exports if the cars are selling abroad.

And how do you manage on that?

My wife works at a different factory. She has a teenage son. We live from paycheck to paycheck.

I simply don't want to figure it out. There are workers who know everything: the export bonus, the quarterly bonus, and so forth. I'm just not interested. Of course, they can make a mistake; someone might have pressed the wrong button. But I simply have too many other interesting things to do. The newspapers have become so interesting, and I try to read them. That's why I feel a bit guilty about the factory.

Do you still work in the same place?
Yes, only now I'm a foreman. We got a raise recently. They cut the number of foremen in the shop from twenty to sixteen and raised their wages.

Do you earn more than the workers?
Less than the workers on the assembly line. They make about 200 rubles plus about seventy in bonuses, though I'm not completely sure about those figures. But with the raise, the foremen are catching up. Some foremen now get 185, without the bonuses, and the senior foremen get 200. That's pretty close to the workers' wages. In my instrument section, however, wages are low, less than what I make: 170, and that's with the bonus.

There are worker-operators and there are "sliding" workers, who fill in when someone is absent and are paid a bit more. There are usually four sliding workers in a section of about twenty to twenty-five workers. In practice, three usually work regularly on the assembly line as operators, and only one is one duty. But the foreman doesn't write that. It would be stupid. He writes that all four are on duty. For the three boxes in his report where it says he has no operators (since the sliding workers are doing that work), he writes the names of three workers from a different shift and a different section. In this way, over the course of the month, they earn the foreman 80 rubles, which he splits with them.

Are there many women on the assembly line?
That depends on the line. Where the body is welded and the fenders and hood attached, there are only men. It's hard, dirty work. Women work, for example, where the upholstering is done, and where they install little things that require dexterity, like small light bulbs. Our technology is dated, and we glue on a lot of rubber seals and insulation. Only women can do that well.

Do they earn the same as men?

Yes, except that there is some work that women don't do. It's hard work, so it's better paid. So you can say that men earn a little more.

Do women work the night shifts?

Yes, though it's illegal. And they get no special benefits. Of course, if they're pregnant, they're put on what is called light work.

What sort of women come to work on the assembly line?

Usually, they come when they are young. When I started at the factory, girls were coming from the villages. After military service, the men usually didn't return to the village. They'd go to some big construction site, to build the Baikal-Amur railroad in Siberia, or they'd come here. So potential husbands were scarce in the village. The girls left not just for Moscow but also for nearby cities. They'd come to Moscow if they had a relative or friends here already.

A girl would work a while on the line, get married, take maternity leave and stay with the child. Afterward, she'd get a job in charge of a storeroom at some factory; that is, she'd try to get some decent work. If she couldn't find any, then she'd come back to the assembly line. But generally, after having a child, they look for easier work.

Can you say anything about their cultural level?

They have all completed high school, that is, ten years of school. As far as I know, they like the cinema most, and some go to the film festivals. In the dormitories, there are inevitably photos of actors on the wall. They don't go much to the theater. It's hard to get tickets to good performances.

Some girls who end up here originally came to Moscow to study at some institute of higher education but failed the entrance exams and are ashamed to go home.

My wife used to work at a very old ball-bearing plant in the stamping shops. Young girls who hope to enter some institute often work there. After a few weeks, some might lose a finger or a hand. That happens a lot there because the equipment is in terrible condition. It's old. You're supposed to insert the detail using special tongs, but the women are in a rush and do it by hand. The older ones want to earn more, and the younger ones simply want to have a smoke. If the machines ran normally, nothing would happen. They insert the detail as the press rises, but unexpectedly it falls, crushing their hand, because it is out of order.

Is there any protest?

It doesn't go beyond shouting. It's smoldering anger. They don't see any way out. The traditions of struggle have been destroyed, and there is no experience. I think this is especially true of Moscow. There are no working-class traditions here. People come from the village. As far as I know, most cases of collective protest are over delays in paying wages.

In our factory, management once announced a "black Saturday," a working Saturday, and about 100 didn't come out to work. They were sick of it. One young worker united them. Actually, it happens quite often that workers don't come out to work on such days. Of course, it's frightening to do that individually. So some fifteen workers will agree among themselves to meet in the morning at the factory and go together to the movies.

One time, as I said, it wasn't fifteen but 100 workers. Management wanted to run two lines that Saturday, but there weren't enough workers. The next day the foremen were writing down the names of the instigators. It was arbitrary—they just put down whoever had shouted the loudest, for example. The administration decided to fire seven people. They also threatened to dock everyone else's thirteenth month [the annual bonus of one month's pay for over-fulfilling the plan].

So the workers decided to complain to the central committee of the Union of Workers of Automobile and Agriculture Machine Construction. They wrote a letter and collected signatures on the line. One foreman tried to grab it, so they hid it.

This was about seven years ago. I wasn't yet a foreman. I also signed, even though I worked that Saturday. The workers really got scared when I came to sign. They thought I was working for the administration. We all went together to the union's central committee here in Moscow. We told the officials how hard the work was, how we were forced each month to work nights and days off. They gave us understanding looks, "Can you believe that? And at such a renowned factory, too! What a disgrace!" Of course, they heard this every day from workers seeking justice.

We waited for a commission of inquiry to come. Actually, I think they tricked us. They said it was a commission from the union central committee, but it was only a commission of the factory's union committee. We appeared before it; I made a lot of noise. I told the administration that they were seeking guilty workers, when it was the administration itself that regularly violated the law. We said that we didn't care if they violated the law by setting overtime, but don't dare punish those who refused to work. In the end, they didn't fire anyone.

But they gradually managed to isolate the guy who had organized the action. The foreman would come up to him and say: "We called the KGB. They're coming for you, and your mother won't even know where you've gone." Or, "Did you see me walking over there with a man? He was from the KGB. They're interested in you."

Gradually, his comrades began to avoid him. That's why I went up to him and told him that I would raise hell if they took him. I wouldn't abandon him. I wasn't trying to muddy the waters. I was just trying to understand, like you now, if the workers are capable of acting collectively for their rights. In my time, I spoke up and did a lot and received a lot of unpleasantness for it. But I eventually realized that I was alone. I always tried to find allies, but I couldn't. That's why I went to him. The others were frightened. They knew that it would get back to the bosses that they were friendly with this troublemaker. And since, as I explained before, workers always need some favor from the foreman—the mother-in-law is coming, or there's a wedding—you don't want the foreman to be angry with you.

They isolated him. He was also having family problems, and he finally left the factory and Moscow too. Usually, the workers begin to fight when some common interest is threatened. They are solidary for a time, but gradually they get scared and move away from you. It isn't a fate to be envied. This happens because over the course of seventy years, informal relations have formed, that is, we don't live according to the formal laws that regulate worker-management relations, but according to informal agreements. Every worker has some favor to ask or some way to earn a little extra, and every boss also has ways of earning extra, for his summer home, for example. We are all linked together by these sins. And so when a fighter appears, and though you might really sympathize with him, you know you have some sin. Maybe in a burst of enthusiasm you will go shoulder to shoulder into battle with him. But you know that if you continue like that, they will inevitably dig up your sin.

Have your own views about management changed since you became a foreman?

Well, I can understand their psychology better now. I too thought all the bosses were loafers. Now I understand that they are under pressure from above as well as from below. You have to experience that yourself to understand. They aren't loafers but they are forced to bother with things that they really shouldn't be doing. Take our department head, our boss. We aren't fulfilling the plan. The assembly line has been turned off because some part is missing. The director comes into the department and presses the button that restarts the line. Cars are coming off the line and piling up in the department unfinished. What can the department head do? He should be doing his work, but the director is standing there. So he runs out, jumps into a car and drives off in search of the missing parts that some other department or factory has not delivered on time. I feel sorry for him. He's like a little boy when he's in front of the director, who can say to him: "Don't come to work tomorrow." I've personally seen that happen to foremen and senior foremen.

His superiors are pressing him to get things done. He curses them but accepts the situation as inevitable. The boss said to make 100,000 cars, and it's clear—the plan. But then you hear voices from down below, "No, we can't. Only 80,000." He knows that 100,000 cars will get him a summer home built and a medal. And suddenly, someone down there is throwing a spanner in the works. He'd like to crush that voice from below.

He's not really a bad person. I sometimes catch myself with those attitudes when the department head comes and says, "What do you mean—you can't fix that machine? It's nothing. What sort of foreman are you?" I come in and see one of my mechanics smoking or playing dominos. "What's the matter, can't you fix that machine?" I ask. "Give me the parts, and I'll fix it for you," he answers. I know I can't get the parts. But I also know it's easy to make them. But it isn't his job to make them, and the worker demands that I supply them.

So he sits and smokes. He can do that. But as foreman, I'm

responsible and I have no choice but to make the parts myself. Meanwhile, the department head is complaining about other things that I have not done, but I'm busy making those parts. So I begin to think of that mechanic as someone who is making my life difficult.

That's my view of how a manager thinks. He will curse his superiors, but he neither praises nor curses his workers. Rather, he says, "Ah, the people, I feed the people." You know, it's the idea that the workers are stupid, that if you don't chase them to work on their days off, they will die of hunger. The department head is like a military commander going to battle. Say some part is missing, and the line stops. He says to the foreman: "What do you mean you don't have any parts? What's this?" "That's for the left side. We need the part for the right side." "Nonsense!" he answers. He knows he could be prosecuted for it, but he takes the risk. He's a real leader. And so when someone says to him, "But that part doesn't fit specifications," he's ready to wipe him off the face of the earth. And he does.

That's how it is on all levels of management. Very tough. Any manager can be called in by his superior to be yelled and cursed at in the foulest language.

Can the department head use foul language with workers?
No, he can only yell at them in a friendly way, except of course in the privacy of his office without witnesses. They are very afraid of witnesses. They could be accused of violating the Leninist principles of leadership. And department heads have a lot of enemies looking for a pretext to hurt them, although everyone knows that everyone routinely yells and swears. Of course, he can curse his immediate subordinate, the foreman, without fear.

And can the foreman curse the workers?
He can, but it is a subtle question of judgment when to yell and when not to. The foreman senses if the worker will let him get away with it or if he will answer back in kind. It's important for a worker not to show he's soft—that he's really tough—or else the foreman will walk all over him. If the foreman knows the worker is tough, he'll be afraid of losing face. He'll only choose weak people to vent his wrath on.

When did you become interested in social and political issues?
When I grew up in the 1960s, I believed Khrushchev had done

away with Stalinism, that we had freedom and that no one was imprisoned unjustly any more. Then we heard that Khrushchev had "retired." [Khrushchev was forcibly ousted in October 1964.] Hints began appearing in our school textbooks that he had not been such a good leader. Also at that time, my father bought a radio and sometimes listened to the Voice of America. There I heard that Khrushchev had been forcibly removed. I was really surprised. And I began to see that our papers can lie. Still, I listened to the foreign broadcasts mainly for rock music, and what I heard on the newscasts left little impression.

But then I came to the factory and I understood that there was a great gap between what I was seeing there and what the papers wrote; that is, I finally got a glimpse of real life. At the same time, I was hearing on the foreign radio that people were being arrested. I began to take more interest, and it seemed to me that what they were saying on the Voice of America was really about my life, while what was written in the papers was something else—lies. So I simply rejected the regime; I began to feel they were bad people.

I wanted to share this with my friends at the plant. They listened to me patiently and asked questions. But I saw that it didn't really concern them. They didn't care that someone was arrested, someone was beaten or died in camp. They were interested in beer and soccer. I wanted things to change.

One of my first small attempts at protest was my refusal to come out to work on a Saturday. In 1970, when we were still at technical school, it was the hundredth anniversary of Lenin's birthday, and they organized a *subbotnik.* [Originally organized under Lenin, these were formally voluntary working Saturdays; people would clean streets, beautify their neighborhoods, or work a shift and donate the money to a political cause.] We sang songs and collected the dirty rags and rusty iron from the yard. Some *subbotnik!* No one thought to keep the yard clean all year round. I couldn't understand what this had to do with Leninism.

A year later, when we were already at the factory, they organized another *subbotnik* in Lenin's memory. I really lost any taste for it. But we came out to work on the assembly line. It was announced that the first secretary of the central committee of the Komsomol was coming with a delegation to participate in the *subbotnik.* Close to noon, a group of healthy, strong, handsome young men appeared. They worked an hour or an hour and a half and then disappeared. Then I read in *Komsomolskaya Pravda* that the first secretary had worked alongside the workers on the *subbotnik.*

When next year's *subbotnik* came along, I was already studying at night school while working the first shift on the line. We were supposed to come out for the night shift. Well, I was studying, and after all that had happened on the previous *subbotniks,* I decided with a group of friends that we weren't going. But the foreman found out about this, and the pressure began—from the administration, the party organizer, the trade union. Each in turn came over to talk and pester. It was very strong pressure.

In the end, I decided it would be simpler to come out. And it was a strange thing. When I began to work, I was fuming. But the work on the line had been well prepared for the *subbotnik.* The necessary quantities of parts were on hand, and the line ran smoothly. For a change, work conditions were good. Gradually, almost despite myself, I fell into the swing of things and even began to feel joy in my work. It wasn't just my sense of mastery over the machine, but the simple enjoyment of being able to work normally, to do decent work, something that is so rarely given to a Soviet worker.

Kolya Naumov
[December 1989]

When I returned to Moscow and resumed my interview with Kolya, perestroika was already going sour, with the economy entering a tailspin that at this writing still has no end in sight.

After I left the assembly line, I worked as a mechanic in the instrument section. My boss was a moron, a drunk, and a crook. One day, not long after I had begun to work for him, he called me into his office and said, "Kolya, would you like a little alcohol?" Well, I was thrilled that the boss had noticed me. He poured me a glass, added some water to it, stirred the mixture, and repeated the operation for himself. "Let's drink," he said. I drank and thanked him. But he hadn't touched his glass. So I said, "What about you, Ivan Fedorovich?" He said, "I'll sit a bit. I don't quite feel like it right now." I got up to leave, but he told me not to hurry and offered me a cigarette. I sat a while longer and finally said I really had to return to work. "Of course," he said. "Go ahead. I'll drink mine in a little while."

Satisfied with myself, I told the story to the manager of the storeroom, a desperate alcoholic. He told me that Ivan Fedorovich often invites him into his office for a drink while not drinking himself. "I know he's testing the alcohol on me—wood or grain. But I figure, if I croak, I croak." So the bastard kept me in his office while he was observing the effects of the drink!

That was fourteen years ago. I was just a beginning mechanic. When I saw how this person, who got drunk everyday and sold the factory's tools right and left, ran his shop, I began to think to myself, "If I became department head, I could put things in order."

My time finally arrived. I became foreman. For two or three years I worked like a dog. I killed myself running about the factory from the time I arrived in the morning until six or seven in the evening. I kept telling myself, "Just a little more effort and you'll have everything running smoothly." I paid left and right out of my own pocket to get things done.

Three years passed. By then, I had established my ties, I knew who to pay off with some tool, who with money, who with alcohol. And gradually, instead of working, I began to read a few pages of a magazine or a book. Sometimes I spent almost entire days reading. And my mechanics began to say about me what I had said about Ivan Fedorovich, "He's a lazy bastard. He only reads or plays chess." Of course, no one knows that I sometimes take a nap for half an hour. That would be a big scandal. But my mechanics say, "He doesn't do anything. He's a boss. And so why should we work?" To my face, of course, they appear to respect me.

Why were you unable to change things?

Where does one start? Before I became foreman, there was one instrument section under Ivan Fedorovich. Actually, he was senior foreman, but he called himself head of the instrument department. The problem was that all the machines stood in one of the divisions of the section, and when it was divided, Ivan Fedorovich got the machines, and we got nothing. But I have twice as much work as he does. To get something milled or cut, I had to pay his workers with alcohol or money.

You mean you didn't have access to the machines for repairing the tools?

He wouldn't let me use them. I went to the chief engineer, to the director of production, and explained the situation. They said they couldn't give me the machines because if they did, they would have to set some kind of plan for them. I asked how come Ivan Fedorovich had machines. They said that they were not officially there; he kept them illegally. He didn't want to have any trouble with Ivan Fedorovich, who is a relative of the factory's director. It would have drawn the director's attention to them if they took away or divided up his machines. And no one wants to remind the director of their existence at the factory any more than is absolutely necessary.

Why was the section divided in the first place?

We weren't meeting the plan, and they decided to make two sections with two bosses because it is easier to manage smaller sections.

Did they increase the number of workers?

No. But the increase in managerial and technical personnel is a rule, even under Gorbachev. They added two bureaus to the accounts department at the factory.

And how many workers was Ivan Fedorovich left with?

Two. And imagine! He had a factory car and driver. When he drank himself into a stupor, they'd load him into the car and cart him home.

Why did he have the car?

Sometimes we have to bring parts, instruments, polishing materials, and so forth, from the warehouse, which is a few kilometers away. When he needs something, he takes the car, but when I need something, I have to ask him. He says, "I can't give it to you now." Of course, I know why he can't: his driver took the car to fill it up at the factory pump and then drive it around to the employees' parking lot to sell it. He's always driving somewhere on private business. So in asking for the car for half a day, I was actually taking twenty-five rubles out of his pocket. I would have had to give him a present equal to that amount.

Of course, I couldn't. So I made a formal complaint. The director of production called me to his office. He got all worked up, shouted that Ivan Fedorovich's behavior was outrageous, impermissible. He called in the department head, Ivan Federovich's boss, and threatened him with the direst consequences if it happened again. The next day I went to Ivan Fedorovich and asked him for the car. I told him I had spoken to the director of production. He replied, "You complained, did you? Out of my sight! Now you'll never see that car." He has the director behind him.

In the first years, I was really burning with desire to put things in order. I would go to the department head and make suggestions. He would answer, "You know what? My headlight is broken. Do you think you can fix it?" So I found a turner, paid him out of my own pocket in the hope that the department head would help me in return. I came back to him and told him my ideas about improving work organization. He said, "You know, the handle fell off my car." Or, "I need a hole made in this detail." All he was interested in was his car or his summer cottage. He didn't give a damn about my suggestions. He didn't even hear them.

I think that Mikhail Sergeevich [Gorbachev], before he became general secretary, must have had thoughts similar to mine before I became a foreman. And now everyone in the shop hates me.

Surely, you exaggerate.

Well, maybe a little. For example, we have an automatic screwdriver. The longest it can last is two years. In 1983 I filled out an order for a new one. Six years have gone by, and we still haven't received it.

Your workers blame you for that?

Well, yes. I repair the tools, because I am conscientious. Ivan Fedorovich has probably already thrown away ten wrenches, while I'm still working with the same one, because I repair it. I'm sure that I've received many times fewer tools than he has because I take care of them and repair them. But life is good to him, he receives tools and sells them, earns money for alcohol and bribes some clerk to write off the instruments as worn out, and his workers are satisfied.

What do you do when you need to use a machine?

I secretly ask one of his mechanics—they all secretly hate him—and I pay. In my opinion, I pay them too much. Sometimes, I go to the director of the accounts department and ask them to pay, and they do. But sometimes I pay out of my own pocket.

The workers try to do the work when Ivan Fedorovich is not looking, because he wants things to go badly for me. He wants the higher-ups to see that he can work better than me. Meanwhile, the machines stand idle in his shop. Complain as I might, no one will help. Sometimes, to get a detail ground, bored, or milled, I have to spend the whole day running around the factory asking the machine operators. And the department heads keep changing. Just when I have finally explained the situation to one, another one comes and gives me jobs to do.

How many workers are there in your section?

Five. Actually, I am supposed to have eight, but I could theoretically manage with three. Periodically I go to the accounts department to complain that I can't manage with the number of workers I have. I also inflated the value of the equipment.

If I officially should have eight, I get five. When I said I could manage with three, I meant three skilled workers who really want to work and maintain the equipment. In practice, because wages in the shop are so low, I know I can't get capable, motivated workers. They'll send me an alcoholic who can't get a job anywhere else, an invalid, or a pensioner. And it takes eight of these weak, unskilled, unmotivated people to do the job. Sometimes it is less trouble for me to do their work for them.

Why are wages so low?

Compared to the assembly line, for example, the work is cleaner, less strenuous, there aren't any drafts. So I get cooks and barbers and I have to train them. But no sooner are they trained than they quit and someone else is sent. I'm the most skilled and experienced person. There is no job I can't do. So in the end, I say to myself, "If I'm so experienced, they can pay me for my experience. I'll read the paper. If anything happens, I'll make sure the job gets done." That's how I've come to justify my reading.

Why didn't you try to organize your shop into a contract brigade?

[Under this system, the brigade contracts with management to furnish a certain quantity and quality of work by a certain date in return for the materials, tools, and a total wage package which is divided among its members. Thus, any economies of labor and materials mean higher wages.]

You might ask why Gorbachev hasn't been able to organize a market. I have tried. The head of department of accounting always answers, "Kolya, I'll think about your suggestion. It's interesting. But right now I have to calculate these things here." And she is constantly calculating and recalculating. Wage rates are constantly changing. Either it is a new model or the speed of the assembly line or something else. Or maybe she just doesn't want to be bothered with me.

I go to her about once a year with my request. To go more often would risk getting her angry, and I depend upon her good will. I mentioned, for example, that she sometimes gives me money to pay workers in other shops to do jobs for me.

Not long ago, I paid a couple of workers from another department to help me steal a drill press that we desperately needed. I keep it hidden in a hole I made in the wall. This is one of the sins that you have to commit if you want to do your job. But any administrator who wanted to take revenge on me could use those sins. That is why I'm not at the forefront of the rather small group of people fighting for change at the factory.

You mentioned that Ivan Fedorovich sold instruments. Have you done that?

No, I give them away. Not expensive ones, of course. Anyway, I don't have his connections. But workers come to me and say, "Kol, I really need these flat-nosed pliers." It's not a big deal. Everyone does it. For the majority, if they don't carry something off, even if it's only a rusty nail or a bolt, it's as if the day has been wasted. Their feet don't want to carry them through the gate (laughs). I'm kidding, of course, but there's a measure of truth in that. And it's considered natural to use factory equipment during work time to make things you need at home. No disgrace is seen in that.

There are some thoroughly corrupted elements. But most would like to change things if they saw a way. Attitudes are changing. Last summer, I sat in on a meeting between the director and workers in the red corner [a place for meetings on the shop floor] of the assembly shop. The issue was the work schedule for 1990. Until then, there had never been any discussion with workers of schedules. This year, the administration proposed that the labor collectives decide what labor regime they preferred: two shifts of seven hours and forty minutes or two of seven hours and fifty minutes. [The work week is forty-two hours.] In the second case they would have fewer "black Saturdays." Most shops had voted to have less. Some even proposed to work eight-hour shifts in order to reduce working Saturdays to a minimum.

Management wanted to keep the old schedule. With seven-hour and fifty-minute shifts, the second shift would finish work well after midnight. Even now, with a seven-hour, forty-minute shift, workers quit a little early in order to catch the suburban trains. Moscow is growing, and there are people who travel an hour or an hour and a half to work. The time to get washed and changed is not included in the work time. Of course, there are also some lazybones like myself who just want to leave a bit early (laughs).

Management calculates that they can produce 2,500 cars on each of these Saturdays. That's because the assembly line can be idle for entire days. They need the Saturdays to be sure to meet the plan, since they can't guarantee a regular rhythm of production.

So in order to get the work collectives to change their minds, the director decided to meet with them. I can still see his hulking figure. He barely gets the words out from behind his teeth. He's tired. Instead of the planned 120,000 cars for this year, we will make only 60,000. He's tired from running around to the ministries and Gosplan [State Planning Commission], asking them to "correct" the plan down to 60,000. He can't admit to the workers that he lied to them and to his superiors when he accepted the plan. That's probably why his tone is so sad and disgusted.

He blames it all on the factory's reconstruction and expansion, which are behind schedule. Some say the mafia is standing behind him warming its hands on the huge construction project. Lately, management has been laying the blame on the poor training and lack of professionalism of the adjusters of the machine-assembly works.

Anyway, at the meeting in the red corner, the workers become aggressive. Someone asked, "Why does the speed of the assembly line vary?" It happens that a whole shift is idle, and the next day they speed up the line to make up for the lost time. Then the next day, they are idle again, because the departments and factories that supply the line are in any case late with their deliveries. The director's answers show management's inability to organize production in a normal way. They only make the workers angrier. They call him a liar. They propose to make cuts in the white-collar personnel. They believe that they will be able to raise their wages that way. In the end, they voted for the seven-hour fifty-minute shifts. After that, the director was afraid to organize a meeting with our department.

A recent trade union conference was similarly stormy. One of the issues raised was the purchase of machinery in France and Italy that turned out to be completely unsuitable for the factory. At the conference it was alleged that this occurred because the director's son was sent instead of engineers and workers who would be working on the machines and who knew the specifications. The director defended himself by arguing that he wasn't even in his post when this occurred. Nothing came of all this, of course, but even a little while ago such a discussion would have been unthinkable.

The press and officials often blame workers for everything. That's pure demagoguery when you realize that workers have no say in how things are run. As for the technical and administrative personnel, it varies really. There are bastards and there are honest people among them—a few real fighters who want to improve things have appeared lately at the factory, and they have the workers' support. But generally, the workers see them as parasites, and relations have become very tense. This is not only because the workers see the number of technical and administrative personnel growing and their wages rising faster than those of workers, but they see a lot of corruption.

The factory's new car model is a big seller. The employees have their own separate waiting line for purchasing cars, and several dozen are now sold each year compared to maybe ten in previous years. Of course, to start with, the price is enormous, something like 10,000 rubles or maybe more, I don't know, and the average worker is somehow convinced that no one could come upon such a sum honestly.

The obvious corruption starts when the employee whose turn has come wants special treatment for his car. In order to get it painted with metallic paint, which is in short supply, he shells out some 500 rubles to the appropriate department head. He does the same thing to have four-point welding instead of the usual two, to have two coats of rust-proofing instead of one, and so forth. He even pays management for a safe, enclosed place to leave the car overnight while it dries out. After all, it's a very good car, and the mafia is well informed about everything that goes on. More than one such car has been stolen right at the factory. This spread of corruption provokes a lot of anger among the workers.

I think sometimes of leaving the factory. But I don't know. There is a potential there, and in the end, I love these people. I love how they keep their wonderful sense of humor even under the most adverse conditions, their native intelligence and resourcefulness.

I sometimes think of the workers in my home town. Incredible people. They'd arrive at work in the morning bursting with energy and go to tremendous lengths, organize the most complicated operations, running great risks, including a jail sentence, just to get the money to buy some vodka at the end of the day, to sit around with some comrades who will hug each other, maybe end up punching each other's lights out, and then hug again and make up. If this talent and energy were put to a positive use, it could perform miracles.

I'll stay for now. I'll manage whatever happens. The religious values I inherited from my mother and grandmother give me stability. But I'm worried more about you, with your socialism and faith in the workers. How will you survive disappointment?

Mariya Tkacheva and Lyuba Mineeva:
Two Generations of Workers
at the Optical Factory
[October 1990]

My meeting with Mariya and Lyuba was arranged by Galya, a journalist friend. Galya was originally from Lytkarino, a town about an hour from Moscow, where her parents had worked at the optical factory. Along with her parents, Mariya and Ivan, Galya invited a younger couple, Lyuba and Sergei. Lyuba works with Mariya at the optical factory. Sergei is an electrician at a Moscow warehouse.

[MARIYA] I was born in a village in Tambov province. My parents, who were poor peasants, told me how they worked for rich peasants, not for wages but for satin ribbons. And they were lucky to get even that work. There was typhus. Whole families fell sick, and many died. My father died around the time of my birth. My three brothers all died: one at the front and another from burns when a kettle overturned on the stove. After my last brother's death, my mother and I were all alone. She worked her whole life in the *kolkhoz* [collective farm] and although she had lost her husband and sons and was sick herself, she received no assistance from the state. Only later did the state pay her thirty-six rubles a month for the son killed at the front.

Life in the village was very hard. My husband left for Lytkarino and enrolled in the technical school there in a carpenter's course. When he came for me in 1950, he was living in a dormitory, in a room with six others. The superintendent of the dormitory was very angry that he had brought me, but where could we live? We had no money to rent a private room—my husband was earning seventy rubles a month, and I was unemployed. My mother couldn't help, since she herself was so poor. All we had to our name was a broken-down bed and some spoons, not even a frying pan.

At night, we hung sheets for privacy, and during the day we hid everything away, because women were not allowed there. The superintendent would shout at us. He wanted us to leave, especially after

I gave birth to Nina. Sometimes she cried at night, and one of the lads would come over and offer to rock her. "Let Masha, at least, get a little sleep," he'd say. That's how we lived.

When they called my husband up to the army, I was given a room seven meters square in the dormitory. There I had my second daughter, Galya, while my husband was away. I took my two months' maternity leave in the village and then returned to Lytkarino with Nina and Galya. Soon after, I brought my mother.

Then I went to work, and the work was hard. In the morning I took the children to a nanny who lived a kilometer away, and I picked them up in the evening. After two days, Galya got sick. I slept in the hospital with her. My mother took them to the village for the summer. It was a hard time. There were all kinds of food, but there was no money. No one went to the *kolkhoz* market. I don't even go now, since it is so much more expensive than the state stores.

When I first came from the village, I worked paving roads. It wasn't so easy to get a job in a good shop at the factory. Eventually, I got work in one of the factory's shops polishing copper parts. We were mainly women, and the work was dirty. Polishing makes a lot of dust. There were no masks, and the ventilation would almost immediately get clogged up. But I didn't even take my vacation; I took compensation instead.

In 1959, I got a job in a shop that makes military optical equipment, and that is where I worked until my retirement a few years ago. I also got my husband a job there, as an optical mechanic. When we began producing night-vision equipment, we worked almost twelve hours a day. The shop had a lot of trouble mastering this new production. Sometimes, when my girlfriend and I were walking home, we'd say, "Let's hang ourselves from this birch tree. Tomorrow they'll say that two friends died from overwork." We got filthy from the putty. The lenses were cleaned with ether, which was not officially considered harmful. We'd walk into a store, and someone would remark that we smelled like a hospital.

[GALYA] She spent her whole life in that ether. That's why workers there have such a high cancer rate. It's harmful work, and they don't even receive extra pay for that. I remember how Mama would come home and tell us about the anarchy at the factory. They are supposed to clean the apparatus with alcohol, not ether. But the administration steals the alcohol. The supervisor doesn't even try to hide the flasks she is stealing. I used to ask, "Why are you silent?" And she would only answer, "We're helpless."

[MARIYA] Yes, the supervisors and the bosses sold alcohol. Workers didn't get any. The workers had nothing to steal. Who needs pieces of metal? There were very expensive light bulbs, but they were carefully controlled. In order to sell this alcohol, they disregarded our health. The whole administration lives off this alcohol, and they live well. Even when one of them got caught at the exit, the affair was hushed up. They take away carloads of the stuff.

We didn't like our supervisor. We were all afraid of cutbacks or transfers, so we were quiet. Workers were afraid of losing their jobs. I, for example, loved my work very much, even though it was complicated. The doctor once asked me what kept me there. She told me that I shouldn't be working with ether. But I continued to work there all the same. I once broke my arm and had to go to hospital. My first thought was, "How can I not go to work tomorrow?" I was afraid even to think about that.

My work was varied. I assembled four units a day. First you prepare a whole pile of parts, screws, lenses, bolts. Then you finish machining the eyepiece to the exact measurements. This is not mechanical work, like on the assembly line. You have to concentrate. The objective is very complicated, five lenses, each one with a mounting and a ring. It's very complicated work. Where I was working, we were almost all women. The guys worked only on the lathes.

Are there some jobs that only women or men do?
No. There were men doing the work I did.

If there was a lot of work, we got paid well. But there was a limit. I could go as high as 230 rubles, but the supervisor would never give me 250. If I made more, he would just put the units aside for next month's plan.

You mean that you were capable of producing and earning more that 230 rubles?
Of course. We would willingly have stayed past five, until seven in the evening—who wouldn't?

During the review of piece rates, they would read off the list, "This detail is worth so much; and this one is worth so much." We'd ask,

"Why are you cutting the rates?" Well, we'd argue and argue; we'd demand. But this was spontaneous, unorganized protest.

How did you finally move out of the dormitory?

The factory allotted us a one-room apartment, thirteen meters square. We built it ourselves, working at the construction site on our days off and after work. After a while, we went to the director and explained that our children were growing up and that it was crowded in one room. We didn't really expect anything, but all of a sudden we got a call at work informing us that we had been allotted a two-room apartment. We were told that we'd have to work a certain number of hours for it.

Those are the conditions in our country—that one works overtime on the construction of the apartment building. We left the girls with my mother and went to build. Now we have a three-room apartment, although there are only the two of us.

The factory gave us a plot twenty by thirty meters, but it is five hours away by electric train, and the land is marshy. The first time we went, we could hardly put our feet on the ground. We built a little shack, and the girls and I dug drainage ditches and pulled out the stumps. It was horrible in the beginning. They gave you a plot and left you on your own, without any help or equipment. Eventually we built a *dacha*.

What sort of town is Lytkarino?

It has a population of about 75,000 and six defense factories. We have a fine palace of culture, beautiful woods. The Moscow River is nearby. It is a very green, very pretty town. Our factory has a good polyclinic.

And you are now retired?

I got sick and was given disability leave. I had an operation in 1980 and returned to work in 1982 until I became eligible for my pension in 1985. Maybe I would have continued but I was ashamed after I returned from my illness. They understood that I had to work off the rest of my time until my pension, and they were careful not to let me lift anything heavy. The objectives are very big. So I worked until my pension, and I would have gone on working, but I was ashamed. Actually, I did work two months longer, until I had a fight with the supervisor. She yelled at me for missing work one day. I was very insulted. After all, I was sick, an invalid. So I quit, and now I sit home.

[GALYA] Mama took her departure from the factory very hard. She cried so much.

Did you have a good collective at work?

[MARIYA] We worked together well and didn't fight. The whole brigade used to come over to our place. We would visit each other, have tea, and share a bottle. Yes, it was a friendly collective. It's good when you're working. Now they've forgotten me. It hurts sometimes.

Is your husband also retired?

He took his pension this year. He has diabetes. When I ask him how he feels about it, he says, "I haven't thought even once about work." But I suffered a lot, because I loved my collective and my work very much.

In your view, has the Soviet regime done anything for the workers?

Yes, I think so. I came with nothing and all the same made my way in life, became a person. I earned something. We raised our children, put them on their feet. Galya finished the pedagogical institute and is now a journalist. Nina studied two years, but she had trouble with her vision and had to abandon her studies. Now life has taken a turn for the worse. Perestroika began, and where it will land us, no one knows.

Were there any changes when Andropov came to power in 1982?

In those days, when we were given time off to compensate for overtime, they warned us not to go into Moscow because everyone was being stopped and asked why they weren't at work. The police would drive up to a line for wine in front of a store, put everyone in a bus, and drive them to work in the fields. In general, I liked that; there was order. I don't like it when people can just walk away from work in the middle of the day. How can I walk away? If I leave an hour earlier, I make it up later.

[At this point, Ivan, Lyuba, and Sergei arrive and the conversation continued around the supper table.]

[GALYA] If I worked at the factory, I would know that ether is

toxic. I would tell them that I am supposed to work with alcohol.
What if you all went together to complain?

[LYUBA] But the workers don't believe that they can change
anything.

[MARIYA] You can't change anything.

[LYUBA] You see what our ignorance leads to? A lot of people
work with ether. If they were all given supplements for hazardous
work, it would cost the state too much.

And your trade union? Hasn't it changed at all?

No, the trade-union committee is concerned exclusively with its
own well-being.

Why don't you elect a new one?

New people would behave in the same way. They would look after
themselves. If a good, talented specialist happens to get appointed
to head the department and he tries to change things, the apparatus
either forces him out or else transforms him into one of their own.
What you need is a revolution. Otherwise, nothing will change. Our
state is a big machine, and the larger the mass, the more inert it is.

My impression from the people I work and socialize with is the
same: we are expecting it to get even worse. Maybe there can be
some progress in the economy, some improvement in the food or
clothing situation. But a change in the apparatus—we don't believe
in that. As far as our trade union is concerned, I have heard nothing
about it during the past year. The union movement is completely
unpopular.

What do you think about the miners?

I think they're great. [The 1989 coal strike is described in Part
IV.] But nothing like that will happen in Moscow. Even if some
factory takes the lead, the others won't follow.

Is the length of continuous service a very important lever in management's hands?

Very important. If you don't have the twenty years, you don't get
full pension.

I finally left that shop last year. I wanted to improve my education,
change my profession, and become a member of the engineering-
technical staff. I have been at assembly work a long time. My fingers

hurt from turning the screwdriver, and my neck aches constantly. We also work in the dark, since the apparatuses we make use infrared rays for night vision. We receive no extra pay for harmful work conditions. They are supposed to give us juice for the dark conditions. Anyway, I enrolled in evening classes at the institute and I asked the head of another shop to take me on. He agreed to take me on as a foreman. But when the head of my old shop heard about this, he called and explained that I'm an uncompromising person, one who tells the truth and should not be taken on. The other department head told me directly, "I got a call from your shop. You always tell the truth, and I don't need that kind of worker."

[GALYA] I can't understand why, when they are surrounded by such injustice, people don't unite.

[LYUBA] That's fine in theory. You should work for a month where I work, socialize with the people, and you would see things differently.

Are women different from men in that respect?

A woman will do anything, tolerate anything, to earn her wage. She's like an ox, especially if her husband drinks, since she has to earn a living, she has to feed her family. So if they pay her, she'll try to maintain normal relations, no matter with whom.

Women will shout, speak their piece, but that's where it ends. There is no solidarity. For example, we demanded six extra days of vacation as compensation for working in the dark. It was my turn for vacation, and I went to the director, to the trade-union committee, everywhere, and they finally gave me the six days. Then there was a meeting, and someone complained that I got twenty-one days of vacation, while he got only fifteen even though he had been at the factory much longer. No one defended me, even though they knew that, thanks to me, they would have the extra six days too. They almost devoured me.

[MARIYA] Now that you've left them, things are bad. Who will speak the truth?

[LYUBA] When I was there, the boss was afraid to insult people. Now they say she has really become impudent. But in this country, women don't like people who they think consider themselves better or smarter. The women didn't understand me. When I was fighting, I wasn't doing it for myself, but for the whole section. If it had been just for myself, I would never have been able to say, "Why didn't you give me my bonus?" I would have just let it go. They have a hard time believing someone would make a fuss for someone else's sake.

I've been fighting for how many years already? Sometimes, others did fight with me. But in a crunch I was always alone. One time, another woman came to my defence. As a result, she also fell out of grace with the supervisor. Of course, in their hearts, they know I'm fighting for them, but they are afraid of the supervisor. They're afraid the same thing will happen to them that happened to me. They're afraid to lose their place. In their hearts they probably appreciate me. Among themselves they will approve of what I do, but those who will say that to the boss's face are very rare. That's because they understand that they are powerless. Or maybe they aren't as stubborn as me.

Our Soviet woman has a very hard life. She has to earn a wage and then run around to the shops to find something to feed her family. All her free time and days off are lost in that way. I have to stand in a different line for each product. I have to get to the store before it opens to buy milk. I have to go to another store for cereal. I have to go to Moscow for meat. Some women are surprised, "And she even reads books! When does she have time?" I read at night. I can't see what kind of problems your women can have when there is everything in the stores.

[IVAN] I worked in the same shop. Military production is on the decline now, wages are down and life is getting harder. People don't know where to go. Management sends workers to construction sites or to other shops. They are paid only the average wage. If the plan goes up, they will be called back to the shop.

So workers aren't being dismissed from the factory?

[LYUBA] No, that's not allowed by law. But you can be offered a transfer to a job where conditions are worse, where you'll have to work as an apprentice and learn a new profession. You'll earn less. A worker will tolerate everything, lose everything. [In fact, Soviet law allowed dismissal for economic reasons, though management was obliged to help find other work for the employee. In practice, however, given the chronic labor shortage, workers were hardly ever dismissed for economic reasons.]

They say the economic reform will allow management to fire workers.

I don't know how that will be decided in the apparatus. I can only say one thing: a worker will put up with anything. There is a sense that there is no way out. A lawyer might explain that management has no right to do that, that the law doesn't allow it. But at the factory they'll tell you something entirely different, "We don't need a worker here anymore; so you will work less hours." Or else they'll say, "I don't need your kind." Single mothers who replaced women on maternity leave are being laid off when the original worker returns. There was a case last year in our shop where a fifty-three-year-old woman, with only two years left to her pension, was cut. She had to work as an apprentice in another brigade. Of course, she was deeply hurt and cried a lot.

[IVAN] Not long ago I worked in the shop that tested products. There were a lot of pensioners there. They were all told to find other work. Some managed to find work, but others had to leave the factory.

[LYUBA] As for the reform, judging by what I see at our plant, I am convinced that they will sell off the factories.

Will that make things better or worse?

Well, workers who do good work will get a good wage. There's no reason to fire them.

Why do you think that? In Canada, conscientious, hard-working people are laid off every day.

Even if they work well?

It happens all the time when management decides that it's more profitable to replace workers with machines or to move production to another country or if demand falls.

But on what basis can they fire you if you do good work?

On the basis of the fact that they are the owners and you are hired labor, and if they don't need you anymore to make profits, they won't hire you. [Lyuba shakes her head in disbelief.] Do workers understand how their wages are calculated?

There are piece rates: so much for the assembly of a certain apparatus. I know that in the course of a month I have assembled a certain amount, and I can calculate how much I should get. But there are some types of production where people can't calculate.

[IVAN] Like where I worked. I would get an order worth a specific amount of money to fulfill in the course of the month. But besides that, there was day-to-day work, like repairing a burnt-out lathe or changing a light bulb. We are supposed to be paid for that too. We make a record of those jobs, and at the end of the month we take it to the boss. But he can calculate the payment for that work as he likes. It can be twenty rubles or 150.

A lot depends on the person. We had one supervisor who always stood up for the workers. Apparently, that's why they got rid of him. The new one paid less or nothing at all for those odd jobs. We would complain that we received nothing for that day-to-day work. He'd say, "The wage bill has been spent. The shop doesn't have the money to pay. We'll pay you next month." But next month he wouldn't pay. We go to the shop chief, and he would say, "We don't have the resources."

[LYUBA] Work—but do it for free.

[IVAN] In the end, this money is lost. In the final analysis, we also have the *progressivka* (bonus), which can be 40 percent of the wage. The boss can give you more or less. If you displease him, he can give you nothing that month.

We had the following case. We came to work at night, since this work couldn't be done during the day. That night, a large quantity of materials worth a lot of money was broken in one of the sections. The next morning, the department head called us out and said, "You were working; you must have broken them." And we lost our bonuses. Our bonuses were big, around 150 rubles. The bosses have an interest in depriving the workers of their money and taking it for themselves. I was mad and complained to the conflict commission.

Who is in that commission?
The shop chief, a trade union person, and a representative of the public, three or four people. I got my money. And the boss said to me, "Okay, we'll return the money to you, but you'll regret it." Next month, I was not paid my bonus. He came into our shop and said, "Why are these cigarette butts lying on the floor?" And I lost my bonus because of the unswept floor. So, if the boss doesn't find me to his liking, he can deprive me of my bonus each month. But if I

had given in that time, I might never have had to worry about my bonus in the future.

Do you have a lot of idle time at work?

[LYUBA] Yes, but the stoppages aren't recorded as such. We can go home, and at the end of the month, when the supplies suddenly appear from God knows where, we work day and night. We can even work twenty-four hours in a row.

I'll give you an example of how I worked last August. The details are delivered to the brigade, and we share them equally. I worked more quickly and ran out of supplies. No more came. So I went to the department head—the supervisor was on vacation—and told him that it was only noon but I had no more supplies. I said that I worked faster than the others and I needed more. He answered, "And where do you think I can get them?" I said, "Then record the stoppage for me and pay me for the time I am idle." His eyes popped out—to pay me for idle time is not profitable for him. No worker had every made that demand to him. The worst thing you can do in the factory is to be too smart. It's a very bad thing to know how things are *supposed* to work. You're immediately labeled a troublemaker. So he told me to go home. And I worked like this all August. I would come at eight, there would be no parts, and I'd return home. I wasted a lot of time walking. At the end of the month, parts came in, and we worked until midnight. The idle time was never recorded.

How do you manage to put in such long hours?

The Russian people can bear anything. You see, they are all on piece rates. If they were on hourly rates and there was no work, they'd have to be paid anyway. But with piece rates, if you don't hand in the output, who is going to pay you?

Can you explain how these piece rates work?

[LYUBA] In the course of the month, you have to assemble whatever the plan calls for, say, 1,000 units. I assemble opera glasses. I could assemble the entire 1,000 in a week or so if I worked day and night, since I can do forty in a shift. But that depends on how regularly I receive the parts. Besides, the parts are often defective. It is hard to assemble binoculars with defective parts, but we do what we can. There is quality control, but it's really a fiction. There is no control on incoming parts, only on outgoing products.

For example, a controller in the mechanical shops spot-checks the parts made there and sends them on. I might get 10 percent defective parts, but since there can't be 10 percent defective production, I have to assemble the unit as best I can. I have to use my skills and ingenuity to put the binoculars together and have them pass inspection.

Over the last two years, at least until recently, the press was reporting a lot of conflict over the poor organization of production: overtime, black Saturdays, management's failure to respect workers' rights. Has there been any echo of that at the Optical factory?

No. We consider the stoppages and overtime normal. You get time off to compensate for the overtime, plus you get wages for it. As for the administration's responsibility to supply workers with materials and parts on time, well....

Did you have elections to administrative posts in your factory?

In some shops the leadership is elected, including the shop chief. But not in ours. [The 1987 State Enterprise Law provided for elections of administrative staff, though the elected directors had to be confirmed from above. This law was replaced by a new enterprise law in 1990 that rescinded that right.]

Are things better where the administration is elected?

Certainly. The workers there support management.

Then why don't you try to have elections in your shop?

No one in our shop opposes the head. He does nothing bad—and nothing good either.

What do you think of the protests last August when tobacco disappeared from the shops?

We had protesters in our town, too, who blocked traffic. But I don't think they were entirely correct. They closed off the road in the evening and prevented the workers from getting home after work. The bosses don't care how you get home. If they had done it in the morning, that would have forced the bosses to do something.

What do you think happened to the tobacco?

They created an artificial shortage. Supporters of Brezhnev, or enemies of Gorbachev, or enemies of perestroika.

What's the situation in the trade sector in Lytkarino?

[MARIYA] There's nothing in the stores. We have to go to Moscow. Only four months ago, there was milk, chicken, eggs. Now the stores are empty, but everything is for sale in the street. The whole city is in the hands of the trade mafia. The police know all this.

What do you think about the cooperatives? [Small private enterprises were legalized in 1988; a significant portion were really partnerships employing hired labor.]

[LYUBA] Our cooperatives are nothing but swindlers.

[IVAN] The cooperatives have destroyed the country.

[LYUBA] We never buy clothes in the cooperatives. I would rather sew them myself or else wear old clothes. But there's no cloth. It's insulting. The cooperatives charge 100 times more than the thing is worth. And the work is of poor quality.

What do you think of people who make money from buying and selling?

It's dishonest. I work at a state enterprise and receive a state wage. I can't afford to buy from the co-ops. But they were supposed to have been created for us. Take a look at the shop windows. One dress costs more than my entire wage!

[IVAN] Seven years ago, you could walk into a store and find everything, refrigerators, irons.

What sort of people go into the trade sector?

[LYUBA] A person who wants an easier life, since we constantly have shortages, and such a person can always get things. [*Dostat,* "to get," is a major preoccupation of people in the economy of shortages. One "gets" things in various ways—by rushing over to a shop when one has heard over the grapevine that a delivery has arrived, by bribing the salesperson, through connections, etc.] Some, however, like that work; for them it is a vocation.

People are constantly accusing them of being crooks.

[IVAN] That's basically true. A young person sees that his friend working in trade can get certain things, while he, working at the factory, has nothing.

[GALYA] Ten years ago, no one went into trade. The service

sector was held in contempt. Those people were considered servants. Now it has become prestigious; they are "businessmen."

[LYUBA] A friend of mine came across two men in Moscow selling Opal cigarettes. He asked them where they got them. They answered, "From a shop in Lytkarino." It turns out that the cigarettes were delivered to Lytkarino, and the shop manager sold them for a ruble a pack—they cost fifty kopecks—and now they are being sold in Moscow. Yesterday, a truck delivered vodka to the store in Lytkarino. They unloaded twenty cases in the courtyard. Four cars were waiting and carried it off. They paid the director, and it disappeared.

But the first thing that the new Russian government did was abolish the People's Control.

And rightly so. [The system of People's Control was administered by the trade unions. Its aim was to was fight corruption in the trade sector but it was ineffective.] Last year, the Central Trade Union Council conducted a campaign of People's Control, and it yielded nothing. The director of the stores just ignore them. They have no real power.

What about the police?
[IVAN] The police are all bought off.

How long do you think people will tolerate mafia domination of trade?
[LYUBA] They are totally submissive and passive by habit. And they don't understand how things work. I constantly run into this. I express myself correctly, and they have totally different expressions.

I don't know. I've spoken with many workers, and we seem to understand each other quite well.
That's not the mass of workers. You haven't seen that. For example, the administration was distributing electrical appliances. [*Raspredelenie*, "distribution" or "allocation," refers to the sale of consumer goods and food, often at subsidized prices, in the factory, usually by the trade union committee.] We had a choice: we could receive coupons or else opt for a system where the worker would receive a postcard when the appliance was available for him. I said that we should do it by postcard, since you have to go to the store

only once and are sure of getting the appliance. With the coupons, everyone gets one, and you have to go every day to check, only to be told that there aren't appliances. But the workers shrugged their shoulders and thought to themselves, "What sort of nonsense is she spouting?" Our workers fight among themselves.

[LYUBA] The town is based largely on *limitchiki*. People come from different regions and live in dorms. Then they get married and receive apartments. Different people, various nationalities. And they say to themselves, "Thank God, I have escaped from the back woods, the provinces; I am living here now and that suits me." They are mostly from the village, youth who have gone through the technical schools. Many have no rights at all. When they first get here, they keep quiet because they don't have a permanent residence permit. They have to work five years in order to be able to live permanently in the city. Once they get the permit, the question of an apartment arises. If you fight with the administration, you won't get one. So they try to keep peace with the bosses, even if they are dissatisfied.

Some of the workers, like you, are from the local population. Are they more able to stand up for themselves?

Yes, they have nothing to fear, even if they quit the factory. They are registered in the city, they have an apartment. They can always find other work. But if a *limitchik* quits, he won't be hired by another enterprise.

The level of consciousness is often terribly low. I'll give you an example. My brother's wife is older than me. As a child, she lived through the war in Bryansk. She lived in dugouts, in terrible conditions. When she finally moved to the Moscow region, she had running water, indoor plumbing, central heating. And she constantly says to me, "Why are you battling. You go to the toilet at home, you have water." You see, she needs only the minimum. But that isn't enough for today's youth.

What do you think of Gorbachev's leadership?

[LYUBA] When I first heard him, I was very impressed. I listened to him for a whole year. There was forward movement in relation to the government and the KGB. But then it was all empty talk, blathering. We got sick of that dish and we no longer believe him.

There were elections to the local and republican soviets last

spring. [These were the first elections based upon universal suffrage. In the 1989 elections to the Supreme Soviet of the USSR, one third of the seats were reserved for "social organizations"—the party, trade unions, the Academy of Sciences, and so on.] Didn't they make a difference in Lytkarino? Who did you vote for?

[IVAN] There were several candidates, but the workers had no idea who they were. I personally didn't vote. I saw no point. Before the elections, you'd see a notice, "Meeting with candidates of such-and-such voting district." But why go? You might ask a concrete question, but as usual, they'll promise anything to get elected. People already don't believe what is promised in elections. We had elections. What changed? There is no sign of improvement.

What do you think about Yeltsin?
[MARIYA] The people are for him. But apparently, they aren't letting him show what he can do. [Following the spring 1990 elections, Yeltsin became chairman of the Russian Supreme Soviet and effectively head of the Russian government, which at that time was still subordinate to the government of the USSR.]

Why do people trust him?
He is taking another path. He has his own plan.
[IVAN] Maybe they see that he is against Gorbachev and that things might be better with him.
[MARIYA] We hope things will get better. If not this year, then maybe next year something will be achieved.

Kolya Naumov
[November 1990]

This conversation took place in a period of heightened worker activism. Gorbachev's economic reforms were failing, though real economic distress among most workers was still relatively mild. Shortages had become acute in the shops, but distribution at places of work was expanding. Though production was declining, few believed the threat of unemployment was real since industrial labor was still in short supply.

In the spring of 1990, anti-bureaucratic sentiment translated in many places into victory for liberals, who presented themselves as the most consistent champions of democracy, in the elections to the local and republic soviet.

The factories were also witnessing a period of heightened worker assertiveness, an example of which is discussed in this interview. But while the economic crisis in its initial stages helped to mobilize workers, it was at the same time creating conditions—a growing dependence on the internal distribution system and on management and general economic insecurity—that would eventually undermine the new-found sense of confidence and militancy.

Did your factory take part in the celebration of the anniversary of the October Revolution this year?

Everyone thought no one would go. But our director probably got an order from the city or district party committee to send a contingent. Our shop was ordered to send thirty people. So the shop director ordered all foremen to come with two people each and warned us rather gently of possible consequences—that we would lose our bonuses or be passed over when consumer goods arrived. About twenty went.

You didn't go?

No. If I had gone, it would have been to Popov's demonstration. [There were two demonstrations in Moscow that year. Gavril Popov, who had been elected mayor in the spring elections, was a key figure in the liberal movement. He resigned as mayor in 1991 under the pall of widespread corruption charges, reputedly one of the richest men in Russia. Prior to that he had been the rector of Moscow University.]

Last year, you said that the system made it impossible to change anything fundamentally. Since then, has anything happened at the plant?

I can't say nothing has changed since perestroika. I told you that I've been waiting twenty years for like-minded people to appear at the plant. Whenever I thought I found them and got close, I got burned. Either they turned out to be not what I had thought or they ended up going back to school or becoming administrators, or else they got in line for apartments or cars and became cautious.

Then Lena Maltseva appeared on the assembly line. It was back when Yeltsin was still first party secretary of Moscow province. She was a young girl; I don't know where she came from. She began to write letters to Yeltsin, complaining about how the plant was working badly, production was arrhythmic, and she demanded it be organized better. I sympathized with her though I could see she didn't understood production too well. You see, she blamed management, but it's the system itself that is rotten. The administration, in turn, began to say that she was mentally unstable, crazy. But she spoke out at meetings and she assembled a group of people around her.

What sort of meetings?

To tell you the truth, I'm not sure what they are. They might actually be union meetings, but the administration sits there and tells workers how badly they work: "We're building apartments for you, and you drink," and so on. Maltseva started answering back. Then she wrote up a set of demands and collected signatures: new union elections, wage increases, better organization of production, and better work conditions. She read these at one meeting during the wage reform and proposed a strike. This was during the wage reform, when one month there was no money for bonuses. [One of Gorbachev's first major reforms sought to reduce bonuses in take-home pay and making them harder to get, and to introduce requalification tests for workers' skill levels. Bonuses could make up to 40 percent of take-home pay.] The administration explained that the bonuses would be paid next month, but the workers didn't seem to hear. They demanded their money and asked how they could live. We really do live from wage to wage.

On payday, when they saw there was no bonus, about forty workers struck on the body assembly line. Management came, and the two sides yelled at each other, until gradually the workers returned to work. Two workers continued to strike for about twenty minutes longer and were fined for the cars that got through. They lost their bonuses.

So I began to talk with Lena, despite the angry looks I got from the head of the shop. She probably thought at first that I was a provocateur sent by management. But there was no real movement. Just small explosions. There wasn't any real unity behind her in the shop.

Another activist is Sergei Novopolskii. He was always an energetic guy, a brigadier on the final assembly line. He's self-assured, with a loud voice and a neck twice as thick as mine.

What does a brigadier do?

The brigades were an idea that appeared under Andropov. [In fact, the brigade system was first introduced under Brezhnev, but in most cases it remained a formality.] The idea was to put the foreman under the supervision of the brigade council, which would participate in the allocation of bonuses to the brigade members. Where the brigadier is a genuine leader, the foreman really does consult with him. Sometimes the brigadier is the one who is really in charge and he allocates the bonuses on his own. But he is still a worker—he isn't freed from his regular job. It all depends. Sometimes the foreman will be someone straight out of the institute who doesn't know anything and so takes instructions from the brigadier. Otherwise, the brigadier is superfluous.

There are probably many reasons why a worker might decide to become a foreman. Workers don't get much information about what's happening in the plant. For example, one reason a worker might join the party is to have greater access to information; you somehow are closer to the administration. There is a sense of power, of being *khozyain* [master, translated variously as owner, boss, person in charge, as in the "master of the house"], and one wants to know what is going on. A foreman goes to regular *operativki* (operational meetings) with the administration, where he gets information. In addition, as I said before, when you have power and information, you can get more; for example, knowing when scarce consumer goods arrive for sale at the factory. Even before perestroika, some things were sold in the factory. I remember once there were sheepskin coats. But compared to what is going on now, that was nothing.

And you don't mind, as a foreman, having to give orders?

Not really. Workers who become foremen usually already enjoy some authority among their fellow workers. Some workers become foremen and, after a few years, become workers again, and then they might once again become foremen.

I met a miner from Kazakhstan who he had been appointed acting director of his mine after the strike, but he eventually went back to

being a worker when he realized that he couldn't achieve anything. Does that happen much?

Yes, we have a guy here who was a department head and then became a mechanic.

You were telling me about Novopolskii.

Perestroika has unbound the workers, and they've become bolder. I first noticed Sergei at party and factory meetings. I'm not a member but I go for information. He spoke more forcefully than the others, but more importantly, he made sense.

Novopolskii is in the party and he is also a member of the STK of the assembly department. Its chairman is Yuri Solovev, who is his pal. The chair of the party committee, Rybakov, is a coward and follows the administration's lead. But Novopolskii is crafty. He tries to keep good relations with management, so they don't try to get rid of him, as they eventually did with Maltseva.

One day, for example, he told me that he had found somebody to be chairman of the trade union committee. He said that he had searched carefully for an independent person. He had checked to see if the person already had an apartment, was he waiting in line for a car, what his wages were. So he got that person elected. You see, even the head of the shop doesn't enjoy the kind of authority that Novopolskii does.

He's a very rare worker. Plus, he has the support of Yuri Solovev. Solovev is more educated and sort of acts as his theoretician. I'd say that Solovev is more after an idea; he thinks more in terms of higher politics. Novopolskii doesn't give a damn about that. He knows there's a shop, a factory, that he's working there and has to defend wages, organize production decently. But Solovev is also capable of speaking to workers and giving them direction. Together they can achieve a lot.

Unfortunately, Lena Maltseva wasn't able to find such a comrade. And I'm a coward. I try to help: I put them in contact with people, I support them, but that's all, because I'm not strictly a worker and I'm somewhat to the side. If I were a worker, it would probably be easier.

Besides Novopolskii and Maltseva there was also an activist called Timur, who was in opposition to the director. I think he was head of a lab at the factory. He had ties to *Komsomolskaya Pravda* and was a participant in the Komsomol movement. [The Communist Youth League, one of the main supporters of reform at the start of perestroika, finally disbanded after many of its officials went into business. The movement's paper is now independent, with a liberal-democratic orientation.] Incidentally, he was the object of the same kind of slander campaign as Maltseva and Novopolskii.

They said that Maltseva was always making trouble and not working herself—she was often sick—and that she'd been on the assembly line only a year and a half and already she was telling people what to do. Some workers believed the slander, especially about Maltseva.

Well, one day last January, I suddenly learned there was going to be a demonstration after work.

You hadn't suspected something might happen?

Well, the country was clearly moving toward ruin, and this had its effect on people. Also, as I said, people grew bolder under perestroika. There was Maltseva formulating demands, and Novopolskii spouting ideas at meetings about how to transform the factory. He was constantly organizing meetings in his shop. He and Solovev, for example, were constantly making demands for a new procedure for the allocation of the consumer goods sold in the department. Things had become very lively.

Maltseva had become acquainted with the producers of a television program for youth and was feeding them information about the sins of our director. Then suddenly *Vremya* [the main evening national news program] accused our director of irresponsible management because of a contract he had signed with a German firm to cooperate in the production of some sports cars. The factory didn't live up to the terms and had to pay millions in penalties. Then an article appeared in *Komsomolskaya Pravda* about how our director had ruined the factory, sent relatives abroad who brought back goods, made bad deals. It was a blow from the apparatus against the director (laughs). The atmosphere was hot.

But the main thing was that we had adopted a plan for 1990, and it wasn't being fulfilled. Of course, we still got our bonus, because the director, as they say, "corrected" the plan; that is, he persuaded the ministry to lower the target. But the assistant director for production, who had opposed the original plan as unrealistic, was removed from his post. He continued to show up at the factory but didn't work. That's how he showed his protest. Usually when a director says to someone: "Tomorrow, you aren't working," that person will sit around until the director finally says: "Okay, go to work." But that didn't happen. And so one of the demands at the meeting was to reinstate this assistant director. It is the same psychology as in Yeltsin's case: if the bosses punished him, he must be good. [Gorbachev removed Yeltsin from his post in the Politburo and as Moscow province party boss at the end of 1987.]

So Novopolskii, this Timur, and the assistant director agreed among themselves and posted notices, though at the mass meeting, the assistant director remained behind the scenes. The meeting was formally called by the STK of the assembly department.

When I learnt about the planned demonstration, I was worried for Novopolskii and Maltseva that no one would show up. As usual, I was late in leaving—I usually arrive late and leave late. There's always something to do—to write, to fix, some instruction to give, or a newspaper to finish reading (laughs). And when I got outside to the square in front of the administration building, it was empty. I was so upset. I thought only a few had come and then simply left.

I thought it over and went to the conference hall. People were milling in the corridor outside. I reached the doors, but they weren't letting people in. It was already packed. People had come from all over the factory. Novopolskii said there were 700 people inside. The rest listened outside through the loudspeaker system.

What about the second shift?

It was working; there wasn't a strike. The demands were formulated: removal of the director who hasn't justified the confidence placed in him and election of a new one; reinstatement of the assistant director of production; an inquiry into the German deal and the penalties; election of a new factory-wide STK, since the present one is a tool of the administration; improvements in the organization of production. A number of speakers called for a cut in administrative staff. Maltseva proposed that *limitchiki* be granted equal rights with permanent residents of Moscow. Sergei also called to reject the proposed 50 percent rise in the prices of the cars.

I was a little puzzled. But he said that if all enterprises made unjustified price hikes, wage gains would soon be wiped out. Maybe it also had something to do with the fact that at that time workers in the plant were beginning to sign up to buy cars, because it had become possible to resell them at double the price. You see, the new model was in high demand, and as perestroika picked up, with the growth of the cooperatives and the underground economy, there was a lot of money around.

All that began about a year and a half ago, but it totally passed me by. I didn't need a car and I didn't have any money. Then suddenly at an operational meeting, the shop chief says, "One of our mechanics bought a car, and the traffic police sent us a report that he sold it." As a result, he said, the union committee decided that no more cars would be allocated to our shop. Someone asked how much one could make on such a deal. When I heard the answer—10,000 rubles—I couldn't believe it. I thought 2,000, maybe 4,000. Then all of a sudden everyone began to put in for a car. People kept asking me if I had taken a car. They offered to find me a "client," promising me 10,000 rubles. That's if you have to buy the car with money advanced to you by the "client." If you have your own money, you can make 30,000 or 40,000. So I turned out to be a fool. Here I am reading all these newspapers and I didn't even know what was going on in my shop. Of course, that's not the kind of thing you learn from the newspapers.

In response to what was going on, the administration prohibited the sale of cars to employees who didn't have a driver's license. But we all work together and know perfectly well that you can't buy a car on our wages. That means that if you were a worker at the plant and had a car and a driver's license, you must be a thief. So these thieves could now sell their old cars for crazy sums, and since they had licenses, they began to buy new cars. And then there are people like me, who didn't steal. I haven't got a license, so I can't buy a car. I found it a little strange. Anyway, Sergei has now bought a car. (Laughs, then whispers) And I have too. (Aloud) No, why should I whisper. I'll explain.

Someone approaches me and asks if I want to make 10,000 rubles. He said his relative wanted to buy a car. I was reluctant at first but he kept pestering and I finally gave in. I offered him 2,000 for his "services." He agreed—he's a very brazen guy. So we went to his relative who turned out not to be a relative. I probably would never had made a request for a car, but this guy really took me by the hand. People who have been there only two years are asking for cars, and I've been at the plant twenty years and never asked. Of course, nowadays in the plant, people are signing up for everything, furniture, carpets, television sets, refrigerators.

The director also changed the procedure for selling cars. He decided that only those who work on Saturdays and other days off are eligible for cars. So after a Saturday, the shop is allocated a certain number of cars, and the supervisor and brigadier in each section decide who will get them.

How did the workers react to this decision?

At first they weren't happy, but now when the director says we won't be working on the coming Saturday, workers themselves ask the department head when the next *subbotnik* will be, because practically everyone in the shop is waiting in line to buy a car.

And not long ago workers were rebelling against the "black Saturdays." Now you're saying they've been bought off?

You can say that again! Look, I've been working here all my life and I have five rubles in the bank. Everyone's in that situation. Now, all of a sudden, you have 15,000. In a word, I bought a car.

So quickly? You bought a license, and the administration didn't check?

They stopped checking because everyone knows these workers aren't buying the cars for themselves, but to sell.

Now, you'll have to work a lot of Saturdays, I guess.

(Laughs) Seriously, I often work on Saturdays, since there are two shifts on the assembly line during the week and they alternate on Saturdays, when there is one shift. Our shop services both shifts, and I'm responsible. So in a way, you can say that my turn didn't come that quickly. But the guy who arranged everything else went to the union committee meeting and did a lot of shouting on my behalf.

What about the police?

Well, the law forbids you to sell for one year. But in fact, you go straight to a notary and make a gift of the car. Of course, the transfer of money in return isn't notarized.

But you can be cheated. There was a very unpleasant episode.

One of the guys who supported Lena when she organized that strike has now been arrested. He had made a deal to give 2,000 rubles when he got his car—I think that now to get a car, you have to give a bribe. But when he got the car, he changed his mind. They began to threaten him, and he went to the police. They must have informed the police about him, because when he sold the car, he and two others were nabbed. He got several years.

So the sale of cars is a big source of corruption among the workers.

Yes, and besides cars, they are speculating in all sorts of other goods. [In Soviet law and popular consciousness, buying goods and reselling them at a higher price was considered "speculation" and a crime. When this became legal or semilegal under perestroika, most people had a hard time accepting a practice that is considered quite legitimate under capitalism.] A lot of workers are selling, though you have to be careful around the factory since the economic police are watching. A while ago they were selling gold earrings in the shop. The adjuster who helped me get the car, won the right to buy the earrings in a lottery, but it was fixed, since the girl had made a mark on one of the tickets so he'd know which one to pick. He paid 500 rubles for the earrings and was immediately offered 1,250.

The whole thing is idiocy, and I'm tired of it. I want everything already to be sold at free-market prices. They sell us French perfume, we resell it at double the price. The workers fight among themselves over French perfume.

But some necessary things are also sold. We get packages of food containing buckwheat, canned goods, noodles, chicken—things you can't get anywhere in the store. I wouldn't be able to feed or dress myself without the factory, so I won't leave it. I was talking with a guy about going to work for a cooperative. He said that it made no sense, since even if you earn 700 rubles a month, you can't buy anything with the money. You have to go to the free market and all the money disappears. Here in the factory, you can play the fool and, if you have good relations with management, not work, and dress and feed yourself. You can even do some selling and make money.

Nowadays, people come to the factory but they don't work. They come only to buy goods. Before the holidays, you can hear people saying, "What a day! I stood in line and got sausage! I stood in line and got liver!" They arrive at work and immediately begin running to the different cafeterias, drawing lots, dividing up goods. These sales occur almost every day.

But the assembly line is running. Those workers can't walk away.

A certain number of packages will be allocated for workers on the assembly lines, say five for thirty people. And they start playing around with pieces of paper for a lottery. A guy will ask me and four others to participate in the drawing for a fur hat. We don't need the hat, so if one of us wins, we let him buy it and he reciprocates by showing "a little respect."

Meanwhile, management allows all this to happen and publicly cries over the decline in work discipline.

There can't be any discipline in these conditions. People pay no attention to work. Look, they're selling winter boots for seventy rubles when they cost 400 in the shop. Why should I work, when I can make money by selling these boots? You're right, workers on the assembly line have to work all the same. But our technologists are constantly busy with these sales, taking people off the line who have cars to go pick up chickens or whatever else. Nothing at all is organized. Someone has to leave his work to go to the central warehouse, another to load and unload the goods, someone does selling, someone deals with the papers. It's a nightmare.

And all this is in the last months?

Yes, it was never like this. You used to be able to buy boots in the store. Sometimes a shipment of boots wouldn't be sold out for three or even five days. The mayor has forbidden shops from selling directly in the factories, but they have found a way around it, saying it's an exchange of products with the factory. Many speculators bribe the factory guards to get in and during the sales they instruct workers on what to buy for them.

Everyone is talking about the terrible shortages, but if you consider everything that is sold outside the state shops, I would estimate at most that there are only 5 to 7 percent less goods than before.

To return to the mass meeting in January, what were the results?

Our director got scared. No one had expected such a huge meeting. So he wrote an open letter in which he proposed that the enterprise's employees themselves decide whether he should stay or leave. A referendum was organized. But the administration let it be known that the director had only a month and a half to go until he was eligible for his pension. People thought that they might as well let him work the last few weeks. But he tricked everyone and didn't retire. Of course, it wasn't only workers who voted in that referendum, but managerial and technical personnel too.

At the mass meeting, a conciliation commission was also elected, including Maltseva, Novopolskii, Solovev, and the chairman of the factory union committee. They met several times. But Novopolskii tells me that management is now laughing in their faces. You see, the commission was taken seriously when management felt that the workers were standing behind their leaders. Now they figure that the leaders would have a hard time mobilizing the workers again.

And do you think that the internal allocation of goods has something to do with it?

It plays a role. People who are in line for something good don't want to fight with the administration. You can imagine what we have come to when the director threatens to punish workers by not letting them work on Saturdays. Of course, the workers should be demanding that a certain proportion of the plant's production be set aside for them unconditionally. But they apparently feel that if they demand that, they might not get a car.

III

ORGANIZING

Vera Lashch
Co-chairwoman of the
Union of Work Collectives
[May 1991]

The work-collective councils, or STKs, were created by the 1987 Law on the State Enterprise. In most cases these elected self-management bodies remained subservient to management. In the summer of 1990, a new Enterprise Law virtually abolished them, reflecting the increasingly liberal orientation of the economic reforms. However, with the growing number of conflicts in the enterprises over control and ownership, a movement of work-collective councils emerged. The Union of Work Collectives (UWC) was founded in Moscow in December 1990. Vera Lashch was elected co-chairwoman.

Despite a promising start, by the summer of 1992 the work-collective movement seemed to be at a dead end, at least in Russia. In August, Vera Lashch left the movement. Most of its activists, under strong pressure from the neoliberal government and media and lacking firm support from below, had retreated from their initial demand that the enterprises be transferred to the full economic management of the work collectives. Now they were fighting so that at least some share of the property set for privatization be distributed among the workers.

The Enterprise Law of June 1990 was a step backward in the development of self-management and producers' democracy. Strictly speaking, the UWC was born in reaction to that law. On the other hand, the Russian Republic's new Law on Entrepreneurship embodies the basic ideas of our organization. So we have been trying to explain to the work collectives how to go about applying this new law.

You say that the Russian government is more favorable to the interests of the work collectives. But last fall it adopted the "500-Day Plan" that called for massive privatization and virtually ignored the self-management rights of the STKs. [In March 1991, in the heat of the coal miners' strike, the UWC took public positions strongly in support of Yeltsin and the transfer of enterprises from USSR to Russian jurisdiction.]

Yes. We are far from idealizing the Russian government either. We don't worship anyone. We are simply trying to analyze carefully all the new legislative proposals. And not just to analyze, but to insert something of our own. We have a special legislative group participating in the commissions of the Russian and other republican parliaments. We are trying to monitor all this to make sure the laws correspond to the interests of the work collectives.

We know that the Russian parliament has already made a lot of errors. It has adopted laws that contain statutes we don't like. Still, our experience in dealing with the Russian parliament leads us to conclude that it's more flexible and amenable to our influence and more often acts in the interests of the work collectives.

What is the level of activism in the enterprises around the issues that concern your organization?

Representation of the work collectives at the congress was quite broad, even though it was not well publicized. Our goal was not simply to attract as many enterprises as possible but to create a union of people who shared the same basic views.

Our organizational work has involved setting up regional unions of work collectives. Over the last month and a half, regional organizations were created in the north around the city of Norilsk, in Lvov, Lutsk, Volgograd, Rostov-on-Don. One will be created soon in Zagorsk. Regional councils also exist in Moscow and Leningrad. Our numbers are growing. The Lvov organization, for example, includes two very large enterprises. So I can't really say exactly how large our union is, since the numbers are constantly changing.

Our council of representatives, the highest elected organ after the congress, has held several meetings to consider how the congress's resolutions were being carried out. Unfortunately, the results are not comforting. We noted the growth of hidden, illegal privatization of state property by the *nomenklatura* [elite state planners and administrators] of the ministries and the party apparatus. There has been much talk about nationalizing the party's property, but in fact that's just a very small part of what now could fall into the hands of the party apparatus.

There are still no laws governing privatization. ["Privatization" was and remains an ambiguous term in contemporary Russian usage. In its broadest sense, it means removing the enterprise from the central states direct control, or "de-statization." This might or might not involve transfer to individual private owners.] But they aren't waiting for laws. The ministries form concerns or associations of enterprises, or transform enterprises into joint-stock companies on conditions advantageous to the *nomenklatura*. All sorts of new private enterprises are set up by ministries and state enterprises. Ministry employees will use their power and connections to create the most favorable circumstances for these new enterprises at the expense of work collectives.

This creeping privatization is a source of great tension in the enterprises. Our task is to get a law passed on this question and then to force a review of all the previous decisions regarding state property.

But do rank-and-file workers support the idea of self-management?

Yes, of course. They understand perfectly that it is not simply a question of managing or not managing. The issue of property is being decided *now*. If we don't start thinking about the processes taking place in the enterprises, we will simply find ourselves deprived of our property.

Think about it: a worker spends his entire working life at an enterprise, and now, on the eve of market relations, he leaves with nothing but his minimal pension. After a life's work! Meanwhile, a director who has just been appointed, on the basis of a ministerial decree—such scandalous facts have occurred—is personally, along with other top management, designated as owner of the basic plant and resources of the enterprise.

I was at the February Congress of the powerful Scientific-Industrial Union, which is really an organization of enterprise directors. It was depressing. I always fought my own director when he violated rules in the enterprise but I've never saw so many directors in one place. And I understood something very important. They find this period, when there are no laws regulating privatization, very much to their advantage, and they want to prolong it as much as possible, so that when laws finally appear, there will be nothing left to privatize. Part, even perhaps the largest part, will again fall into the hands of party functionaries. At present 99 percent of our directors are party members.

When an enterprise is formally privatized, management becomes responsible to someone. At present, management is in practice responsible only to itself. The ministry concludes a contract with the director under mutually advantageous conditions, the enterprise pays a good percentage of its income to the ministry, the ministry assigns the director a very nice salary in return, and if he manages badly, he is given another well-paid job.

Why do you think there so little coverage of your movement in the press?

Unfortunately our papers, even the ones sympathetic to the Russian government, don't write very much about us. I think many people are interested to know that the state's property is ending up in hands other than those of the work collectives. We used to see Western films in which your industrialists bought legislators to defend their interests in parliament. At the time, that didn't mean much to us. But at the congress of the Scientific-Industrial Union, I saw these directors talking with politicians as if they were already owners, those who set the tone, not only in the economy but in politics too.

I don't doubt that that is the case in the West. But our directors don't own the enterprises. That doesn't bother them—on the contrary, it's often said that our national property is in practice no one's, but our functionaries live off it very well.

The democrats want privatization, the transfer of the enterprises to private hands. At a recent meeting with the miners, the head of our Russian government said, "Russia will be saved by entrepreneurs." They are playing here with our directors, as if the latter are really entrepreneurs or capable of becoming them. I worked more than twenty-five years in industry, first in a factory producing measuring devices and then in a rubber factory. I can tell you that administrators weren't appointed mainly for their competence.

Of course, the democrats say that it doesn't matter if the directors aren't competent, since the market, a cruel master, will weed the incompetent ones out within a few years. Maybe so, but why should the workers have to suffer this? Why should they stand by while new experiments are conducted on their backs and the economic recovery is postponed for several more years? Why should they let this happen when other paths are available?

Wasn't one of the official goals of perestroika to make workers the masters in their enterprises in fact and not just in name?

Yes, the workers don't want to be cogs anymore. There are some branches of industry, for example defense, with which we have strong links, where the educational and skill level is so high that the workers sometimes have a much better grasp of things than the administration. They can't remain submissive cogs, and you have to be deaf and dumb to underestimate this factor.

The tension in the enterprises is colossal. Today I'm going to a conference of a work collective at a cybernetics plant. The collective is trying to stop the administration from adopting a charter without its agreement and, more generally, from keeping the employees away from the enterprise's property. But the ministry is pushing hard. The director is already working on contract for the ministry and so is practically invulnerable as far as the collective is concerned—it didn't hire him. That's the irony: the director is paid out of enterprise funds, but the ministry sets the salary.

We know why the conservative press ignores us: we have touched their most sensitive nerve—they don't want to attract attention to the process of hidden privatization. At a recent meeting of politicians and public figures, a member of the party Central Committee admitted to me that when they published the 1987 Enterprise Law, they didn't realized they were creating serious adversaries. So they changed tactics and now consider the path of self-management a dead end.

On the other hand, we are seriously trying to talk to the democrats. But our experience has been disappointing, even though, after all, we are trying to apply the laws of the Russian Republic, which we consider the most progressive. We recently met with the Russian chief prosecutor. We wanted to know how the Russian laws would be applied, given the existence of Union laws that often contradict them. He thanked us at the end and said that the meeting had been an eye-opener, as he had never looked at things from our point of view. *Rossiisskaya Gazeta* [a daily paper at the time very close to the Russian government] sent a reporter to cover the meeting. But when I phoned to ask when the article would appear, she said that her boss had decided to do an interview only with the chief prosecutor.

In other words, our point of view wouldn't get across. That's the sort of blank, impenetrable wall we meet on all sides. The press writes of privatization, the market, market relations. But where and to whom will all this property go—that's never discussed.

Have you thought of setting up your own press, perhaps with other elements of the labor movement?

That's one of our goals, but we're poor. We receive no material support from anyone. A large number of member enterprises pay dues, but the sums are very small. If a collective wants to join our UWC and pay dues, it must first obtain the director's signature to be able to draw money from the bank. That gives you some idea of how complicated things are. We haven't the money to buy paper or rent offices.

Your congress called for the transfer of enterprises to the work collectives. But would the collectives have the right to sell the enterprise afterward?

We proposed several types of transfer: full transfer of property rights without redemption, leasing, and others. But in each case, the work collective gets full management rights. The collective should have the right to choose the form of property. For example, it might decide to form a joint-stock company and include among the stockholders its suppliers or clients. The collective should have the right to decide these things. After all, the workers have invested so much in their enterprise and received such miserable wages in return. Is there anywhere else in the world where wages constitute only 2 to 16 percent of the total cost of production?

If the collective decides it does not want to own the factory, the government Committee for the Management of Property will decide its fate.

It's obvious that you oppose the bureaucratic variant of privatization. But your positive attitude to the democrats is less clear to me.

Even when laws on privatization are adopted, each collective will have to analyze its own situation. Only the work collective can decide what's best for its enterprise. That's why I emphasize that the basic issue is that the work collective obtain full management rights. Then it can decide about property.

We are prepared to cooperate with any political organizations that defend the interests of the work collectives, of the workers. Many have contacted us, but in every case they have one goal: to direct us, to exploit our potential force. They aren't prepared to help us solve concrete problems.

Our starting point is the question of property. From the answer they give, we can tell all we need to know about them. We can see who is only interested in foisting their own slogans on us. But there are people who really want to help us. Only they are very shy. You see the result: these problems aren't discussed anywhere in the press.

When we talk of self-management, we are referring to this transitional period. For now, we have a vacuum of authority. The parliaments cannot agree among themselves, and meanwhile, the people's property is being grabbed. For over seventy years—and I was brought up with this idea—it was supposed to be the people's property. It belongs to all of us.

So after this transition, some arrangement other than collective property and self-management might be decided?

Possibly. But our system already exists. To be sure, it isn't a very rational system of management; we don't really know what we have invented here. The task is now to create, at least for the majority of people, conditions for the transition to a market economy. This is necessary not only for their economic welfare but also to reduce the social tension. When Pavlov revealed his program, he stated very calmly: "So what if there are 30 million workers unemployed?" Maybe in the West you are more accustomed to unemployment, but for us it is something horrible.

We already have interruptions in the delivery of materials and components to enterprises. It's no longer just administrative posts that are being cut—those people as a rule manage to survive quite well. But they're starting to cut at the level of production. The textile industry is not getting enough cotton. These workers are mothers, heads of large families. In the Soviet Union, a family can't live on just the husband's wage. Imagine having worked all your life from the age of sixteen, knowing only that work and nothing else, and all of a sudden being out of work and unable to provide for your family.

It's a terrible force that will take to the streets. I doubt that our politicians and authorities really understand this. The miners have demonstrated, just a little, the potential of this force. But they are only one sector. Imagine if they all they came out together?

What are your relations with the trade unions?

That depends on the trade union. We have good relations with the IMU, which has shown us in action what it stands for. As for the official unions, we first want to see what their real goals are. You might have seen the May Day celebration organized by our Moscow trade unions. What a pitiful spectacle! There were no demands around property issues—just calls to defend wage labor and nothing more. Defend, defend, and again defend! One has to wonder who they are defending, when they don't even ask the right questions. And even the positions they do take are inconsistent. We want to keep a respectful distance for that kind of union.

Some say we are trying to substitute ourselves for the unions. But our functions are different. Our work-collective councils decide the fundamental issues relating to the development of their enterprise, the introduction of new forms of management, issues of property. The trade unions defend individuals against illegal acts and the like.

To what extent are conflicts over property in the enterprises growing?

You can't imagine how many phone calls we get. There just isn't enough time, even though regional councils are already functioning in a number of places. They tell us, for example, that the director has handed them a new charter, that their enterprise is now part of a concern, or that the director has signed a ten-year lease to rent out a building to some organization and is charging no rent for several years. Meanwhile, space is going for $300 and $400 a square meter in the center of Moscow.

They ask very concrete questions and want answers. But you can't resolve these problems from Moscow. The collectives need legal help and economic expertise. We want to create our own scientific association on industrial and territorial self-management in cooperation with specialists in the area. We can't manage without skilled help.

Maybe you think I'm distorting things to convince you of the correctness of our cause. But I assure you that the conflicts in the enterprises are very acute and the tension is frightening, simply frightening. We try to keep things under control, to channel the conflicts into a legal path, but it's not always possible to act calmly and cautiously when you face such massive illegality.

Take the conflict at the Kirov Factory in Leningrad over its transformation into a joint-stock company. Yeltsin was there, Pavlov too. It seemed like everything was resolved. But as soon as they left, the local authorities, the local party apparatus, started to get involved. And again things began to unravel. There is a union there and an STK but the situation was stagnating so the workers formed a strike committee. [Workers' committees and strike committees are generally elected exclusively by blue-collar workers, while STKs were elected by all employees, including management.]

This is a huge collective with 40,000 people. If they want to, they could turn out all of Leningrad. Someone in the executive at the local level is provoking this. I don't doubt that it's precisely this stratum of corrupted local officials or the party *nomenklatura* that is behind this. After all, the issue was already resolved at the highest levels.

A delegation from the Kirov strike committee came here recently, and I organized a meeting for them with the chair of the Committee for the Management of State Property. Still, they had to come back again because when they returned to the factory, the administration began to play around with them again, proposing totally unacceptable conditions. These workers have already advanced to the point where they ask themselves, what will we get and what will Russia get? And they see that Russia gets nothing. A part goes to the labor collective and the larger part to the [Soviet] Union, that ephemeral entity, whose basis and contents are not even clear. And they say, the enterprise is on Russian soil, so why can't we give anything to our own state?

At Zagorsk, where there are also many defense plants, the problems are equally explosive. Conversion is not going as it should, and the enterprises are losing highly skilled cadres; they are creating conditions to totally destroy this branch and its great potential.

At the Volga Auto Factory in Togliatti, a conflict is raging over the administration's plan to create a joint-stock company. When the workers learned of this last summer, they declared the factory the property of the collective. The director agreed to call a factory conference but he also invited all the auxiliary services, who voted as management had instructed them, giving its plan majority approval.

This decision was disputed by the workers, and a commission on privatization was set up to propose different options. Once this commission finishes its work, a referendum will be held, but only among those employed in basic production. So here the workers have understood that these questions require careful preparation. But it was only their mobilization against the administration's machinations that allowed them to reach this point.

Do your activists come from all strata of the enterprise, workers and factory intelligentsia?

Yes. But workers, by their nature, prefer action. They are much quicker to form workers' committees, strike committees. As soon as they see that the administration is not cooperating, they want to react strongly. But this is not always the shortest route. You can't always resolve things in one leap. Laws are being passed, and if we don't analyze them and try to modify them before they're passed, it will be much more difficult to change things afterward.

The authorities would like to push our problems aside, but the situation is coming to a head. The president could pass ten decrees to forbid the movement, but that wouldn't do any good. Our leaders are sawing off the branch they're sitting on. They're busy with other matters. They should come down to earth and see what is worrying the masses. Their behavior is inexcusable. They're driving people to despair, people who don't deserve such treatment.

I can't imagine another people so long-suffering as our Russians. We have suffered so much! We have built so much on sheer enthusiasm, on symbolic wages. We thought that was how one should live. I was born after the war and I used to say to myself: How lucky to be born in the Soviet Union, in Moscow, in such a period without wars! Everything was so good that one could almost envy oneself. And now it turns out that those values, the ideals we served, the ideals they taught us, are completely wrong. And it turns out that we are not at all a well-off generation, that our generation may have to live through something more terrible that the Patriotic War [World War II], that our economy may suffer more damage than during the war.

You understand, each generation has its own problems. But it's hard to get used to these new ideas after that sense of well-being. But everything is relative. We didn't know that things were so good where you live and so bad here. And then there are those regions where they are inciting national sentiments, playing on them. I have the constant sense that someone is dividing us so that the leaders can exploit us and resolve their own problems. It's a very unpleasant feeling.

I can't say what will happen to us, even in a half year. I feel that the calm among the miners now is also temporary. Even after the signing of the agreement on the transfer of the coal mines to the jurisdiction of Russia, I think they will have to return to these issues many times.

Grigorii Artemenko:
Railroad Worker
[October 1991]

I met Grigorii Artemenko on the last day of the Second Congress of Work Collectives in Moscow in October 1991. The morning following the congress I accompanied him to a cemetery, where he paid respects to his "bard," Vladimir Vysotskii, a poet-singer who died in 1980. We got there around 10:30 and found perhaps 100

people standing by the grave. This was not a special occasion—only an example of the unique respect and affection Russians, and Soviets generally, have for their poets.

Afterward, we went to my apartment where this interview took place. What struck me most about him is his honesty, the absence of any posing or false modesty. Few people have left me with so deep a sense of principle (which has nothing to do with dogmatism).

I operate a container-crane at the Odessa Mechanized Loading and Unloading Railroad Depot. I'm also a deputy in the Odessa regional soviet and vice chairman of its agricultural commission. Finally, I am chairman of the work-collective council of our railway division, and here, at this Interrepublican Congress of Work Collectives, I was chosen by the Ukrainian delegates to head a committee to organize a founding congress of a Ukrainian union of work collectives. I live with my family in the village of Nerubaiskoe, not far from Odessa.

My grandfather on my father's side was a Cossack who came to the southern Ukraine when the region was being brought under Russian rule during the reign of Catherine II. He received a land grant, but families in those days were very large, and as the years went by, the land was divided up into small parcels.

My mother's father was of similar background, but he was a very rich peasant, with over seventy hectares and hired workers. He graduated from the agricultural school and was an exemplary farmer. When the October Revolution occurred, he didn't take sides or participate. He felt that it was a peasant's business to grow wheat. Both the Whites and the Reds bought and took from him.

In 1919 or 1920 dekulakization occurred [redistribution of the land from the rich peasants, kulaks, to the poor and landless peasants]. The land was redivided according to the number of mouths in the family. But since he had nine children and a wife, as well as his mother and father living nearby, he got a decent piece of land. It didn't take him long to get back all the land that he had once owned. His better land had been given to local fishermen, and they leased it back to him in return for half its yield. His farm was very successful; he even bought a steam-powered thresher.

In 1928, when talk of collectivization was in the air, he realized that he should sell the farm and go off somewhere. But he couldn't abandon his land. So as soon as collectivization began, he voluntarily joined the *kolkhoz*. And since he was respected in the village, no one thought to harm him during dekulakization. He soon became brigadier and then agronomist, that is, the chief specialist. He moved up very quickly, even though he was very skeptical about the collective farms.

Despite everything, in 1933, he was hit by the new wave of dekulakization in the Ukraine and strapped with a tax five times the norm. He was forced to sell everything he had. That year my mother, his daughter, got married and came to live where I am now. My grandfather wasn't allowed to work on the land and became a worker on the streetcar lines. But in 1935, as the collective farm was going to ruin, he was brought back and made brigadier of some neglected section. He soon brought it into shape, but they forced him off again and he went back to the streetcars and never went back to the land.

When the war broke out, all his sons volunteered. None returned. He was left with one son who had been too young to go to war.

My father's marriage to a kulak's daughter turned out to be a reckless move, even though he was a *kolkhoz* member and a valuable and conscientious specialist. In 1937, he was arrested during the harvest campaign as a wrecker, a kulak sympathizer married to a kulak daughter. Amazingly, however, the court acquitted him. In 1941, he went to war and was captured near Kiev together with practically the entire front. He was transported to Poland but escaped back home. The German occupation authorities learned of this and warned him that if he tried to leave, his family would be shot. I was born in 1942. When the Red Army returned in 1944, they offered to free him from military service so that he could work in the *kolkhoz* as a specialist. But he refused and went to the front. He considered it a holy war, a war against enslavers. He had seen much injustice and cruelty under the occupation. He was killed in the fall of 1944.

My mother, who was left with three children, was arrested in 1946 and sent to the camps in Kolyma. Very influential relatives lobbied on her part, and she was freed in the late fall of 1948. We had heard she was dead and were already living as orphans. She had already sold most of what we had in 1946 to keep us from starving, and whatever remained was stolen while she was in the camps. She returned now to the *kolkhoz*, where we lived very poorly. She was a very proud woman and never asked for help. Sometimes at school they would give us a few meters of cloth for clothing, but even that was done reluctantly, as we were children of an ex-convict. Until 1958, I was barred from the Pioneers [young children's organization] and Komsomol. My older brother worked as a tractor driver in 1954 for a year before he was called up for military service, and that allowed us to eat a bit more decently. That was the first time I tasted butter.

I graduated from the Ukrainian-language rural high school in 1960. I was very good at sports and I wanted to go to the military academy, but the *kolkhoz* chairman asked me to stay on and follow in my father's footsteps, promising to arrange my admission to the agricultural institute. But the following year when I was to be called up for military service I asked him about the institute. He told me to first complete my service and then he'd think it over. I was enraged and left the *kolkhoz* and the land forever.

I got a job as an ordinary worker in a city construction enterprise. After a year there, I had accumulated two years of work experience and was eligible to enter the communications institute. [Under Khrushchev's reforms, in most cases one needed two years of work experience before one could be accepted to an institute of higher education.] But I had to feed my family and I had to leave before long. A new railroad station was being opened, and I got a job there as a stop operator. However, since I had a decent education, they offered to send me to locomotive engineer's courses. I also managed a storeroom for a year. Then they offered me a job in the electrical shop, where I attained the highest skill level and became brigadier. After fifteen years there, I worked on the assembly of the container crane and stayed on to work as its operator.

I was a member of the trade union committee for a long time. When I started working, we had 1,150 workers. I worked on the collective agreement and was in charge of its fulfillment. There were constant conflicts with the administration over this. One of the division administrators once said of me, "Artemenko, of course, is an evil, but he is an evil to which we have to reconcile ourselves."

Other workers got themselves fired for the kind of things I said and did against the administration.

I was an informal leader of the collective and always felt the collective behind me. That's the only reason management made concessions. And my influence went beyond my division to the entire collective of over 1,000 people. For example, at the conferences of the work collective, when I criticized the shortcomings of management, the other delegates always backed me up. Over all these years, I've never heard a careless word addressed to me. Very often in collectives, unfortunately, people are called by nicknames. But they call me not only by my given name, but also by my patronymic [a more formal, respectful form of address], which is very rare.

What were the conflicts with management about?

The most basic issue was constant violations of the work and rest regimes, overtime, and so on. We also had constant conflicts over wages, over a raise for one or another worker. We were never able to raise wages for everyone at the same time, only for individual groups.

What was the occasion for the raises?

Intensification of work, mechanization, increased workload. For example, when I began to work as a signal operator, there were three of us in a brigade plus an locomotive engineer. Now it's all automated; there are no more signal operators. In my own brigade now on the container crane, there are six people doing the same volume of work that used to be done by half the section. At the Lesotovarnaya station, 120 people do less than the six of us.

Is your equipment Soviet-made or imported?

It's imported, but we also use Soviet equipment. But its quality is poor—not so much because it is poorly assembled, but because the design is faulty. The cabins are very narrow. Work conditions on the loading mechanisms are very poor. On the imported equipment, the worker has all the conditions for productive work. The capitalists insist on this with a view to their own profits. Our bosses don't care what the workers' conditions are. People working on our equipment often get sick, since the insulation and heating are very poor. All these machines stand in the open plain, eight kilometers from the city.

Besides my union activity, I was chair of the parent's committee of our school for twelve years. It's a big school with 1,000 students. Our settlement's population is 10,000. I saw directors come and go and did my best to keep the new ones from interfering in the life of the school's work collective.

What was your attitude to perestroika when it began?

To tell the truth, positive. Before perestroika, I felt that there were no perspectives—that the only aspiration anyone could have was to go off somewhere else to earn more money. Yet, it was clear that the regime was coming to an end, that big shocks were in store for it. Those who say that there was no need for perestroika are wrong. But the crisis was not so much in industry. Sure, it had problems, and the technology had fallen behind, but it could have gone on that way for a long time. The basic crisis was in agriculture. In the West, the people who leave agriculture are the least successful farmers who are unable to make a go of it. Here the most intelligent, the boldest abandoned the land, the most active people. This was because of the dictatorial regime on the collective farms. Don't believe people who say that Franco or Pinochet were the biggest dictators. The *kolkhoz* directors were much worse.

But weren't they working under orders of the district party secretary?

True, but these secretaries were themselves recruited from among the directors. They didn't appear out of nowhere. At that time, you could observe among the middle management, especially the farm directors, a growing indifference toward production. They let things slide. And the higher-ups began to understand that they couldn't force them to work. So they started to offer the workers an extra carrot, explaining that because the Russian worker is smarter than any engineer—which isn't true—they didn't have to pay the engineer anything. Yet they constantly spoke of the need to raise the prestige of the work of engineers, doctors, teachers.

They also said it was necessary to cultivate in workers an owner's attitude to work. But they forgot that you have to respect an individual. Besides, if you have no property, how can you feel that you are the owner of anything? As owner of the whole country, I couldn't go up to the Kremlin and feel that I was master in it. Our whole people was lumpenized [as in "lumpenproletariat"; déclassé], from the simplest worker to the general secretary of the party. Yes, Brezhnev himself was lumpenized, and that's why he became corrupt. He gave himself all kinds of awards and greedily took everything they offered him, because he himself had nothing. Officially, he earned only something over 1,000 rubles. He was a pauper like the rest of the people.

Of course, a crucial factor was also that the idea had died by that time. There were very few principled people left. And those who did not believe looked around to see how they could secure their old age. And the stealing began. Look at how easily politicians in the West leave the public arena, because they can return to doing what they did before. But if a regional party committee secretary was dismissed, who was he, what could he do? It was a very frightening prospect. He became a nullity and couldn't even find work. When the secretary of our district committee, who was an engineer by training, was fired in 1983, he ended up working as a mechanic in an agricultural college.

So the regime began to decay, and this was felt above all in the agricultural sphere, which, after all, is fundamental. People can't work when they're hungry. At the same time, the village was being mercilessly exploited and continues to be exploited to this day, despite the democrats having come to power.

The tragedy of the village is that, on the one hand, the bureaucracy doesn't want to give land to those who would take it, and, on the other, there are very few who know how to farm. Very few people know how to manage large pieces of land. Yet, grain cannot be grown on two hectares. Management was centralized; thinking people weren't needed.

A bourgeois stratum has appeared, a collective farm aristocracy that doesn't care about the land. I'm talking about the managerial level, whose ranks have greatly swelled.

So, on the one hand, I do think that the people on the farms should be given the chance to decide for themselves what they want to do. But I agree with the proposal that the farms should be symbolically divided up and each person given a share, so that he will know that if he does want to leave, he will have three, four, five hectares. This would also allow them to get rid of that scum, the aristocracy. The possibility of earning some sort of profit would force them to do it. They would start to organize themselves into cooperatives, since they could not exist on their own. They would become the real owners of their surplus product and not have to give anything away for free to people who did not earn it. This would allow for progress.

You have to make use of what exists. And there is a lot of experience. There is one farm that was headed by a famous chairman, Digusarov, who created an association of peasant farmsteads that works quite well. It is a cooperative where each has a specific part of the work and is responsible for it from beginning to end. And they have a very high income. But I don't think all the farms can take this path.

I've been told that at the start of perestroika workers began to work more conscientiously because they believed that real change was coming.

That was very noticeable. People took hope. When the old leaders made speeches, especially Brezhnev, people switched off their televisions. Whatever they said was immediately of great historical value. In institutes of higher technical education, instead of studying their own fields of specialization, people studied quotations from these speeches. And any speech, even that of a worker, was considered better the more quotes it had and the more times the general secretary's name appeared. But with Gorbachev, people stopped studying his speeches and began to read them, people who before would never have opened a book of a general secretary's speeches. At that moment, he could have achieved a great deal. Using the party apparatus, which was a well-oiled machine, he could have rapidly forced through reforms. Forced the bureaucracy, that is. He could have easily taken apart the collective farms, reorganized them into cooperatives, associations. Discipline was still strong.

But already in 1989 the crisis began to emerge. A little later, the Law on Cooperatives was adopted. Its main negative feature was that it allowed the creation of cooperatives attached to state enterprises, and it made possible the transformation of non-cash credits from the enterprise's accounts into cash sums that were paid to the cooperatives, opening the way for large-scale theft from the state. And when the borders of the country were opened, people began to export anything they could, exploiting the growing difference between the dollar and the ruble. Massive theft of the nation's property began, and people soon lost any incentive to work. The more hours a worker put in, the poorer he got, because he had less time to stand in line.

When did you join the party?

I joined in 1987. I believed in the reforms. I believed that the party could be reformed only from within. And I had a phenomenal career. Literally three months after joining, I was elected to the district party committee. Two years later, I became a member of the regional committee.

As an activist, didn't you feel pressure before perestroika to join the party?

On the contrary, even if I had wanted to, they wouldn't have accepted me. The party didn't need people like me.

How did you come to be elected chair of the STK?

When the issue arose of electing a work collective council, it was already assumed that I would chair it. My brigade proposed me, and when the conference came around to electing a chair, my candidacy met with such applause that the director said we could forego voting.

Who was this director?

The 1987 State Enterprise Law allowed collectives to elect directors. This, of course, was a knife in the heart of those directors who refused to take people into account. A feudal lord would not have dealt with people the way these directors did because even a feudal lord was interested in the results of the serfs' labor. Not so the directors. For them the main thing was the plan. Go beyond plan— that's good. And in general, he considered that there is no such thing as an irreplaceable worker, only a worker not yet replaced. This director had been elected by the collective before the elections of the work-collective council.

We work together, imagine that! There have been few disagreements. And if there is some drunk or someone who violates discipline, the STK itself demands he be called to order.

What happened at your depot during the threat of a general railroad strike in 1990?

At that time, the collective was very agitated. The demands concerned wages, conditions, respect for labor legislation. It was also a revolt against the disciplinary code on the railroad. The initiative, in fact, came from the Odessa railroad, especially the Odessa sorting depot and Kotov depot, though we were not exactly spectators ourselves. To be honest, I took a very moderate position. You see, in our conditions, we could only harm ourselves with a strike.

An arbitration commission was set up very quickly. Management understood that this was no laughing matter. The workers were very determined. One can say that the majority of demands were met. The workers didn't get everything they wanted, but the main thing was management's willingness to make concessions quickly. This softened the workers' determination. I myself was among those who said that since we had met understanding, why rush to break down an open door.

Much changed in our lives. Particularly harmful has been the practice of distributing goods in the work collectives starting about a year and a half ago. The shops were short of goods, so they began to sell them at work. The STKs were charged with this, and management saw how it was destroying them.

You can't distribute fairly what doesn't exist, and it's hard for a pauper to be honest. So, of course, someone at some point would get something that he shouldn't have, or he got more than he should have. It was only natural, all the more so as the country by that time already had forgotten the meaning of sin. All the moral foundations had collapsed, and only the police remained to keep people honest. But the police were the first to be corrupted, and no one was left to watch over this herd. People lost all sense of morality.

We get a list that says, for example, that the collective of 800 people will receive one refrigerator this year, or two televisions each quarter, or two suits, or thirty towels. Well, how are you going to divide them among 800 people? By lottery? But that is unjust also. And most of these goods slipped out "on the left," through the back door.

At the fifth general assembly of the regional party committee, I said, "Comrade Communists, I am turning to you, my party comrades, with the following conclusions. Let us analyze the work of the regional executive committee, or at least certain of its departments. Let us take the trade department. The person in charge of it is a Communist and member of our party's regional committee. The head of Odessa's wholesale consumer trade administration is a Communist and member of our party's city committee. The managers of all the warehouses and local wholesale consumer trade administrations are all Communists. Yet speculation is in full bloom. Let us evaluate the work of these people. I consider that people who facilitate these processes have no place in the party." The hall greeted my words with stony silence. Although in that hall there were many genuinely honest people, they were unable to speak up.

Do you think that the practice of distributing goods at work was done with the conscious aim of undermining the workers' solidarity?

I don't think it was accidental. There were much easier ways to go about it, if they really wanted to introduce some order. I am not even talking about rationing. They should have allowed us to buy only with money we earned at work, that is, only people in the state sector would be allowed to purchase in state shops. People who work in cooperatives would have to buy at the free market. The state could have set aside a certain amount of goods for the market, and with the large salaries that they earned in the cooperatives, they could have paid the high prices for them. This wouldn't have been difficult to organize.

So you are saying that this mafia, which was the real power, had its representatives sitting in the regional party committee.

And undoubtedly higher. So I did what I could, I spoke out, so what? Unless you are acquainted with the underlying, hidden processes, you can't really understand what's happening. For example, from September of last year, freight deliveries started to slow down. Everyone was talking about the bottlenecks at the overloaded railway depots. In fact, the freight could easily have been unloaded and sold. They were just waiting for the prices to rise on January 1.

Take our depot. To organize the orderly shipment of freight, we need twenty-five container trucks. But we are given only eighteen. Do you want to tell me that in a region as immense as that of Odessa they can't find seven more trucks? Obviously someone is interested in slowing down freight deliveries in order to maintain tension in society. Besides, the depot gets paid for storage. It's pure profit.

I have my own point of view on the new, post-Communist Party soviet power. I could observe this directly in our region, but I am sure the same tendencies are at work everywhere. Before, there was a two-tiered territorial administrative structure—party and soviet, with the soviet being the subordinate organ at each level. The party regional committee would receive a directive to look into some matter, and it would pass it on for action to people in the soviet executive committee who were acquainted with that area of activity. They would investigate and report to the party committee, where it would be examined and slightly modified, and the question would finally be decided at the regional party committee plenum or maybe only in some department of the regional committee. An instruction would be drawn up and passed down for execution, "Carry this out or lose your party card." Loss of one's membership reduced a person to a nothing. When the system still existed, it worked quite efficiently.

When during the election campaign I told the people that I would fight for the full power of the soviets, I had no idea that I was calling to destroy the state machinery. After the elections, we didn't even give the soviet's old executive committee a chance to find the documents for us and prepare a proposal for new rules to govern the soviet's functioning. We immediately created a committee to organize elections to a new executive. We wanted a clean break, considering ourselves the first democratic soviet. When the new executive was in place and began to work, do you know what it felt like? It was as if Vesuvius had erupted, and all the lava had fallen on a single person. Such a huge chunk of power fell on the new executive committee that it destroyed it. It turned out that the executive committee couldn't function because it didn't have people with professional, administrative experience. There was no one. Not only didn't these people know how to manage, but they didn't have the authority, they lacked the mechanisms to carry out their decisions.

And the party apparatus had stepped aside?

Yes, it stood aside and took an oppositional position vis-à-vis the soviet, sometimes making use of its old levers of influence. And its main lever was the special telephone system that linked it to all the key posts in the region. So they could destabilize the situation if they wanted through the party organs. That's why in soviets like that of Lvov, the question of who was the real power arose at once: the shadow party committee or the newly elected soviet? It was a very difficult situation, though we didn't see this at once. We thought that we would make a few adjustments and everything would run smoothly. We struggled but we couldn't carry anything out. At present, I am convinced that if a UFO appeared over the city and sucked all our leaders out of that huge sixteen-story building and transported them to another planet, the citizens of the region wouldn't soon notice their absence. I think that it would have been a lot simpler just to let things go on their own, spontaneously.

I think that it's precisely the work collectives that can furnish the basis for effective soviet power. Way back in 1988, I first posed the question of organizing regional work-collective organizations. If we're abandoning party rule and creating a new system of government, it has to rest upon something. Before it was the army, KGB, the police, the prosecutors. We know what sort of law enforcement we have. And the same goes for the courts. Who can the new regime rely upon if it has to clean out the Aegean stables? We don't have a Hercules among us. We need some force, and this can only be the work collectives. Not the working class. I think the term "working class" was used rather artificially here. In our work collectives, in practice, you can consider the engineer a worker as much as the mechanic or anyone else in the shop. Excluding the administration, of course, though the law gives them their share of representatives.

At the congress, it seemed to me that the worker delegates were generally more militant and determined. The engineering and technical personnel, not to speak of the administrators, tended to be moderate and to approve whatever the Soviet leadership proposed.

You raise a real question. I don't want to idealize the situation, since that too is very dangerous. But all the same, I hope that the collectives will become the basis for effective soviet power. Those people, who did not want this, who didn't consider that the work collectives had a place in their structure of power, began immediately to block these processes. That's why it was only in 1990 that the STK movement really got off the ground, at least in Russia.

But as early as 1988, I tried to create some sort of regional organization and failed.

Of course, you have to take into account the inertia in the workers' thinking, the passivity, though we certainly have no right to blame people for that. Now we hear some saying that the people are no good, that they aren't the kind of people that we need. But the people have been constantly deceived. And yet when they went to vote in the elections for the Congress of People's Deputies of the USSR in 1989, and for the local soviets in 1990, they had faith. They went with enthusiasm, because they believed there would be a new regime.

And in addition to all the other problems of the soviets, it turned out that very few workers got elected. And the higher the level of the soviet, the fewer the workers. About the only worker in the Supreme Soviet was Sukhov, the taxi driver from Kharkov. Already during the elections campaign, violent criticism of worker leaders began. Maybe those worker leaders who had been put forward by the apparatus deserved this. But there were informal leaders too, and they started to stick them with the insulting name "Mister I-Approve" [*odobryams*, or yes-men].

The intelligentsia was especially zealous in this campaign. You know, you would think that a guilty person would be careful about accusing others. And these intellectuals should have felt guilty, because they were the bearers of ideas, they constantly praised the system. Ivan Drach, who is now the leader of Rukh [the main Ukrainian nationalist movement] once wrote a poem in which he said, "We don't need the sun, the party shines for us." He didn't repent before the people, he didn't donate his awards to the treasury of Rukh. What services did he get his awards for? These weren't awards earned by a production worker for high-quality work. Yes, workers used to get awards too; they were used to encourage others to try harder, "You see, he can do it, so why can't you?" No, Drach received them for ideological services. These people haven't asked forgiveness.

But they were very zealous in attacking worker-leaders. So when the elections drew near, the old worker-leaders somehow felt guilty, lowered their heads and went off to their factory work. And the new leaders just couldn't break through. There were only a few who weren't afraid of going up to the intellectuals at the meetings and demonstrations and saying, "It's all a lie what you're saying!" I, for example, in those years never approved anything, and there is no reason to call me "Mister I-Approve." And I'm probably unique in the whole of Ukraine as a deputy: I'm a worker, I live in a village, and I got elected in a central city district. But I was able to convince the electors; I told them, "If you want a forwarding agent, elect my opponents. But if you need someone who will defend your rights...." I didn't promise anything I knew that I wouldn't be able to fulfill. I said that I would fight for ecology, try to get our water cleaned up, stop the dumping of industrial effluents into the Black Sea. I'm trying to behave in the regional soviet in a way that won't allow anyone to reproach me.

So when the elections were over, everyone was shocked that there were so few workers. But at the higher levels, some of them asked, "Is this really a place for a worker?" And when preparations began for the Congress of the Ukrainian Communist Party, it was openly stated that workers have no business there. Imagine, this was in reference to a workers' party!

From the tribune of the regional party conference, I said, "We are claiming to be a party of the working class. How can we not send workers to the congress?" Even Gorbachev said, "It is very bad that there are no workers." So afterward, they invited a group of workers. They couldn't entrust the fate of the party to workers. They couldn't do that, since the workers might decide something that would harm their interests. And their interests were always higher, above those of both the party and the people.

And you can see a similar thing today. Our intelligentsia, which has pushed its way into power, which has promised the people everything, gives it nothing. The crisis gets constantly worse. There are already social forces that propose correct ways to get out of the crisis, but the government rejects these. I must say that I was surprised at the Congress of Work Collectives that the president [Yeltsin] invited our leaders to meet with the presidential council. Of course, I hope that these leaders of ours don't let us down, because I'm one of them now. The main thing is that there be no personal ambitions.

Has anything changed as a result of the defeat of the coup?

In Russia you might say something shifted. But in Ukraine every-thing remains as it was. Nothing changed. I am concerned by the fact that full sovereignty was supported precisely by that group of Communist deputies that earlier had opposed sovereignty. This is an alarming symptom.

I don't trust these people, and the course of events over the last year confirms my distrust. A lot could have been done over that year, but they did nothing. And they're now capable of waiting for another putsch, only not from above—I don't think anyone is left who is capable of doing that—but from below. But if people start to come out spontaneously into the street, I wouldn't want to be in this country to witness it.

The delegates at this congress came from enterprises with a total work force of four million. At last year's congress, the figure cited was eight million.

You can't really say that this congress represented fewer people, since last year it was a founding congress to create the Union of Work Collectives and not all the people who came decided to join it. And this year, many were unable to come who wanted to. The congress was organized very quickly. Had there been more time, there would have been many more people. We were poorly prepared. In addi-tion, the enterprise administration was very forceful in its efforts to prevent people from going. Although there is full mutual under-standing between management and myself, I was forced to come as a representative of the regional soviet and not of our STK for the simple reason that my director said, "You're going to the wrong place. You should go to Kiev and not to Moscow." To which I replied, "The road to Kiev passes through Moscow."

Across the vast spaces of the Soviet Union that has fallen apart, the workers have the same goals and tasks. If they don't coordinate their movements, if they don't press together on the state and force it to carry out their will, then nothing good can happen. Each work collective will be privatized in isolation by the *affairistes* of the shadow economy and by the former *nomenklatura*, who will use it in their own interests. I consider that in the existing situation, if you don't blindly reject everything that has happened over these seventy years but try to understand what we really have created that is good and what type of relations can grow out of that, it's possible to create a system of self-management, workers' self-management, regional self-management, and so forth.

Understanding these tasks, I feel my own great responsibility to the workers. If we fail to achieve that which we are called to accomplish, as our grandparents failed in 1918 and 1919, then we will have earned the curses of our descendants, we who stood by in silence, who let the political moment pass.

When those of us from the Ukraine met yesterday after the congress, when we set up the organizing committee for a constituent congress of a Ukrainian union of work collectives, we in fact said to each other that while we are here holding meetings, while we are discussing where to hold the congress—Lvov for some sort of ideological reasons is allegedly not suitable—while we are talking, the Supreme Soviet of the Ukraine, which consists of *nomenklatura*, directors and the like, is making laws. It's building a "directors' socialism" or capitalism that will bear the worst characteristics of the time of Jack London. If we don't intervene in this process now, it will soon be too late. So we decided to forget all ideological dogma, since the workers' movement, after all, is above party allegiance, above nationalism. In the worker milieu, we never judged people according to their nationality, only according to their real capacities. This was always a strict rule.

Why did people feel Lvov was unsuitable? Because Ukrainian nationalism is strong there?

To my way of thinking, I wouldn't say their nationalism is strong. The struggle there is stronger. This is the feeling of an offended people struggling for a national idea. But among such people there is always a handful of rabid nationalists, who, because of their nationalism, fail to see the main thing. This isn't necessarily bad. The main thing is not to allow it to become a mass phenomenon. A small rabid minority can be useful in showing us what we fail to notice. After all, we cannot reconcile ourselves to the fact that 20 million Ukrainians have become Russian speakers. I'm one of them. I know Ukrainian, of course, but I use it rarely, only in my work collective, and only in that part that has remained attached to the language. But the majority at work speak Russian. I have never made a speech in my native language. After all, we are on our own territory. I understand—when I go to Moscow, I speak Russian. But when a

Russian comes to Ukraine, he speaks Russian. Imagine if I went to France and spoke Ukrainian and demanded that people understand me.

In general, I'm hopeful right now. I think that we can have an influence on the presidential elections in the Ukraine. The decision of the Ukrainian Supreme Soviet on full sovereignty places us in a difficult situation. We have to support that decision, because if the worker collectives came out now in defence of the interests of the Soviet government that doesn't really exist, our descendants wouldn't understand us. So in the referendum on sovereignty, we must support the Supreme Soviet, but we know that they came out for sovereignty in order to usurp power in the territory of Ukraine, to move away from the center in order to save themselves. So after the presidential elections, we must demand new general elections and throw them out. If we succeed now in organizing ourselves into a force that can have an influence on the presidential elections, and if we get what we need, if producers appear that can freely dispose of the results of their labor, then people will no longer allow that kind of deputy into the Supreme Soviet. They will elect people who in practice have shown a commitment to their interests.

I just wish that this message could reach the workers. You see how silent our Ukrainian press is. I wish people could hear me and understand how important this is, how important it is to have a massive congress that will unite the worker collectives. The workers must understand the importance of the historical moment. In today's situation Lenin's words are completely applicable: "Delay is like death." If they understand that, they'll know that they must act.

Tatyana Markova:
Postal Worker
[October 1991]

I met Tatyana in Moscow at a session of the Commission for Ties
with the Labor Movement of the Russian Social Democratic Party.
Although this small party is really liberal in orientation—it supports
a "civilized" capitalism—it had at the time a small left fraction, made
up mostly of worker activists.

Tatyana had seemingly limitless energy and tenacity in the face
of tremendous obstacles and repeated disappointments. Women
activists, while fewer in number than men, have in my experience
tended to be stronger and more resilient. It is only in rare moments
that they let some of the pain and even desperation of their situations show.

I first became active during the election campaign to the Congress of People's Deputies in May 1989. Before that I had lived a
simple life. It wasn't as though I hadn't been thinking, but maybe
because of my upbringing, I had been floating off somewhere in the
clouds, far away from real life.

Actually, reality had already struck its first blow in the early 1980s.
I had graduated from a cultural-educational institute with a specialty
in directing. I had big dreams about developing our cultural life
until I came face to face with our totalitarian practices. I was working
as director of a cultural center in Kaluga when I came across a book
about the Rerykhs. [Nikolai Rerykh was a Russian artist and mystic
who lived for many years in the Himalayas.] It was published in the
magazine *Moskva*, which we had in our club library. It had a lot of
material about ancient Eastern philosophy, and although at the time
I was far from any sort of mysticism, I was very struck by the purely
humanitarian side of Rerykh's teachings.

I decided to use this material in a club program, since our young
people adore unusual themes. By chance, news of this reached the
city's party committee, and when I went to consult the magazine
again in the library, it was gone—by order of the city's party organs.
I was surprised. A week later I was summoned to the city's cultural

department and given a good working over. "Rerykh is a closed topic. He's a mystic. How did you dare!?" and so on. I was so shocked that at first I couldn't grasp what was happening.

This was just before Brezhnev died. After his death, life in our club went completely crazy. With Andropov's arrival, they shut down our science fiction society. Under Chernenko, they decided to close the discotheques. Each leader wanted to leave his mark on cultural life, but in just the opposite way of what we needed. But the main blow came under Gorbachev in 1985 when they completely destroyed my work. In addition, my salary was very low, 100 rubles a month. I killed myself for each kopeck but I was a fanatic about my work. I had been promised an apartment, but they assumed that I would go on working anyway, so they didn't feel any need to keep their promise. So in the end, life pushed me out.

After that, I worked at many different jobs, including taxi driver. I have seen many spheres of life but only now have I had the chance to draw general conclusions from this experience and make use of it in my political activity. With perestroika, information began to flow through the media. We learned about our past, about all the negative things. This confirmed my impression that not all was right in our society.

I came to politics in a rather casual manner. I got involved in Tarasov's electoral campaign for a Congress seat. [Artem Tarasov was one of the Soviet Union's first avowed millionaires. A confidant of Yeltsin, he left for the West under a cloud of scandal in early 1991, having been accused of stealing tens of millions of rubles from his firm.] He was chairman of a cooperative in Moscow, a very clever and charismatic figure who aroused a lot of hope in relation to the economic reform. He had large support groups, but the party and KGB tried to block him by fixing the elections. A movement arose to resist this and it eventually assumed other social and political goals.

Soon after the elections, the Popular Front began to fall apart, because it was made up of people with very diverse interests and political views. We formed a social-democratic cell in Kaluga. I became co-chair and was elected delegate to the second and third congresses of the Social Democratic Party. I belong to the democratic center fraction, which doesn't promote any specific program but seeks to balance the left and right to prevent a split. However, I work with the left fraction because I'm very involved in the labor movement in Kaluga.

The party's leadership says it should seek its social base in the middle class. But that's totally detached from reality. What kind of middle class is there with so few skilled workers and when our entrepreneurs are basically recruited from the mafia-style elite of the *nomenklatura*? This so-called middle class is so small and weak that if we adopt it as our social base we'll never win significant support. Whether we like it or not, we need to base ourselves in the working class, the predominant group in society. I believe that life will force the workers to organize and to participate actively in political life, like the miners.

Tell me about your work.

I'm an ordinary postal worker. I deliver telegrams. My own experience at work and that of the broad circle of people I deal with in Kaluga confirms the correctness of my political position. With each new day, it's the ordinary worker who lives worse and worse. The workers are totally dependent on the state system; they are cruelly oppressed by the totalitarian regime. At the factory, the worker is under the thumb of the administration. Through the trade union, which is supposed to defend him, he depends upon management for an apartment, a place for his child in daycare. An isolated struggle is virtually impossible in these circumstances. You have to organize a collective. But when any worker tries to do this, he's simply fired before he really can get started.

When I was active in the Popular Front, my boss called a meeting in my absence in an effort to turn the collective against me. She told them that my political views were very destructive and proposed that I be fired.

On what legal basis could she do that?

In our system, you can always find something. That's the beauty of it as a system of oppression. Fortunately, I had been able by then to form a cohesive group of supporters who were infuriated by this suggestion. When the administration realized that they couldn't get to me through the collective, it tried other means, like depriving me of my bonus for some insignificant detail or transferring me to a more difficult and less well-paid job. These are a few of their repressive mechanisms.

It wasn't easy, but I held out. After two years of hard, painstaking work, I've succeeded in organizing five people in our telegraph section into an independent trade union. To tell you the truth, I don't know how we will proceed from here. It's all very complicated, and I'm learning as I go. There is an awful lot that I don't know.

In Kaluga there are about 600 employees, but the problem is that they are scattered. You have to know what a post office is. We have several branches across the city, in villages, and the suburbs. Kaluga itself is a regional capital with about 300,000 people. A large number of its factories are in the military sector. These are very large enterprises, like the turbine factory, the engineering works, the electromechanical factory, the electrical car parts factory. So the problems of the labor collectives and the labor movement are very acute in our town.

Does the official trade union do anything for you?

My relationship with it is rather unique. As it turned out, they tried to fire my boss for her failure to get rid of me. She then started coming to me for help, and she even took me along to our city postal workers' union conference. There a small revolution took place: they elected a new chairperson. For the first time in the history of this conservative organization, the workers rose up against the chairperson of the trade union committee—who was for all practical purposes a member of the administration—and elected someone of their own choice.

This woman tried to work through the existing structure at first. But they soon put her in her place. She knew that the administration was afraid of me, and we soon found a common language. I suggested that we form an independent trade union, and she agreed. In principle, we could have taken the entire collective with us. But I was afraid I wouldn't be able to do this properly, since I had so little knowledge. Finally I told her, "Valentina Aleksandrovna, I feel that it's still too soon. You go on working in your structure as best you can. On my part, I'll organize my independent trade union. You will pressure the administration from your side, and I from mine, and we will work together."

We are in constant contact—secretly, of course—but she is totally dependent on the administration, which pays her wages and controls her bonuses. Such is the system of state trade unions.

Hasn't the new law on trade unions done anything to correct that?
This law is very imperfect. Thanks to Yeltsin's decree, trade unions can now officially be created only with the agreement of the administration. [This decree of June 1991 was ostensibly directed against the Communist Party organizations in the enterprises, but at the same time it outlawed all political organizations and made the existence of "social organizations," like unions, dependent upon the agreement of management.] Fortunately, we are so politically illiterate, from the administration down to the average worker, that the decree is mostly ignored. But where the administration has understood its import, it has moved quickly to dissolve any independent trade unions.

My present situation is very complicated. Having organized my trade union, having obtained the documents needed to register it, to receive a stamp and open a bank account, I'm not yet ready to make its existence public. I'm trying to fight through the official trade union structures and through the women's council. [In 1987, Gorbachev gave the signal for the revival of these organizations, created after the revolution and subsequently abolished under Stalin. However, they never really became militant organizations and were engaged mainly in charity work. In recent years, they are rarely mentioned by politicians or the press.] The chair of our union committee, who also heads the women's council, isn't formally a member of my party. But she is sympathetic, and we work in close contact. In practice, I fulfill the functions of chair of the women's council.

I'm surprised to hear that the women's councils are still functioning.
Well, they still exist, but as appendages of the administration. Ordinary working women don't know of their existence. I myself was surprised to discover them, even though in the district soviet buildings there are offices with "Women's Council" written across the door. What do the women's councils in our city do? Basically, they distribute necessities. In this period of massive shortages, they manage to get hold of a few goods. But they don't do any political work.

Until recently, work in the communications sector was very poorly paid and attracted only women. What were 110 rubles a month to a man who needs 300 to maintain his family? Last January they finally raised our wages to 250 and we sometimes get bonuses of 50 or 100. In other words, the wage system itself is defective, and we will have to fight to change it.

Here's a concrete example of our situation. I came specially to Moscow to see the conditions of telegraph workers here. Women who deliver telegrams receive 370 rubles a month. Six women are employed to deliver 100 telegrams each day, and they manage to do it on time. In our town, we have to deliver 400 each day—and as many as 600 or 700 on holidays—and there are only twelve of us.

Picture it: we deliver telegrams for a basic wage of 250 rubles a month, and a promised bonus. But one complaint is all it takes to lose your entire bonus. It's quite a feat to live on 250 rubles today, when prices have risen so much. Yet, complaints can come at any time because of the way things are organized. The work load is simply too great. The situation in Moscow, with its big apartment complexes and with telephones in almost every home, is very different from Kaluga, where houses are scattered, there are relatively few telephones and the delivery routes are very long. It might take a whole hour just to reach one's route, while the time limit for delivery of an urgent telegram is one hour. If one urgent telegram is delivered on time, the next one is sure to be late. Hence, the complaints, because the administration refuses to reorganize our work and to spend the money for extra people. So if it isn't the thirteenth month's wage, it's some other bonus that we lose.

We are really oppressed. You have to understand the specificity of communications. First of all, it will never be privatized; it's a state structure. Second, discipline is strict: the regulations covering dismissal are similar to those in military factories. Communications also mean secrecy. So union and political work is very difficult.

I don't know how I managed to create our independent union in the face of all the pressure from management. Their arbitrariness has sparked so much anger over this past year. I organized two meetings that very nearly resulted in a strike, particularly in my division.

I remember reading somewhere about six months ago that postal workers were preparing a strike.

That was in Perm. I can tell you about it. As I said, communications workers are generally conservative, the administration even more so, and add to this the pressure from the party organs. So the employees are very downtrodden, and their intellectual level is not high. People with higher education aren't going to work there; it's purely physical work that requires no thought. So things are generally very quiet, even though all around us today political life is seething. Postal workers don't know how to begin, and they have no confidence that they can achieve anything.

Prices started to rise. As a state institution, the administration had some leeway to raise our wages, but Soyuzpechat [the state distributor of newspapers and periodicals] took a large part of what should have been the post office's income and in turn gave a large part of this to the Ministry of Communications, which put it into the state budget. The state then turned around and gave us a small subsidy. In practice, except for that subsidy, the letter and telegram carriers received next to nothing for their work. The Perm postal workers were the first to demand that publishers pay us for delivering their materials. That's when they struck. In Kaluga, I came to an agreement with the old administration that had been trying to get rid of me: we'd stop harassing each other, and they'd write a letter to the Supreme Soviet in the name of our post office demanding an agreement between the publishers and the postal service that would give us our due.

This was the goal of the strike: to obtain a direct agreement between the postal service and the publishers that would exclude Soyuzpechat, which had been receiving money for the delivery work that we did. As you probably know, the Ministry of Communications exploited this movement and ended up taking about 50 percent of our profits.

I read that the ministry even helped to organize the strike.

That was in its interest, because under the new conditions of self-financing, the ministry knew that without subsidies it would soon go bankrupt. So the strike had the support of the ministry, and it was a success. At present the law says that the postal service gets money from the publishers.

But that wasn't the end of it. The money we got from the publishers was placed in the State Bank, and we couldn't touch it. The head of the post office had promised the employees a raise by the New Year, but he couldn't deliver because the money was stuck in the bank. The matter was thrashed out in the higher state organs until April or May. Finally, it seems that the Ministry of Communications was able to get hold of part of the money, since we did get a small raise. And after April 2, we got sixty-five rubles. Now our post office is beginning to get some money, though I'm not sure from what source. All this has to be clarified, since it is possible that we're being cheated. If the postal service is now receiving such big sums from the publishers, where is our money? The publishers have raised their prices tenfold, but our wages haven't risen by anything even resembling that. In principle, we should be receiving the subsistence minimum of 360 rubles, but our base pay is still only 250.

What's your attitude to the present Russian government?

In my opinion, Yeltsin's speech yesterday at the Russian Supreme Soviet showed that after the coup he has simply betrayed the people. Of course, I'm not surprised, since I have been critical of him for a long time. My analysis is more psychological than political. Who is Yeltsin? A former Communist Party member, a man with totalitarian inclinations. I don't want to criticize the entire Communist movement. I am told that in the West there are good people in it, that the movement there is what it should be. But here it's linked to totalitarianism. Yeltsin spent his whole life in it, was a leader there. He's now close to sixty, and one can't expect him to change completely.

My prognosis was that since some 50 percent of the Russian Supreme Soviet consists of *nomenklatura*, we couldn't expect reforms that would improve the lot of the people. And, of course, they made sure they passed laws that served only their own interests, not those of the people.

We can now see this in practice. They passed a law on privatization that suits the *nomenklatura* very well. And those so-called democrats who passed this law are basically individuals who sought to make a political career for their own private benefit on the wave of perestroika. Real democrats, genuinely honest and principled people, are very rare in our political life. Indeed, it would be surprising if they weren't so rare. After all, for seventy years public life has been conducted without any consideration of principle or morality.

This is probably the natural evolution of politics in our country, and my task and that of other political activists who seek truth and justice is to try to influence the course of political life as best we can by whatever means available, sticking to our principles that are so lacking among our politicians. But we are very few comparatively.

You are also active in the women's movement. What are the most urgent needs of women?

The most urgent measures must be directed at protecting women's living standards. The first and main blow of the market reform will be directed against women. They'll be fired first. Services are already being cut and becoming more expensive, undermining our ability to raise our children decently. Look at our young girls and boys. They are growing up like little animals who will later tear us to pieces. The law on privatization also hurts women, because there are very few women economists, people who can orient themselves well in these questions.

What do you think of the private businessmen? For example, how does it feel to watch television ads that offer seats on commodity exchanges for a million and a half rubles?

I can't speak with any authority about Moscow's exchanges, but who run the cooperatives in Kaluga? They're energetic, active people with initiative who were unable to find an outlet for their energy in the old society. They are trying to earn money, as in any normal country, by selling their intellect, their brains. But since we lack normal laws in this country, they encounter tremendous difficulties. And since the moral level in this country is very low, most of the cooperative and entrepreneurial sector is made up of animals, people totally lacking in moral values. At the same time, I have to say that some of them are prepared to help me.

We have been placed in a situation where the main question is survival. It turns out that to survive, you have to live by the laws of the jungle. The system itself created these conditions. But strange as it might seem, during the past seventy years when the human being in us was stifled, some people did emerge with real moral and spiritual fiber. But all those stocks and exchanges and the like—they are lawless. If a barrier isn't erected to contain them, they will simply sweep over society and devour us whole.

Our economy is on the verge of collapse. It would seem sensible to allow ordinary people who have some entrepreneurial talent and inclination to work to turn things around. They shouldn't be taxed too heavily, perhaps at 35 percent. They should be able to freely purchase raw materials and machinery. But our Supreme Soviet has set the tax at 47 percent.

Yet initially there was a good Russian law on small enterprises that gave them a two-year tax holiday so they could get on their feet. This law has been abrogated and replaced by a predatory tax. In addition, ordinary, honest people lack the capital needed to start a business. For example, you come to register your small enterprise and although you have only a few hundred rubles, the functionaries immediately start to rob you of it. To write the enterprise's charter, the city soviet asks 300 rubles, sometimes more. For registration, 1,300. For a stamp, 200. To open a bank account, 200. And these figures are from before the price rise. It's obvious that even if I have the will and the capability, I can't start a business.

And those who manage to accumulate capital, how do they do it?

Only through illegal methods. In my opinion, all the people in our country who have capital accumulated it originally through various illegal dealings. It was easy. Now there is tremendous speculation: They buy cigarettes in Moscow for two rubles a pack and sell them in Kaluga for four. That's not trade. They earn more in a month than I do by working honestly in a state job. This kind of illegal accumulation really expanded under Brezhnev. You could make big money only by stealing from the state or by robbing your own comrades.

Yeltsin wasted a whole year. He could have done a lot for the economy by making laws to promote small business. But alongside the high cost of obtaining all the necessary documents, a whole system of bribes has grown up. I tried to open a small enterprise, part of whose profits would have been gone to support invalids, but I couldn't pay the bribe they were asking. Without it, you have to wait months for the documents. The people who have come to power exploit our flawed legislation.

The situation in the Kaluga city soviet is similar to that in Moscow.

The mayor of Moscow, Gavril Popov, is what we call a "democratic *nomenklaturshchik*," and the chairman of our city soviet, Chernikov, also presented himself as a democrat in the beginning. But he has in fact joined with the old mafia. They've managed to bring all the democratic papers under control, and the papers now are afraid to publish critical information about the soviet. And we, the real democrats, simply cannot get anything of our own printed in these democratic papers. We have to go to the reactionary former Communist press, like *Sovetskaya Rossiya*. Personally, this does not bother me.

The electoral campaign to the Kaluga soviet in June 1991 gives a concrete idea of our political process. These were by-elections in nine city districts that coincided with the presidential elections in Russia. In Kaluga, Democratic Russia [once the main liberal coalition, begun as a democratic voters' association in 1990 and strongly supported Yeltsin, now virtually defunct] has in fact replaced the Communist Party as the ruling party. These are often very educated, intelligent people, former members of the Communist Party, and even before these by-elections they had some eight deputies in the key posts as chairmen of commissions. These would-be democrats decided to experiment with multiparty elections, but it turned out that with seven or eight people running in each electoral district, the dispersal of votes threatened the elections.

So at a meeting of Democratic Russia, they decided to reduce the number of candidates. Of course, their intention was to arrange things so that the elections would strengthen their own bloc. They decided to conduct surveys, and only the most popular candidates would be allowed to run for election. These surveys were then taken at meetings they organized to ensure their majorities.

This "democracy" frankly shocked us. It's up to the voters to determine the popularity of candidates, and if it's necessary to reduce the number of candidates, each party could be limited to one candidate per district. We dove into the campaign with even greater energy. And in effect we won: three of our candidates won on the second round, including myself. But in fact, no one was elected, since too few people showed up to vote on the second round. This is what happens when democrats fight with democrats, using uncivilized methods, hurling abuse and slander. And I think the same thing is going to happen in the coming elections in 1992. [Yeltsin managed to have these elections postponed.] The fighting among democrats will be even more terrible than the fight between democrats and Communists in the past.

What happened in Kaluga during the coup?

The city soviet supported Yeltsin, but I believe they did so only because they felt the coup couldn't succeed and, of course, because they wanted to protect their own positions.

The soviet organized public meetings, and 3,000 people came. The rest were completely passive. They felt that a military dictatorship would be better than what they had. If, God forbid, there is another coup, some people are predicting that it could win.

What is it like for a woman to be active in politics?

First of all, I don't feel I am a genuinely political person, since, in my view, such a person has to be well-grounded in theory. At first, I had a very difficult time understanding things and only gradually did I begin to feel more comfortable.

I recently read *Thais of Athens*, a book about ancient Greece. Thais said that where women are put in the position of slaves, they grow up with a slave's mentality, and the generation they raise will never be bold and courageous. In other words, a society that doesn't understand that woman, that is the free woman, is the basis of everything, of the cultural and spiritual development of the nation, will never be able to rise above the materialism of this world, above purely selfish goals, animal instincts.

As a woman, it's hard for me in the political movement, and not only because men are for the most part merciless toward us and don't understand women's psychology, that women tire more quickly, they are more emotional. But it is hard also because if I have succeeded in raising myself to a higher level of spiritual life and have a deeper grasp of things, I find no understanding. People are so mired in their petty concerns of everyday life that they simply lack the strength to rise above it.

Yesterday you argued with a man who denied that there was anything particular about women's situation that would require special women's demands.

Women are somewhat above men in their spiritual development.

This is not just a question of intellectual breadth. What is the difference between a man and a woman? A man thinks with his brain, with cold, logical reasoning. A woman thinks more with her heart, subconsciously and intuitively. One can't say that women should think like men. This is a fundamental part of the specificity of women.

Physically, of course, we are weaker. And morally, we are more vulnerable. It's so easy to break a woman's soul. This is also why it's harder for us in political life. I am terrified by how our youth are being raised. We're not raising women and wives capable in turn of raising a normal generation, but women who are capable of selling their bodies for money, for trinkets. Economically, too, we're much weaker. Well-paying jobs are generally inaccessible to us.

It's also unacceptable that women should not have any free time for themselves, as men do. How else can you talk of equality? The limited measure of equality that we have is mainly in the sphere of paid work. But there is no equality of opportunity for spiritual growth. Most often in our country women marry not so much out of love, but out of calculation, to have a normal family. But then, because of our low cultural level, women most often suffer from this family life. Either the husband beats her or else he can't understand her desire for spiritual growth, something to which women are more inclined than men.

Are you saying that the family should be the exclusive concern of the woman? Many feminists in the West believe that men and women should share this work equally, with the state assuming much of the burden through expanded services.

That's the problem: in our country, the family is a great burden that oppresses women. I agree with that solution, but, unfortunately, very few here have understood this so far. In general, a man gets married to have a housekeeper who will wash his clothes and prepare his meals. His main purpose is not to have a friend, a loyal companion. And after all, a woman's best characteristics are her loyalty, devotion and understanding. A highly developed woman even has a sort of intuition; she can understand without words. But few people understand these things.

I'm a single mother, divorced. And I can tell you that it is unbearably difficult in this society to raise a child on your own, especially without an education in a field that allows you to earn a decent living. If men could only grasp how hard it is for single mothers to raise normal children, not criminals or moral degenerates—but they think that a single mother can do this on her wage and alimony payments. Alimony is only one quarter of the man's wage, in my case forty to fifty rubles. I receive one quarter less than I need for my son. I'm in constant material need. What does that mean? I can't afford to buy him a toy or a book or sign him up for extracurricular classes that would help him to develop spiritually. A child that grows up under these conditions will not contribute to society's progress. He will live only for his own purely egoistic interests.

My son is sixteen and a half. And I'm amazed that in my situation I was able to raise him not to be a criminal. Yesterday at the commission, when I cited the example of a single mother with a handicapped child who received absolutely no consideration from the government, I was really talking about myself. He has psychological problems. I've encountered so many difficulties with him and received not one bit of support. You can't imagine what it's like. Each day I live in fear that he might get into some trouble. He's not mentally ill, but his nervous system has been seriously weakened as a result of illness, and he's capable of anything. He has stolen from me, and got caught up in some criminal gang—a mass of troubles from which I pulled him only with the greatest difficulty. At least I've raised him not to be criminal. But I wasn't able to help him develop spiritually. I simply didn't have the time. Like all young people today, he wants to dress well, he wants money.

We constantly changed schools, since he couldn't stay for long in any one. I taught him at home for two years. But this was like being sentenced to hard labor, since it's very hard to find work that will let you stay home for entire days and give you a wage that keeps you from starving to death.

Tell me about the women's movement in Kaluga.

It began with a woman's conference in the town of Dubno last March. We sent someone who reported on what happened and brought back documents. Even this little bit of information made me realize that we needed a woman's movement, that we have many, many problems that are specific to women who are about to enter a market. On our initiative, the Social-Democratic Party formed a women's commission. There are seven of us, and today we are meeting for the second time. The next time we meet I will definitely invite you.

In Kaluga itself, I became acquainted with another woman who had also been at Dubno and had begun on her own to organize a women's movement in our town. She was working in the regional soviet social welfare department. She is from Yakutiya and had been put forward there as a candidate to the Russian Supreme Soviet. She didn't make it solely because she was a woman. Even at that time they were saying that a woman has no place in government. After that, she came under pressure at work and had to leave the soviet. She now works as a lawyer in a commercial bank. She returned from Dubno and began to organize the women's movement on her own. It's extremely difficult to be a leader when the movement is only beginning to blossom. She was looking for people, and we found each other.

The organization she created goes by the rather original acronym NOZhI [knives], which stands for Independent Organization of Women's Initiative. For some reason, she dislikes men very strongly, though the situation in her own family is quite good. She's a very decisive person. It helps that she's a lawyer. She has already helped many women with legal advice. Initially, her idea was to create a purely legal defense movement. But when I told her about the women's commission in our party and after we had discussed the problem of privatization, we concluded that it was necessary to develop a movement with a broader profile that could deal with the various dimensions of our lives. It was only necessary to find women who could take charge of the different aspects. And we agreed that I would head the trade union section.

Besides the purely legal defense functions, many questions are arising in relation to the market—dismissals, people being cheated, thrown out of privatized enterprises that are then taken over by cooperatives. I know of one shop whose employees had worked there for twenty-five years. They were fired, and the shop was given to the cooperative that paid the highest bribe. The city government's concept of privatization of the commercial network is not to lease it to the collectives or to transfer it to them completely but to give it to those who offer the largest sum. Unfortunately, this is the most urgent problem at present.

Another problem is the material situation of single mothers. These people are now totally unprotected. There are no state allocations, nothing. Another area of activity is the cultural development of women, basically educational functions.

It has about forty or fifty women, and that's quite good. So far, these are people who come because they need some particular kind of help. But we need people who can help the organization to function. There are only about ten women of this type. However, we understand each other well, and I feel our work will take off. These are very determined people.

I have to say that women are more organized than men. Their thinking is more organized, and so is their practice. Life dictates this for women—you can't maintain a family unless your feet are planted firmly on the ground. I can assure you that when women take up the methods that we intend to use in our work, including strikes, picketing, demonstrations, and even hunger strikes, it will be a very serious affair. Remember when the soldiers' mothers stood in front of the Supreme Soviet of the RSFSR, how they conducted their struggle? True, I was somewhat amused when they said they would lie down on the railroad tracks—but they would have done it. This is pure desperation.

Our problems are extremely complex. And even though the situation is psychologically very depressing, I don't get discouraged because I'm together with women who share my views.

Nikolai Belanovskii
Vice-Chairman,
Byelorussian Union of Workers of
Auto and Agricultural Machine
Construction
[May 1992]

I met Nikolai at the Canadian Autoworkers Union's Family Education Center in Port Elgin, Ontario. He was with a delegation of auto union leaders from the former USSR. Nikolai stood out among this group. At the first session, he was the only delegate to mention participation in a strike as an important part of his biography.

When Nikolai took me to factories in Minsk the following August, I saw workers look up from their jobs and stop to shake his hand. He was someone they knew, respected, and liked. Unfortunately, his union is still very rare among the former state unions, where 95 percent of organized workers are still based.

I was born in 1954 to a peasant family. My parents, unfortunately, got divorced, and I grew up in a family of two sisters, my mother and my aunt, myself and my aunt's daughter. As the only man in the family, I was actively involved very early on in the household economy. At school, I loved sports. After graduation, I started working in the *kolkhoz* and also completed a course for truck drivers. Then I was called up. I consider that I received good training in the army: I completed a junior aviation specialist's course and worked as a mechanic servicing aircraft weaponry. When I returned home, there was really no work for me as a truck driver or mechanic; so I left for Minsk and got a job at Minsk Avtozavod. They make intermediate-class trucks, considered the best of their kind in the Soviet Union, that is, the former Union.

Did you have problems getting a permit to move to the capital city?

Well, in those days, if you were moving to work in a large enterprise, it wasn't very difficult—and I went to work in a foundry shop, where they were short of workers, and I was already familiar with a lot of the machinery. I was taken on as a mechanic for lifting equipment, cranes, tackles, and so on. I got into a good brigade with a very good brigadier, generally a very positive work environment. The collective was a big one—more than 30,000 people at the factory.

I worked like any other worker. Of course, I tried to do my job well. I also participated in competitions on the shop's team and was active in youth tourism, camping, hiking.

Then, in 1980—I was twenty-five—the chairman of our shop's union committee left. I was on vacation at the time; I had recently got married. When I returned home, my neighbors told me that people had come three times looking for me. I was alarmed: maybe something had happened. I went over to the shop, where some people from our Komsomol organization, which I had been somewhat active in, told me that my name had come up in discussions about a new shop chair. This was a complete surprise to me. The younger workers supported me; they knew me at work. They said that I could be trusted.

What was the former chairman like? Did he defend his workers?
For that period, it's very hard to figure out who defended the workers and who didn't. Conditions were totally different. You have to have experienced them from within. Sure, there were very many problems in the foundries, especially the harsh work conditions. But the system that existed then didn't really give you any basis to think things could be different. Meetings were held in a routine, formalistic manner; collective agreements were signed that on paper included improvements in work conditions. Wage issues weren't even formally discussed, since wages were under strict central control.

But there were conflicts. As early as 1970, there was a strike in our steel foundry over wages. That was so exceptional that the whole republic and Moscow learned about it. The system at the time didn't allow for much open conflict. And it wasn't just a matter of repression; it was also people's mentality. I'm trying to understand these things now. We had no information about the outside world, no real contacts, and unfortunately the majority of people felt that things couldn't be otherwise.

I was elected chairman of the foundry shop committee. There

were other candidates, but I got a majority. I began working full-time for the union. At first I found the job very difficult: more than 1,000 people under one roof, three shifts, many problems, including personal ones—housing, child care and the like. They also foisted the allocation of cars and other goods on us.

Exactly three months later I had my first serious conflict with management. We had a new shop head, a man with a long work record at the factory who tended to look at things through the eyes of a *khozyain* (master). A young worker had been drinking and was absent from work, and it wasn't the first time. The shop head wanted to fire him.

But we had, and still have, a system that requires the consent of the union committee for dismissals. On my recommendation, we refused. We had heard the worker out and decided that, as he was young, he deserved a chance to correct his ways. In those days, getting fired for violating work discipline meant a black mark for the rest of your life.

So the shop head came to have a talk with me. In the end he said, "If that's how it is, then I don't need you or your committee." He ordered me to reconvene my committee and get consent. That tells you something about the place of the unions in those days. I simply answered, "If you have the power to force the committee to accept that decision, then convene it—only I won't be there." That's all I could do then. At least I had enough self-control. But I have to give him credit: he thought things over and after a couple of hours excused himself, though he still insisted that I was wrong. And true enough, the worker didn't last long in the shop.

Another conflict arose during a discussion of work conditions. We were listening to a report by the head of the section. Our shop committee asked some very pointed questions about his work. His boss, the head of the shop, defended him in a very crude manner: "I'm the best judge of the section chief's work!" There were a lot of workers there, and I had to answer firmly: "In your own office at your own meetings, you can judge the work of your managers, but here we're looking at things from the workers' point of view, and we're considering how he works with the collective."

Had these conflicts not arisen, and had I not taken these positions, it's possible that I might have become just another committee chairman. Of course I wasn't really conscious of what I was doing. I'm sure I made my share of mistakes, but I intuitively took the path I did. And, in fact, I eventually developed pretty good relations with management. We never again had such pointed confrontations. The shop head ordered his supervisors to prepare carefully for meetings with our committee.

I spent six years as chairman of the shop committee. The foundry department had eight shops in all, with 3,500 people. In 1986 the chairman of the foundry department's union committee was forced to resign on a vote of no confidence at a workers' conference. They elected me chairman.

The union operated democratically even then?

Well, at least among the foundry workers. Votes of no confidence also occurred in the case of secretaries of the foundry's party organizations. You see, foundry work is hard, conditions are very difficult, there is more danger and more chance of injury. The workers figure there's nowhere worse to go from there. And that makes them more open, more independent and demanding. It also brings people together.

Is it somewhat like the miners?

It's comparable. And I'm not only judging by our workers. I've seen the same thing in the foundries of the Tractor Factory and in other places. Their mentality and behavior are different.

Why was your predecessor ousted?

He was blamed on two counts. One, his committee was a conciliatory to management on the question of work conditions. Two, he was dishonest in the allocation of cars. People knew that I had adopted rather firm, critical positions toward the administration, and they apparently felt I could handle the job.

I worked there for three years. It was difficult but good work. We succeeded in solving many problems related to work conditions. For example, the auxiliary workers in the foundries—mechanics, electricians, and so on—had been trying for a long time to get special pension benefits for harsh work conditions. We had two types of special jobs in the Soviet Union. The first type included jobs with "especially harmful work conditions"—in metallurgy, mining, and so forth. People in these jobs could retire with the full pension after twenty-five years. The second type gave certain workers the right to a pension five years earlier than ordinary workers. Auxiliary workers used to be in this second category until 1968. But there was a tendency in those years to cut jobs from the list by changing their job titles.

In 1989, the auxiliary workers finally organized a protest meeting in the street and decided to go on strike. I was present, and they elected me to head the strike committee. But I asked them to wait, as chairman of the department committee, not to strike until I tried other means. We negotiated with the administration but couldn't resolve the problem. Then the government joined the talks. By 1989, the situation had already changed somewhat and the government was paying some attention to these issues when we raised them. After two months of talks, we finally won.

Toward the end of that year, abuses were discovered on the part of the administration and the factory union committee in the allocation of housing, cars, and so forth, and I demanded a full inquiry. Our foundry committee demanded a factory-wide conference. But, of course, the administration couldn't allow that. So the director reorganized the foundry department. Each of the ten shops became a separate department; in effect, our department no longer existed, and so neither did its union committee. The foundry workers wanted to fight, but in the other departments, management, together with the union committees, had a strong enough hold to keep the workers quiet.

Was the foundry department alone in the factory in its independence?

There was also the pressing department. These are the two departments where conditions are the harshest, where the work is the most harmful and dangerous.

Soviet labor laws required that an elected union official be offered another job at the end of his tenure or if his position was eliminated. They offered me a job as assistant director of an administrative bureau. But I knew that once I accepted an administrative position, I would no longer be covered by the legislation that protects workers from arbitrary dismissal.

I had a long talk with the director. My main point was that he was acting against his own interests in seeking subservient unions. After all, when a union committee functions as it's supposed to, most questions get resolved directly in the shop, and the authority of both the administration and the union committee are firmer. But, of course, I didn't expect him to retreat. Since I had already graduated from the institute in economics—I had been studying in the evenings—I took a job as an economist in the foundry shop.

Did you have a work-collective council at the factory?

Yes, but when the new enterprise law appeared in 1990, management dissolved it and created an enterprise council where half the people are appointed by management and half elected by the workers. Anyway, it didn't have much influence. It acted more as a facade for management to continue to decide things in its own interests.

Toward the fall of 1990, I began to think about the creation of an independent union of auto and agricultural machinery workers in our republic, since we didn't have any separate republican structures. There was only the union's central committee in Moscow, which was under the ministry's thumb. In the republic, we only had representatives of the central committee, who had no real power.

Was your idea exclusively a reaction to the central committee's dictatorial ways and its subservience to the ministry, or were nationalist motivations also involved?

It wasn't at all nationalist. Even while I was committee chairman, I had come out against the way the union was organized. The republican structures decided nothing; they merely wrote reports and signed orders from the ministry.

Did you give any thought to reforming the union's central committee in Moscow?

In practice, that couldn't be done from the republics. At the central level, people were, in fact, appointed. Elections were completely formal.

You're saying that it was easier to change things at the local republican level. Was this also a consideration that fueled the drive for republican sovereignty in the former Soviet Union?

Yes, it's an entirely objective process. People wouldn't have been moved to fight for sovereignty if Moscow had not exercised such dictatorial powers. All power was concentrated in Moscow. No enterprise director could decide anything of importance without Moscow's okay. All the major financing came from Moscow. That's not a normal situation.

Then the push for sovereignty was more a democratic than a nationalist movement?

Of course, of course. But it eventually fed nationalist sentiment too. When relations with the center are bad, there is a natural tendency to attribute all problems to the center.

Our republic had a Federation of Trade Unions that united all the branch unions. But it, too, was extremely conservative, and its officials were selected in the same way as Moscow's. One of the reasons we have so many problems with our unions is that the party apparatus consciously placed its functionaries, who mostly had no lower-level union experience, in the unions' higher structures. They brought to their union jobs their own way of dealing with people and their ideological dogma. This had a serious effect on the quality of the unions' work, and it meant that it was impossible for a worker from the bench with different views to move up into the higher positions.

It was only in 1990 that our union and the Union of Radio and Electronics Workers democratically elected central councils in the republic. Aleksandr Bukhvostov, who had been union chairman at Gomselmash [a large agricultural machinery production association centered in the town of Gomel], became our chairman. He had led the strike movement over the consequences of Chernobyl in 1990 and headed the march of Chernobyl victims to Red Square during the party conference.

That's our pain. Statistics now show how child mortality and cancer rates have risen. There was an attempt at the time to suppress these problems in the republic. The protests forced the authorities to deal with them.

How was your republican union organized?

The idea arose in the factories. A conference was held in September 1990 and elected Bukhvostov chairman over two other candidates, as well as a commission to write a constitution. I was also asked to participate. The constitution states, for example, that employers can't be in the same union with hired workers. That point met a lot of resistance both from the union committees in our enterprises and from other unions. It might seem natural to you, but we have trouble even defining who an employer is.

Have the administrative personnel already left your union?

Not yet, but we are constantly raising that question.

In writing the constitution, we had two basic aims. One was to make the union democratic, to get rid of the top-down pyramid structure. The plant organizations had to become the foundation of the union, and all the other structures should serve their interests. I knew from my own experience what it's like when things are the other way around. Labor bureaucrats would come to the plant and issue orders; they never asked how they could help us. We sent them all the dues we collected, and they decided what to do with them.

Those aren't normal relations. Unfortunately, the mistrust of higher structures has become deeply rooted. In writing the constitution, we took this into account. So, for example, only 10 percent of the dues, the smallest proportion of any union in the republic, goes to the central council; 90 percent remains in the primary organizations. We decided to take the minimum needed to support our work. That, at least, is how we felt things should be in the first stages. It makes work with the primary organizations easier. When they have problems, I say, "Excuse me, but you have 90 percent of the funds." We ask and demand that they don't spend the money but create strike funds. We could have created a central fund, but we had to take into account people's mentality.

How do the factory committees use their 90 percent of the dues?

We still face big problems in the lower organizations. Many functions that rightfully belong to the state are still hung around our necks—cultural activities, libraries, sports, swimming pools, and the like—and they are maintained by our membership dues. For the transitional period, we're demanding that the state assume part of the costs. At present, the government gives us 6 percent of the social insurance fund for maternity and sick leave, funerals and recreational activities. But we're trying to get the system reformed. We don't want to administer these things ourselves, but we want to be able to control how the government administers them.

So many of our unions aren't what they should be, because they're kept so busy with social insurance, sports, child care, and the like that they can't pay the necessary attention to the price of labor, which is the primary issue.

How much resistance was there to this drive to renew the republican union? And did you have much support from below?

Of course, there was resistance, mainly from the structures above the plant level. However, I can't say there was much pressure from rank-and-file workers to reform the union. Of course, they sent delegates and made some suggestions.

Then, the changes are due mainly to the efforts of a group of activists from the factory committees?

To a very large degree. That's because you can't really expect independent actions from workers or individual shop committees in an unreformed system.

After electing a chairman and a constitutional committee, we moved on to the second stage: formulating demands for a collective agreement and organizing a founding congress to adopt the demands. The congress adopted the demands in even stronger form, something quite unusual in our republic, as well as a plan of action. I was elected vice chairman. The chairman and vice chairman are the only two officers in the union.

The biggest problems at first involved breaking the old mentality of the enterprise committees. They were used to waiting for instructions from above. We put moral pressure on them; and we can do that because our authority among the workers, who can see the sort of things we are doing, is rising. The rank and file are beginning to ask a lot of questions of their committees. Many of those people haven't been able to change their ways and are being forced to leave. Others are trying to change.

Another complex problem was to clarify our relations with the Byelorussian Federation of Trade Unions. It was supposed be a coordinating center that dealt with issues that couldn't be resolved by the branch unions, but instead it had grown accustomed to ordering around the branch unions and running them. When we and the radioelectronics workers adopted our new constitutions, the federation tried to plug into that process and tell us what to do. But we were able to break the old relations and force them to recognize that it's the branch unions that create and finance the federation, which should deal only with those issues that the branch unions assign to it.

Were the processes in the radioelectronics union similar to those in your union?

In our work over the last year and a half we realized that we saw things in the same way, so the two unions formed the Association of Industrial Unions. Each branch has over 250,000 employees; we're the two biggest unions of the twenty-three in the republic, and that's not bad. Representation in the federation is one delegate per union, regardless of size. Since we were a very long way from being a decisive force in it, we decided to form our own association. We are still in the federation, although it's conservative and holds us back. Many of the leaders in the other branch unions are close to retirement; many were high party functionaries in the past.

The Federation of Trade Unions is to a large degree responsible for the April strikes. [Belarus–the former Byelorussia–saw a series of large-scale strikes in April 1991 that were set off by the price increase of April 2. They coincided with the second month of the coal miners' strike.] The growing discontent among the workers was already evident at the federation's plenary session in February. I spoke there and proposed concrete actions. At my own union's plenary session, we decided to put the following demands to the government: stop inflation—prices were rising rather quickly, though the government denied it—and adopt measures for the social security of the population. At that stage, however, we were only a few months old, and the government didn't pay much attention to us, preferring to deal with the federation.

Discontent continued to grow. At a meeting of the federation council, I said very bluntly that if we didn't put forth concrete demands with specific dates for fulfillment, demands that we were prepared to back up with strikes, the unions might find themselves overboard. My proposal to set March 28 as the deadline for a government price freeze and social guarantees was adopted. The next day I opened the paper and read the federation's declaration. It seemed okay until I realized that there was no deadline for the government's answer.

It was the old style. And that failure had a big influence on the further course of events. The government seemed ready to negotiate. But how? "Well, you see, we just can't pay for these things...." Had there been a strike deadline, we could have turned to the rank and file and mobilized them to exert pressure.

Meanwhile, without waiting for the government, our union began to negotiate with the plant directors to raise wages and pay compensation for the rising cost of meals in the canteens. The radioelectronics union did the same. But there were universal engineering plants located not far from ours in which the unions did nothing. On April 3, the day after the price increase, their workers pointed to the gains in our plants just across the street.

At the Automatic Lines and Kirov engineering factories, the workers spontaneously poured out into the yard and held a mass meeting. Representatives of the Workers' Union and of the Popular Front arrived. [The Workers' Union was set up a just few days before the strike by workers who had links to the Byelorussian Popular Front, a liberal nationalist movement.] They tried to convince the workers to strike and offered to lead them.

After a couple of hours, the meeting broke up. But a wave of agitation was already sweeping through the other factories as strike rumors reached them. Of course, had the trade union committees been up to their task, they would have systematized the demands and openly declared their support for the workers, and there probably wouldn't have been any strike committees and all the rest that followed.

But the next day, since the administrations had not adopted any measures to calm the people, the workers of those two plants came to work and then went to the other plants to ask support for the movement. It proceeded in a very chaotic manner, with groups here and there striking, but not whole plants. Not much happened that morning, until a conflict over wages, not directly related to the price increase, arose on the assembly line in our Avtozavod. Aware of the agitation in the other factories, about 4,000 or 5,000 workers downed tools and went to see the administration. Neither management nor union representatives came out to speak to them. So someone said, "Forget them. Let's go to Government House." That gives you an idea of how amorphous our union structure is, how totally unprepared to react intelligently to events, or to react at all. That's why their authority is so low.

So they began to march in columns, in their overalls, to the central square. They included most of our foundry workers as well as several thousand workers from our Tractor Factory. When news reached the others that the Avtozavod workers were marching, they also began to form into columns and move, but, as I said, only groups of workers, not whole factories. In some factories, the union committees began to wake up and went together with the columns, but very timidly. In the Tractor Factory, the union committee itself suggested the election of a strike committee. But then the two committees began to fight among themselves. The marchers had no clear goals except to raise their wages to compensate for the price increase.

The coal miners' strike had been going on for a month. Did it have anything to do with the Byelorussian movement?

I don't really think so. Incidentally, our union supported the miners. We were the only large union to do so openly and to condemn Gorbachev's behavior. But the miners' situation was more complicated than ours. All the media were reporting on the "excessive" demands of the miners, blaming them for stopping production at other factories and warning of a heating fuel shortage. This was a psychological campaign to get people to take positions against the miners. We evaluated what was happening as an attempt by the government to smash the labor movement. We didn't pass judgment on the miners' demands, but we placed full blame on the government for its refusal to negotiate. Its pretext was that the miners were demanding the government's resignation. But the government's response was totally irresponsible and destructive, motivated by narrow political interests.

Our central council voted to give the striking miners 10,000 rubles, which we sent to Donetsk. But none of the major media reported this. I personally gave the resolution to the Byelorussian correspondent of *Trud* [at the time, the central trade union paper, with upwards of 18 million readers], but they didn't publish it, which shows that it was a long way from being a union paper.

In not supporting the miners, The VKP [General Confederation of Trade Unions, the interrepublican union federation] simply betrayed the labor movement, because if the miners had been crushed no union would have been able to raise itself up after that. The coal miners have a most powerful argument—coal. If an engineering factory strikes, the government can just say, "Please, go right ahead. You'll be the ones without wages. We'll just transfer your orders to another truck factory."

What were you doing when the workers began to move on April 4?

I was at the other end of town, when I got a call from someone in our factory. "Nikolai, the factory is moving, and we don't know what to do. There's no one here." When I arrived, they were within 500 meters of Government House. I talked with workers I knew and asked what their demands were. I asked them to ensure order and to watch out for provocations. There were special forces police waiting in the square. The government was in session.

We organized a group to stop the column when it reached the square. But instead of stopping, people began to move toward Government House. It was a very dangerous moment. I managed to climb up on a lamppost to shout for them to stop. I yelled that it was a provocation, that they would destroy the cause that they had come for. Luckily, there were some of our foundry workers that knew me and they stopped, stopping the crowd behind them some twenty meters from Government House. The police would never have allowed it to be seized.

There were about 5,000 people in the square, maybe more. A spontaneous meeting began. Parliamentary deputies from the opposition, from the Popular Front, came out. The workers' demands were purely economic, but these people, along with people from the Workers' Union, wanted to exclude any leaders from the official unions, saying that they were phoney, and the like. They wanted to let only their own people get to the microphone.

I was on the tribune all the time but I avoided a confrontation with them. I merely asked the workers to send up their own people. The people from the Popular Front and the Workers' Union made the mistake of telling the workers that their demands were wrong, that they wouldn't achieve anything, that they had to change the political system. What they were saying might make sense, but you have to consider where the workers were. And they grew wary at once. They were being insulted by these people, who told them theirs were "sausage demands." That's no way to behave. You don't just appear and say: "Let's decide it all over again." It ended with the crowd electing delegates who went to hand the government the demands. After that, the people went home.

That evening, the negotiations between the unions and the government that had begun before the strike, resumed. Earlier that day, the authorities had convened all the directors in the city and all the union presidents and talked and talked, but again nothing was decided. I asked to speak and demanded an immediate decision from the government. I warned that if they didn't inform the people of measures adopted on wages and social guarantees, they would come out to the square again. And that's what happened. When they finally published a decision, the strike wave had already spread to the smaller cities and isolated plants.

When I spoke to the crowd on April 4, I told the workers to take the strike seriously and avoid provocations. I told them that they should entrust the leadership of the movement to their union committees, and if those committees refused or were unable to lead them, then to elect strike committees. I was later accused of undermining our own trade unions, but I considered what I had said to be quite proper. I advised the workers to maintain order, to guard their plants, and so forth. The workers began to elect strike committees. It was all quite spontaneous, including the formation of the city strike committee. The lack of experience of struggle was evident.

And so on April 5, the Minsk workers again came to the square, but in a rather more organized manner, groups of workers from the different factories. Throughout the republic, the movement was quite peaceful, except for Orsha, where the workers blocked the railway line. The factory administrations adopted a neutral position, and there were no open persecutions, though, as usual, there were threats that people would be docked for being absent.

The city strike committee included people from among the leaders of the Popular Front, and I feel that they needlessly heated up the situation. For example, our Avtozavod struck on the first day, April 3, and then didn't come out anymore. The administration there had raised wages and introduced compensation for the price increases in the canteens. Most workers were satisfied with that, which shows that their demands really were economic. But these Popular Front people drove up to the factory and shouted, "Strike-breakers!" and the like. They were demanding that the party committees be put out of the enterprises, that the government resign, that a special session be called. Many workers didn't accept this politicization of the city strike committee.

After that, there was a pause for negotiations, but they broke down. On April 10, there was a big demonstration on the square with about 50,000 people. But really, how could the government resign? And since the enterprises were meeting the workers' economic demands, the strike committee was forced to suspend the strike. But it was resumed on the April 24, when the strike committee announced that the government was dragging out the talks, that it would not agree to calling an early special session of the parliament or to evicting the party committees from the factories. But only the tractor factory and one other plant came out that day. The rest only sent representatives to the square. And the meeting decided that they would not come any more.

But on the morning of April 25, at the tractor factory, people gathered in the yard and a mass meeting took place. It was the anniversary of the Chernobyl accident. When I arrived, the workers weren't listening to anyone—not to the administration or to the union committee—and they were even expressing their lack of confidence in the strike committee, insisting on going to the square again. When I spoke, I told them that they couldn't act like that, that they had to trust the people they had elected. But since it was the anniversary of Chernobyl, and since we had asked the government to establish a national day of mourning, which it had refused to do—a disgrace!—it was decided to go to the square. I proposed that we go in an organized manner, to first return to the shops, organize the columns, prepare black armbands, slogans, and so on.

At the same time, Bukhvostov, our union's president, had gone to Gomel, where on the union's initiative a mass meeting was organized. In Minsk, more than 50,000 people marched. The columns included the unions, strike committees, and factory administrations. The Popular Front joined in with its banners. The demonstration had the coloring of a protest against the consequences of Chernobyl, and this time it was organized.

The demonstrators were mainly from the Tractor factory, the others sending only small groups. Avtozavod, our other large plant in Minsk, didn't go. The Tractor factory is more militant. The divisions among the strike committees could already be felt. The city strike committee insisted on political demands, while not all of the enterprise strike committees agreed with that, so they decided to send only groups of representatives to the demonstration. The city strike committee accused them of betrayal.

How did the movement end?

On April 24 and 25, in the town of Orsha the workers went onto the railroad tracks and shut down the line. This movement was led by a certain Razumov from the Instrument factory. He was very radical and spoke about the need to change the government and the political system. This winter their regional trade union council joined our Association of Industrial Unions, and he is now saying that we should not have strikes, as they lead to instability and things only get worse. That's the sort of transformation that occurs. He's now the chairman of his factory's union committee.

How did it end? Well, the government refused to carry out the political demands. Meanwhile economic demands were being met in the plants; the people stopped coming out, though many union and strike committees did express their lack of confidence in their administrations. There was no clear program of action. The only ones to kick out their party committee were the Motor factory workers. The positions of the city strike committee didn't correspond to the workers' thinking, and that most of all explains why the strike committee subsequently failed to win majorities for their political demands, such as evicting the party committees. It's true that in the heat of the events many workers did vote for these demands, but afterward this support evaporated.

I think that a fundamental error of the leaders in the strike committee in those days—and it might have been the influence of the Popular Front or the Workers' Union—was their desire to keep members of the union committees and Communist Party members out of the strike committees. But these were precisely the people with experience in organization and in working in the collectives.

Things might have been different if at that time the Popular Front and Workers' Union hadn't put forth such radical political demands, and especially if they hadn't tried to keep the unions away. In fact, they wanted to destroy the existing union structures. But one can't say that everything in those unions was bad and that they enjoyed no support among workers. That wasn't true, especially on the level of production. Those attitudes of the Popular Front and Workers' Union helped prevent the processes from working themselves through to the end. And as time goes on, this problem grows more complicated.

Besides the economic gains, what would you say was the most important positive consequence of the strikes?

The experience pushed consciousness forward and allowed the emergence of potential new leaders. Many of the people in the strike committees were temporary phenomena, products of the crowd, people who spoke louder and criticized stronger. But there were also sober people.

I should also mention that the strike committees often also included representatives of the union committees, and many strike committees, especially in the periphery outside of Minsk, were, in fact, led by the chairmen of the factory committees.

At the Ball-Bearing factory, the members of the strike committee were elected to the new trade union committee. We're working closely with them, teaching them the ropes. It's a pleasure to work with these new people, since our views coincide. You see, after we created our new republican council, there was a gap between the republican structure and the plant committees. We wanted to pose things in a radical way and to speed up the changes, but we had to deal with the existing plant committees, who often don't understand our approach and try to smooth over the problems with the administration. But things are changing. In several factories, there are already people that don't share the old outlook. The workers have confidence in them, and we can work with them easily.

But it's a complex issue. For example, at the Tractor factory, the plant committee got mad that the shop committees were inviting us directly and not going through them. You see, on the one hand, our constitution affirmed the priority of the primary organizations, but, on the other, there is an urgency to change things. We can't just walk into the plants and order the committees around. But we do say openly—I say this at all union conferences—that it makes no sense for there to be both union and strike committees in the factories. To my view, the strike committees have only one task: to win the confidence of the majority of the work collective and to come to power in the union committees, to reform them. If there are two organs, they split and weaken the workers.

The union committees should be in charge, and that if the strike committees feel they aren't living up to their task, they should force new elections and run. I can't work openly with a strike committee to help it overthrow an existing union committee. However, we do invite their representatives to our assemblies, something that gets the plant committees angry.

Many of the union leaders who came here with you say that the new worker organizations are power-hungry, not serious, and infringe on union jurisdiction. Why is your attitude different?

My attitude is positive. Their emergence is healthy and forces the union committees to be on their toes. Much of their criticism of the union committees is well-founded, but they often make this criticism in such a way that it fails to win them support among the workers. After the strike, many factory committees adopted a position of criticism and rejection of everything. In many plants, they have already fallen apart.

The same is true of the Workers' Union. These were politicized people, and at the time of the strikes, there might have been an opening to form a strong workers' party. But they too adopted a stance of criticizing everything, including the unions, which they wanted merely to destroy. Sure, many factory committees are conciliatory and bad. But words aren't enough.

What about the republican strike committee?

The Minsk committee doubles as the republican committee, but we've hardly heard anything from it in half a year, and it's the same in other towns. In Minsk we tried to find a common language with the strike committee, but then representatives of the International Confederation of Free Trade Unions came to Minsk. They met with us and with the strike committee. The strike committee was trying to establish new independent trade unions, and they told the ICFTU not to trust us, that all our reforms had merely been cosmetic. Theirs was a two-faced, disloyal policy, especially after we had done a lot to help them. So we distanced ourselves from them.

As I said, I support the existence of any worker organizations. But the republican strike committee hadn't even yet got on its feet when it called a press conference to announce the creation of free trade unions. This caused some of their members to leave them. It's really a crude struggle for power by leaders of an organization that hasn't come close to power.

What about the Workers' Union?

It doesn't really exist anymore. It has become the Confederation of Labor, which is very embryonic. It allows dual membership in the old and new unions, which, to my view, is not normal. They reject the idea of strikes and have taken up exclusively the issue of privatization, demanding that the workers get property in some form of other. That's their only activity. Naturally, the government likes their position on strikes. The president of Belarus spent two hours in discussions with them, though they represent only 600 people— we are several million. After the talks, he pointed out with satisfaction that the confederation has a different approach than the old unions. I can understand him: they don't give the government any trouble.

But there are also the small free trade unions promoted by the Minsk strike committee. They are closer to us and to the industrial workers. At Avtozavod, the factory committee refused to hold new elections, and the strike committee formed a free trade union with about 150 members.

You mentioned the influence of the Popular Front, in the city strike committee. What is the political weight of that organization?

It has a presence in the republic, but it isn't a mass movement, largely because of its extremist positions on the national question, its extreme attitudes toward the former Communist Party members, whom they see as criminals, making no distinction between ordinary members and those who actually held power. We have quite a large number of ethnic minorities in our republic, and the Popular Front has alienated them.

Did Gorbachev's March 1988 referendum on the preservation of the Soviet Union really reflect public opinion?

At the time, yes. [Of the 178 million eligible voters, about 59 percent participated and over three-quarters voted for a reformed Union.] The Popular Front called for a no vote. They failed to consider people's attitudes at time. But even today, a majority feel that sovereignty is stupid. Those of us who are more politicized, who are closer to the political and economic processes in the republic and who saw more clearly the character of relations in the Soviet Union, might not think so, but ordinary people see that they used to be able to travel, to take vacations without any problems anywhere in this vast land, and now things only get worse, while the television shows people killing each other.

But do you feel that there should be some sort of political structure above the republics?

No, I don't. I don't see at present the kind of attitudes upon which it would be possible to build a structure that would reflect the interests of all the republics.

Are you referring to the Russian leaders?

To a large degree, they forced the process of sovereignty, since the representatives of the other republics couldn't get the Russians to create equitable solutions to their problems. They hurt themselves and others by trying to resolve things by force. The result is conflicts that don't get resolved, squabbling over the division of the army, and so on. The Russian leaders put economic pressure on the other republics by limiting exports to them, though they had promised they wouldn't. So the other republics reacted in kind; the Russians exploit the fact that they possess the greater part of the raw materials.

The Russians took a lot of steps that undermined mutual confidence, and that to me is the most terrible thing. They did everything without consulting others. Some of this was intoxication with power. You remember how Yeltsin behaved toward Gorbachev at the Russian congress after the putsch? Gorbachev was speaking to the congress about the party's responsibility in the attempted coup, its lack of vigilance, and so on, when Yeltsin walks over to the dais and hands him a document ready for him to sign suspending the party. Many people didn't like that, and I was one of them.

You haven't mentioned the question of property. But surely the way that's resolved is going to be decisive for you.

That's a very complex issue. Parliament has yet to adopt a law on privatization. In the factories the administration is trying to force the process and remove the enterprises completely from state control. For example, some have become leased enterprises. But, in practice, the old managerial structures remain intact; it's the director who unilaterally decides what to do with profits. In our general collective agreement with the government, as well as in the enterprise agreements, our union has insisted that all decisions on changing the form of property of the enterprise must have the agreement of the work collective. That's the most basic issue. And we have intervened to stop the administrations' actions in this area.

Our second position is that, in face of the chaos that reigns in the area of privatization, the state must adopt laws to regulate it. One possibility is the allocation to each inhabitant of a share of the national property. In some enterprises the workers say, "It's all ours; you should give it to us." This is not right. In reality, it was the whole nation that built the factories. The part that was built from profits [under the perestroika-inspired system of "cost-accounting"] is a different question: that part, one could argue, does belong to the work collective. But what of the pensioners who put fifty years of work into the enterprise? A flexible approach is needed to this complex issue.

In our discussions here, the Canadian union members explained that property is power, control over investment, jobs, and so on. That's why it seems strange to me that you and your colleagues don't seem to have a clear position on it.

We're trying to understand the issue. There are many hidden shoals here. The tendency in the republic now is toward leasing arrangements and the creation of joint-stock companies from the state enterprises. We're trying to analyze the consequences of each variant.

We see the tendency of government to pull out of the economy. They say, "We've given you full autonomy, so your fate depends on what you yourselves can earn." But we want the government to resolve the problems of exchange between enterprises in the different republics, because that's threatening production.

As far as the free market is concerned, I'll tell you in all serious-ness that in our union we understand that this race to the market will only bring harm to the workers and to society. A market poses cruel conditions. We are aware of what has happened in Eastern Germany and Poland. They are striking examples of what not to do. The Polish reform was a terrible mistake. They opened their borders and flooded their market with imports. In practice, they exported jobs to other countries and deprived their own workers of the possibility of working and earning money to buy those goods. Production there has declined over 20 percent.

Reconstruction requires huge investments. Our enterprises are now approaching the edge. During the first half of this year, the government still supported them, but now there is a shortage of money—the workers can't even get paid. Before coming here, we sat down and analyzed the economic situation, the state of relations between the republics, the issue of conversion of military produc-tion—we have many plants now producing for the warehouse.

Do you think workers should demand direct power in managing the economy and their enterprises or should they aspire to be simple wage laborers who try to influence things "from the outside" through their unions?

I don't feel that our old system was as black as many people like to paint in today. There were also positive aspects. And I am opposed to rolling everything back so that we find ourselves forced to fight all over again to recreate the good things we had. Such a danger does exist.

Our union is discussing the appropriate forms of worker influ-ence in the economy. I think that form has to be the struggle for political power. Nothing else except the law will force the entrepre-neurs to invest where we want them to. The other option is open confrontation directly in the economic arena. But can we afford to constantly organize protests, strikes, occupations? Each protest is a great responsibility. If only one person is killed, it is a terrible responsibility to bear.

What has your union done in the political area?

There are many small parties in the republic, but none of them suit us in their views and functioning. We see that the workers really have no political representation. They are an undefined political force today, and no one can say who they will follow tomorrow. We're seriously discussing the formation of a workers' party, one that workers would really support. In effect, it would a variant of the Swedish model.

Our union helped to collect signatures for a referendum that will force new parliamentary elections. We slept through the last ones, and as a result, directors and party bureaucrats got themselves elected. About 40 percent of the deputies are people with absolutely no ideals or principles, weathervanes who shift with the political wind. I've proposed that we start work in the enterprises to draw up a list of candidates for the new elections—to do it methodically, take a good look at prospective candidates, and give the workers a chance to know who they are voting for, so there will be fewer mistakes.

But to be objective, I have to say that although we're trying to force new elections, the present government has moved ahead quite a bit over the months. They were pushed forward by the labor movement and by the more radical positions we've adopted. I'm not saying things are good, but there has been some progress. However, if the economic crisis continues to deepen and the plants shut down, then all movement will come to a stop. And that can happen especially because of the economic conflicts between the republican governments.

Your unions generally have "softer" relations with management than ours. Can you explain that?

In our country, we can't adopt a classic stance of unions against employers. In fact, we're pushing our directors to form a union of employers. They aren't yet prepared to unite, and it's very hard to deal with each of them separately.

One of the areas of cooperation is our efforts to get the government to change its tax policy, which places the entire burden on the state enterprises. But the most important problem is the supply of raw materials and parts from other republics. It's a frightening situation. We see production coming apart and we can't stop it. In the large factories, where the directors have been in place for a long time and have access to all government offices, they work out their own solutions and try to deal directly with the government. But the majority of enterprises, especially those outside of Minsk, are waiting for our proposals, at least during this transitional period. We call the directors to meetings, and they ask us to help them resolve the problems.

Our problem is that we can't let production collapse. Of course, if I were just an economist and not a trade unionist, I would have to say that we have plants that just aren't up to the mark and really aren't needed in our republic. But I know we have to find work for people in other places or else convert these plants to useful production. Unfortunately, the crunch will surely come. The question is how to make the change in the interests of people—how to ensure that the losses are kept to a minimum.

IV

THE INDEPENDENT MINERS' UNION

Aleksandr Erokhin: Mine Mechanic, Member of the Executive, Independent Miners' Union [October 1991]

The coal miners' strike of July 1989 embraced all four major Soviet coalfields and over 400,000 workers. It was the first mass collective workers' action since the Novocherkassk strike in 1962. It also gave rise to the first independent workers' organizations, the strike committees that subsequently transformed themselves into permanent workers' committees, as well as to the Independent Miners' Union (IMU), founded at the Second Congress of Miners in Donetsk in October 1990. This union, which unites only a minority of miners—the majority remain in the former state union—is the largest and most influential of the alternative unions that have arisen over the past years.

In the fall of 1991, Aleksandr Erokhin was a member of the executive of the IMU. His responsibility, among other things, was to serve as liaison with various institutes and social scientists who might be of use to the union. I found him to be the most open, thoughtful and sensitive of the miners' leaders that I had met. I tried to contact him in Moscow again in the summer of 1992, but he was back in his western Siberian village, no longer a member of the IMU leadership. Somehow this did not surprise me, given the loyal position toward the Yeltsin government that the Russian IMU leaders had adopted (as detailed in Aleksandr Sergeev's interview of July 1992 in this part).

I was born in the Kuzbass in Myski, where I live today. ["The Kuzbass" is short for Kuznetz Basin in Western Siberia, a coal and metallurgical center.] My father, a truck driver, died when I was three. My mother brought us up alone in very difficult circumstances, but she refused to give us up to a boarding school. I should be there now helping her, but I'm here.

I was doing well in school when I went to work after the eighth grade, though I had already been spending my summers working in our truck garden so that we could feed ourselves. I got a job in a brick factory in hellish conditions. The heat and dust were terrible, and it was all manual labor. Legally, I was too young to be doing that work, but no one cared. I fainted once; the older workers had to drag me out.

I worked there that summer and into the fall, returning to school in time for the mid-year exams. In our school we weren't taught to think, only to earn grades. I managed that like everyone else, though my grades suffered. I completed high school and enrolled at the Siberian Metallurgical Institute, working at the same time at a factory. I worked three shifts in a row and then got two days off. I had an agreement with the management, who let me start late sometimes when my studies held me up. Eventually I was promoted to more responsible work, and then it was my studies that suffered. I got married at that time. We lived on my wage of 100 rubles a month plus a fifty-ruble stipend—in those days that was enough for one person.

I graduated as an economist-specialist in the organization of metallurgical production and went to work in a defense plant as head of the production-organizing department. Later I was promoted to assistant manager of production and planning, and soon after we moved out of the dormitory into a two-room apartment.

Everything would have been fine, but I was young and green and had a restless character. My work often took me to Moscow, where I was able to observe many things. I realized that something was very wrong in those ministries. I was dumbstruck at how our economy was being "managed."

This was in the second half of the 1970s. I kept coming up against outrageous things, such as theft and falsified production reports, and I fought against them. I was a Komsomol activist, editor of the factory's Komsomol wall newspaper. I tried to use it to improve things, to ridicule the abuses.

Once, when I was working in the sub-Artic, I came upon a large-scale theft operation. I warned those involved, but it did no good. In the end, they were given long sentences in the labor camps. But the highly placed organizers hardly suffered at all. This set me to thinking. At another factory I again found falsified production reports. The administration forced me to ask for a transfer. I would come to the plant, and they would say that there was no work for me that day. I wasn't fired, but I wasn't paid for the idle time either. I was alone; there was no trade union to back me up. I had already understood that our trade unions were anything but trade unions.

After that, I worked at a planning institute for a long time, then as an electrician, a carpenter, a mechanic, and in other professions. In 1983, I was again forced to request a transfer. I was director of the production bureau of a metallurgy plant. Everything passed before my eyes. I analyzed and compared: things on paper were totally different in reality. It was all documented. I raised hell again, and in the end the whole nest was cleaned out. But both the administration and I grew sick of fighting each other. They organized all sorts of intrigues against me—the Communists were strong at that time. It was then that I began to write poetry. Apparently, my soul needed this safety valve. I still write, though there is little time.

What did you write about?

About reorganizing our life, about what needed to be done. I understood that I was merely fighting against the symptoms. We had absolutely no information. Yet, there had been the massacre in Novocherkassk and other similar events. In Novokuznetsk too, in 1975 or 1979 there was some sort of strike movement in response to food shortages. The authorities quickly brought in supplies from another region. Obviously, people had begun thinking well before the miners' movement arose. It didn't appear from nowhere.

So people were thinking even then, but it was difficult to fight. People were afraid, and there were many betrayals. I remember one Communist, also a department head, who had been the victim of injustice. Three of us, all administrators, met and shared our dissatisfaction. But they quickly got wind of this and separated this lad from us. They told him that they had evidence of some illegal doing—it was impossible to do one's job and not violate some law—and that if he continued, they would put him in jail. So he testified to what was the opposite of the truth.

Many people were thinking, and many lives were broken. Until the miners' strikes, the struggle was always an individual one. Of course, the aspiration to organize was always there, since it's easier to fight together. Attempts were made but they didn't succeed until the miners' movement appeared.

How did you end up in the coal industry?

In 1983 I was more or less forcibly transferred from the Ministry of Ferrous Metallurgy to an open-pit mine in the Kuzbass belonging to the Ministry of the Coal Industry. People wondered about this strange "transfer" from one ministry to another. I was no longer in management but worked as a mechanic-electrician. Although I had decided not to "make trouble" in this new place, I couldn't suppress my nature. The chief engineer or director would come around and tell us that we had to do some special work or work overtime—one of the frequent "emergencies." I answered, "Guys, you have your own jobs. Why act as overseers here? If I don't do my job right, then punish me. There are rules and laws." But here, as everywhere else in the country, it was disorder and bedlam.

How did you react to the start of perestroika?

Like everyone else. There was some movement, expectation of change. Then there was a lot of talk. But I can't say that my immediate reaction to that was negative. No one was in a position to judge what lay behind it. The least one can say is that when glasnost was proclaimed, information finally began to arrive. Of course, it was only partial. Even today it remains limited, though people need information to understand, to be able to take positions. That was the main benefit of perestroika. None of our strikes would have been possible without it, because information is light. Without it, it's like in a dark room, you don't know where to turn. The development of consciousness that has taken place over the past years is based on that above all else.

What led you to get involved in the IMU?

When the labor movement began after the coal miners' strike, I wasn't the delegate of any workers' committee or even a member of my own mine's workers' committee. When the Workers' Union of the Kuzbass was born [a political organization formed in October 1989 by delegates from the workers' committees, now defunct]. I arranged to get some time off in return for overtime and went on my own to Novokuznetsk to see what this union was. My consciousness had evolved. I saw that no matter how many wrongdoers were dismissed or jailed, nothing really changed. In fact, some who should have been sentenced, whose abuses were fully documented, were actually promoted to jobs in Moscow or given awards, thanks to the intervention of the party apparatus. In Novokuznetsk I saw that the workers were trying to achieve something and that it was better to fight together. And so I joined the labor movement.

I wasn't formally a member of the Workers' Union but I went to the meetings of my town's workers' committee all the time. They would ask my opinion on different issues, and I helped as best I could. Then at one of the miners' congresses, the town's delegation asked me to speak. The congress appreciated what I said, though of course there was no standing ovation.

The IMU calls itself a trade union, yet practically all its mass actions since the July 1989 strike have had a strongly political orientation.

The further we went, the clearer it became that economic demands would lead nowhere. And so political demands arose. Some say that a trade union should not take on political tasks or propose legislation. But how can we avoid doing that in our situation? I think the near future belongs to the trade union movement rather than to political organizations that only reflect the interests of limited strata. All the natural laws concerning the unity and the struggle of opposites must be given free sway. Without that struggle, everything falls into decay. We had no trade unions in the past, and you see the result. Yet despite that, those who today stand at the head of the state are merely replacing one authoritarian regime by another. The authoritarian essence remains, and this goes for Yeltsin's government too.

Aleksandr Sergeev
Co-chairman,
Independent Miners' Union
[May 1991]

This interview took place at the end of the second major coalminers' strike. Like the first, this strike, which began in early March and lasted nearly two months in some mines, had a profound political impact. Though it never really became general—the Karaganda strike in Kazakhstan lasted only a few days—at its high point the strike embraced over half of the coalminers.

One of the demands was Gorbachev's resignation, and although this was not achieved at the time, the strike was of considerable help to Yeltsin and other republican leaders in their efforts to wrest power from the central government. The agreement between Gorbachev and the republics at the end of April 1991 to devolve major powers to the latter eventually provoked the abortive August coup, causing the further emasculation of central power and leading directly to the demise of the Soviet Union in December of that year.

Aleksandr Sergeev, a mine electrician from the Kuzbass, was elected vice-chairman of the IMU at its formation in October 1990. We talked in the IMU's cramped office near the center of Moscow.

The delegates to the Second Congress of Miners were supposed to report back on its decisions to the collectives that had sent them. What happened after that depended a lot on the capacities and motivation of the particular delegate. I went back to my mine in Mezhdurechensk and told them I had been elected to the executive bureau. I asked if they needed my help in forming the new trade union in the mine. They said they could manage and told me to come back in a month. When I returned, all they had done was register the union and receive an official stamp, but the union itself had only a few members. They just didn't know what to do. So I explained things to them. Today we have about 300 members in a collective of about 1,500.

But the small number isn't so important. People are wary of

leaving the old trade unions, whose main activity for many years has been distributing various benefits and goods.

Can you be a member of both unions?

Our constitution allows that. But the other union wants to force people to choose. People are afraid of losing sick pay. We explain that sick pay, trips to health spas, and so on, are paid for by state social insurance, not the unions, and that a worker has a right to those benefits whether or not he is a member of the union. And those who leave the old union really do continue to get the benefits.

Can you explain the origins of the present strike?

At the founding congress of the IMU, it was decided to conduct a campaign to sign an industry-wide collective agreement with the state in the coal sector. The congress assigned three tasks to the executive bureau of the union: to organize local unions, to conclude a general collective agreement, and to convene miners' congresses. As I said, the first task turned out to be a difficult one, though the process is moving forward. We have 50,000 members. The number is small, but these are committed people.

We wrote a draft collective agreement and presented it to the [Soviet] government on November 20. The law requires a response within five days; a month later we received the response—negative. The law then proposes conciliation. We requested it and were ignored. So we sent a polite warning: "In view of your refusal, we are forced to examine the possibility of a general strike." Then the government changed. Pavlov replaced Ryzhkov as prime minister. We again submitted the documents. No reply.

Did the government ever explain its refusal to negotiate?

No, they completely ignored us, despite the powerful strike we conducted in 1989. That's the style of the government. So on February 11 through 13 at a meeting of union representatives and of the regional strike committees, we decided to prepare for a strike in the spring, sometime at the end of March or toward the middle of April, and to hold meetings with the collectives to discuss this. The meeting instructed the executive bureau to inform Gorbachev of the situation and to warn him that if he didn't observe the International Labor Organization convention, of which the USSR is a signatory, guaranteeing the right to a collective agreement, if he violated his own Law on the Resolution of Labor Conflicts, the miners would strike.

But then politics intervened. The Ukrainian parliament decided to transfer the mines on its territory to Ukrainian jurisdiction. The miners said, "Okay, you've declared Ukrainian sovereignty and the mines should be transferred. But our basic wage is 300 rubles, and we were promised during the 1989 strike that our wages would be indexed to the cost of living. We were also promised that special pension rights would be extended to all underground workers. We're prepared to forget the smaller points, but we want satisfaction on these." The Ukrainian government invited them to talks. They agreed to the pension demands, but refused the wage demand. So the Ukrainian strike committees decided to come out earlier.

Our union structure is federative. The demands of the strike that began at the start of March in the Donbass and Vorkuta [respectively, the Donets Basin in eastern Ukraine and the Pechora coal basin in the Russian far north] were economic and failed to evoke a response from the government, but from March 15, when Kuzbass entered it, the strike became political. The Kuzbass miners demanded the resignation of the president of the USSR [Gorbachev] and dissolution of the Supreme Soviet. After all, all the economic demands had been promised back in July 1989. Who needs that kind of government?

You have to understand why political demands came to the fore. A struggle for power and influence is going on, and the authorities at different levels can't agree on how to divide up the property. We told them, "Either you divide it up by republic or else make a common agreement for the entire industry."

When did the demand for the transfer of the mines to republican jurisdiction arise?

The Kuzbass wanted this from the start, or at least a majority of the miners did. But there are differences in the political levels of the miners. Some put forth only economic demands at first, but others reasoned that since the republics had declared their sovereignty, the issue of jurisdiction should be resolved.

Has there been discussion of the problems this might create for solidarity among the miners?

Economic conditions are different in the two [Donbass and Kuzbass] basins. Kuzbass coal is closer to the surface; there are many open-pit mines. But we feel that if one republic signs a collective agreement, it will put pressure on the others to follow. People wanted sovereignty. They elected republican supreme soviets that proclaimed their sovereignty. So they have to define their own positions. In the referendum last March, people voted yes both to the continuation of the Soviet Union and to [sovereignty for] their republics. That means there has to be a division of powers.

Will your union divide along republican lines too?
It hasn't so far, but I think that it will eventually. You know, the official unions accused us of splitting the union movement, but they were the first to split up into republican houses, even though this makes no real difference to the workers. What difference is it if you breathe dust in the Donbass or the Kuzbass?

The issue of employment has top priority and it provokes a lot of debate. The government's draft law on employment is very bad. We are demanding first that the government conduct surveys of the mines to determine how long each one can hope to function. This should give the miners a long enough warning of what the future holds. Second, we want social guarantees: unemployment compensation and, if necessary, three years' support while the miners retrain.

Are the Donbass miners satisfied with those demands?
Not really. In fact, some of the Donbass mines didn't strike simply out of fear that they would be closed down. We told them, "What difference does it make if they close you now or in half a year? Isn't it better to fight for guarantees when the mine closes?" But they were in shock, because they had been told that they could be closed if they struck. We told them they'd be closed anyway.

Does your union have any program for the restructuring of the economy in the coal regions?
We have a plan for a social development fund. That's in addition to the employment and retraining guarantees we're demanding from the state. This fund would be used to create new jobs, in addition to what the state will do. Because any state—whatever goals

it proclaims—oppresses the individual, restricts his rights. That's why we have to create nongovernmental structures.

Will these structures belong to the miners?
No, they will be large enterprises created by the funds of several independent trade unions. We have one such project in the Tula Basin near Moscow that will be engaged in construction, but that's only one thing. In this country, no one else has yet bothered to think about these problems. Everyone counts on the state.

Yeltsin has issued a decree on the procedure for transferring the mines to Russian jurisdiction. What will that mean?
Those mines that want it will become independent and only pay taxes to the state. The others will be subordinate to the Russian Committee for Fuel and Energy.

This measure of Yeltsin's is populist. It might well turn out that Russia will take over only the profitable mines—we'll have to see. But even in the Kuzbass, the threat of closures is real. That's why we have to examine closely this issue of autonomy and Russian jurisdiction.

I'm categorically opposed to blanket recipes. We had mass collectivization in the 1930s. Now they want mass privatization at full speed with no preliminary analysis of the situation in the coal industry as a whole. What will the unprofitable mines do? We need time to study these questions. They are holding out to the miners the prospect of becoming owners and masters. But no one knows what will happen after that.

I told the representatives of the Raspadskaya mine [one of the largest in the Kuzbass and in all the former Soviet Union], "Two and a half years ago, they offered you a leasing arrangement to persuade you to abandon the strike. You struck again in 1991 and they let you become a joint-stock company so that you'd end the strike. What will it be next time? You haven't even understood the first change and already you're leaping into another. They're tossing you bones, slogans with no economic basis, just like [the Bolsheviks] in 1917."

That's my opinion and that of some of my colleagues. Incidentally, we are often harshly attacked for those views: "You're wrong! How can you talk that way!"

What are the views among the rank and file?

Opinions are divided there too. It's a complicated issue. One could say that it's a political question and not one for the union, though I was talking with a representative of the official coal union, an acquaintance, who expressed the same fears. I'm talking about people who more or less understand and are capable of analyzing these issues. But someone who has spent six hours at physical labor and has to worry about where to get food naturally doesn't think about these things. They tell him, "Here's your chance to become owner. Until now you've worked without being the owner." And he says to himself, "Hey, maybe that's the truth! Who the hell knows?"

To tell the truth, we don't trust any economists. They offer different and contradictory analyses depending on who's paying. But the questions really are complex. In practice, we're now going through a process of self-education. We take different points of view, compare them, and then draw our own conclusions. But we always start from our union's principles: the workers' interests in the areas of employment, wages, health and safety. None of the programs of Pavlov or Silaev [Yeltsin's prime minister at the time] take these interests into consideration. In principle, that's how it should be, since that's what a government exists for: in a crisis, you have to dump your cargo and do what it takes to keep the ship afloat. But we can't adopt that point of view.

Regardless of all these problems, if you draw up a balance sheet of what has been accomplished, the prospect of industry-wide general collective agreements in the basic sectors is no small matter. The agreements will be concluded by the old unions, and I'm sure they'll distort the whole idea, making concessions to the state. But our union, with only 50,000 members and independent of any other structure, has nevertheless forced the state to recognize the principle of a general collective agreement. And it will be forced to sign such agreements not only in coal but in all basic sectors. This was the practice in the Soviet Union until the 1930s, when the State Commission on Labor took over from the unions the right to determine the price of labor.

The state unions have a chance now to take that right back. But when I look at their ideas, I fear they will distort the whole idea that arose from the workers, and that it won't bring much benefit. We've compared our two draft agreements. As if by coincidence, theirs appeared one month after our founding congress. They don't know how to fight—that is, from the workers' point of view. They been accustomed to being conciliatory, though they claim to have suddenly changed. Well, this is their chance, and we'll see. But a quick analysis of the agreement between the Central Trade Union Council and Pavlov's government reminds one of a carrot tied in front of a horse's face.

There's nothing in the agreement about who will manage. It says to the state: You own 90 percent of the property, you buy our labor power, and you have numerous obligations toward us. Let's define our respective powers. First of all, you are obliged to provide us with work and pay us so that we don't starve. At present, we are on piece rates and we don't get paid for idle time that isn't our fault. This leads to exploitation worse than the Henry Ford era in the West, when he introduced his sweating system. We want hourly wages: 70 percent of the wage should be hourly; the rest—piece rates.

We're saying to the state, "You're the owner; we're the labor force. You must give us work and decent living conditions." We don't deny the collective its right to take over the enterprise as its property. But even if it does, wages and conditions can't be set below those of the agreement. That's true regardless of the form of property—joint-stock, private, state, or collective. A person works in order to feed his family and to live decently, not to feed his neighbor's family or to realize some lofty ideals.

That's the principle: that the needs of the worker, the basic producer of all the value that exists on earth, be he a physical or an intellectual worker, are the cornerstone.

The government will naturally oppose our demands, because they raise the whole issue of the organization of production. They'll say, "How can we pay a miner for what he hasn't produced." We reply, "It's your responsibility to organize production efficiently—you the director, chief engineer, department head, minister and prime minister. I am above all a person. I pay taxes. I elected a deputy to parliament that appointed you. You are supposed to be a skilled specialist at your work, and I at mine."

The other day, when we were coming up in the elevator, a woman asked you if you were going to the demonstration called by Democratic Russia in support of Yeltsin's candidacy for president. You

said that "we miners have our concerns and Democratic Russia theirs." What did you mean?

The IMU adhered to a purely trade unionist position and, for now at least, does not believe it should support any political party. However, there are strike committees that haven't yet become union committees and that more or less adhere to the orientation of the democrats, in the Soviet use of the term. [In contemporary usage, it meant "liberals," some of whom were democrats and many of whom were not.] This is the Democratic Russia movement here.

Do the rank and file support the positions of those strike committees?

I would say so, for the most part. After all, the idea of sovereignty is attractive. The center has ripped us off for a long time, and the idea, in principle, is a correct one. I am also incidentally, a patriot of Russia. I want there to be a Russian republic that is sovereign, but within the Union. Let them divide up their powers. I spoke before the Supreme Soviet about the strike. I told them that I had neither the moral right nor the desire to speak to them, because the Kuzbass at that very time was striking for them to resign. However, as a representative of the IMU I had a professional obligation to inform them.

To put it in the crudest and most abstract terms, we are witnessing a struggle between the Communist *boyars* [as in the Russian higher aristocracy] and the new bourgeoisie, the enterprising people, who used to serve those *boyars* as their ideologues but got tired of it. This new bourgeoisie wants to rise to the top itself.

You mean the intelligentsia?

Intellectuals, economists, and so forth. For us, the workers and the workers' movement, it makes more sense now to support this bourgeoisie, because over the last seventy years the Communists' ideas, that "everything belongs to all and to everyone," or that "it all belongs to the *kolkhoz*," have proven to be unsound in general. Some degree of centralization and planning are necessary, it's a matter of deciding what is rational.

Of course, you can argue whether the Communist idea is utopian or not. My view is that like the Bible, the Koran, or Buddhism, Communism should have its place on one's shelf. When you have a concrete problem to solve, you look through the various books and when you find something that answers your needs you adopt it. But you don't adopt the whole theory. That's unnatural, a violation of the natural course of humanity.

This new bourgeoisie is proposing a system that gives the worker a chance to sell his labor at an agreed-upon amount: "You too are a person, and we give everyone a chance"—though that is really open to debate, here as well as in the West. So while this struggle is going on, we naturally support the new bourgeoisie, because the Communists' foggy, orthodox idea of a radiant future is not based upon concrete reality and concrete forces.

However, we should never forget that once the new bourgeoisie comes to power—that's an inevitable process: either they'll share it with the *boyars* in peaceful coexistence or they'll come to power on their own—those whose capital is now only knowledge will want to transform it into material wealth. They will want to exploit us, since that's how their system works. So while we now support the democrats, we know that the are really a bourgeoisie and we must never forget that we will clash with them. We are already clashing over a number of issues. Therefore, we are creating a union that, for now, is dealing with purely trade union issues and stays out of politics. That, in brief, is why I said that we have our problems and they have theirs.

Do you see the need for a workers' party?

I can't predict what the future holds. My personal view is that a person must first have attained a certain level of knowledge and desire in order for him to define himself politically. The majority of workers today are preoccupied with the problems of obtaining food and drink. So we have to interest them in other things, allow them to feel that they are people. When a worker has felt this, when he receives all that he has earned, when he has extra money and time to read books, his horizons will expand. Then he will be able to define himself politically. To force through the creation of a workers' party now, in my view, is utopian, since such a party would fall under the influence of the right or the left; the United Front of Workers, for example, is really an orthodox Marxist party. But sooner or later, we will need a normal party, either an English-type labor party or a socialist party. There will be one in the future, but to try to create it now would be a waste of time.

But an increasingly open struggle for property is already taking place.

Yes, at the state, branch, and enterprise levels. It's a struggle for economic power. I was struck by how many laws on leasing, joint-stock companies, and the like have been passed in the period since the 1989 strike. Many directors have proposed that the collectives take over the enterprises. We asked ourselves why, and we concluded—we could be wrong—that if enterprises become collective property, the workers will become even more dependent upon the enterprise. It will be theirs, but they won't know how to manage it. So the directors see a chance—indirectly—to exploit the workers' lack of preparation in order to become the real masters of the enterprises themselves. They used to be subordinate to the ministers; now they will be free. And why should they want to become legal owners themselves—they could go bankrupt. But if the collective takes over the enterprise, one day the workers will come to the director and ask, "Where is all the money? Where are our wages?" The director will answer, "Why are you asking me? It's your enterprise; you're responsible for it."

Take a look at the process of establishing republican sovereignty at the level of the enterprise. In principle it is something good. But there are also negative aspects. The republics say to the workers, "We're all brothers; the center is robbing us. Let's take over the enterprises and we'll be rich." Each republic says: "The other is to blame. I'm a good guy." That's the paradox: they want to free themselves from the structures above them and to preserve their own structure to dominate those below them. So it goes all the way down the line. This struggle really exists.

You're right—the stratification is occurring. I can see it myself. They want to exploit our ignorance. In essence, capital is being accumulated and it will flow to those with economic knowledge.

When the workers fully grasp what is happening, will they revolt?

I don't deny that possibility. It's at that point that the creation of a party will be a real issue.

Aleksandr Sergeev
[October 1991]

When we last spoke in May, the miners' strike was drawing to a close. How do you evaluate its results?

The political results are already evident. We demanded the resignation of the president of the USSR, its government, Supreme Soviet, Congress of People's Deputies. All this came to pass in the aftermath of the coup attempt by that government. The Supreme Soviet is to be reformed. The republics have received more power—probably too much; they've all become independent.

The central government will be a coordinating organ with only those powers delegated to it by the republics that sign the economic accord.

What is your attitude now toward Yeltsin's government? Many people have commented on its authoritarian tendencies.

This is a government that has no conception of what to do. [This was two months before the start of "shock therapy."] Its work in the past amounted to scoring political points by criticizing the central government. Now the center is gone; it's time to get down to work, and they're in crisis. So of course, we're dissatisfied with that government, not only with its methods, but we can't even see it working. It's total chaos, and if real steps toward stabilization aren't taken, if some sort of clear administrative structure and reform concept are not established, then I can't predict what will happen by winter.

What about the campaign against the soviets, Yeltsin's appointment of prefects, the usurpation of legislative powers in the regions and localities by the executive branch?

Personally, I agree with that. Take Moscow, for example. The mayor was elected by all the citizens, while the deputies [elected legislators] were each voted in by only several thousand. But even to judge by the experience of the soviets elected in the mining regions, these are bodies with a very large number of deputies, with unclear powers and obligations, and they aren't effective. In the old days, these were secondary structures, transmission belts for the party apparatus. The number of deputies needs to be reduced, and their powers and functions strictly defined. So I feel that new elections now would be premature and that the appointment of prefects is totally natural. The role of the soviets is to control the executive powers.

And you're not worried by Russia's long, sad history of absolute, uncontrolled state power?

Sure I am. But for a transitional period, at least a year, we have to suffer such things. It's true that we struck in the spring against Gorbachev's executive presidency. We're aware of Yeltsin's authoritarianism. After all, he came from the party regional committee structures and bears their imprint. But at present it's simply impossible to carry out democratic transformations. In over half of the regions, the former first secretaries of the defunct party committees are still in power, only now as chairmen of the regional soviets. There is also a tendency for the old functionaries to reappear in the new apparatuses.

In last spring's strike, the miners supported the Russian government against the center. If you aren't satisfied with Yeltsin's economic policy, are you prepared to fight him too?

In the spring, we made it clear that we retain our full political independence. We were very aware that if we supported the democrats, it was in order to overthrow the totalitarian system. But if all they want to do is gain power and change nothing, this will not be. At our next congress, we'll invite representatives not only of our own union but of other unions and of the whole labor movement. In the IMU, we are discussing the organization of a congress of the labor movement. Things are moving in that direction.

How do you evaluate the economic results of the spring strike?

Wages were doubled, and that has more or less softened the effect of the accelerating inflation.

Has the transfer of the mines from Soviet to Russian jurisdiction brought any benefits?

The immediate doubling of wages was one result, since the Soviet Union government promised only a gradual increase in wages. The mines also obtained greater freedom to sell or barter from 10 to 20 percent of their coal output. The rest is delivered to the state under contract. Those mines that have become joint-stock companies are being gradually given the right to shift fully to market relations. A third gain is that the USSR Enterprise Law of 1990, which again gave the ministry the right to appoint directors, no longer applies to us. Enterprises are also freer to change their form of property, that is, state enterprises can become collective or joint-stock companies.

But the miners remain dissatisfied after the strike, though not because wages weren't raised enough or the central government wasn't immediately forced to resign. They realized perfectly well the practical limits of their strike, which was more a protest against the authoritarian system. In general, there's been a big growth of consciousness. The union is growing, though I can't say very quickly. If we had our own mass-circulation paper, we would grow much more quickly.

Who decides what to do with the 10 to 20 percent of coal output that can be freely sold?

The work collective. In rare cases, the director decides, although he can always influence the collective's decision anyway.

How are these earnings spent?

Generally on two things. In the past and still today, mostly on consumer goods for the miners. But in the mines that have been selling their coal for a couple of years now, the miners have realized that this is not the best thing. Now they're discussing the purchase of new equipment for the mines and for construction—there's a big problem with building materials—medical equipment for the town, machinery for the collective and state farms for processing food. Commodity exchanges have appeared, and although the prices there are very high, apparently we will have to sell coal, ore and other minerals through them to buy these things. But the state will have to set quotas and prices. So the issue of free market prices is a long way from being resolved.

Your ultimate goal is free market prices for coal. But wouldn't that lead to the immediate closure of many mines?

If the state needs the coal, even if the market price makes a mine unprofitable, the state has to subsidize it. The problem of mine profitability can only be settled after all miners are guaranteed a decent minimum hourly wage related to skills, regardless of the quality of the coal or the costs of production.

What problems does the market pose for the unity of the miners' movement?

The Raspadskaya mine, for example, obtained its independence two years ago, first as a leasehold and then as a joint-stock company. The miners found that this didn't work in our conditions. When the miners voted, it sounded like a good idea, but they soon realized that they lacked the knowledge to organize production. And they had a series of strikes, which were formally directed against themselves. Some sections of the mine failed to meet the plan and naturally received lower wages; those miners protested against the poor organization of work by the administration that had been elected by the collective as a whole.

So although the IMU did not exist at this mine, they now realize that they need it too. They had taken over the mine without first settling relations between management and workers. That can be done only through a trade union that regulates relations between themselves as workers and as lease-holders or joint-stock owners. It was like Mongolia trying to make the jump from feudalism to socialism in one leap.

How do you feel about the sale of mines to private individuals?

In principle, it's all the same to the union: private, state, leased. But there won't be any sale to private owners, though there may be joint ventures with foreign firms.

Will such jointly owned enterprises allow the workers' self-management?

I'm sure they won't. And I don't think the workers themselves will want to run the mines. The self-management that now exists is only on paper.

But didn't you just say that the miners decide how to spend the money earned from the coal left with the mine? And didn't some mines strike for the replacement of their directors? Isn't all that self-management?

Let's look at this question of self-management. Fifty workers elect one delegate, say Vasya. After a shift underground, Vasya comes to a meeting with the administration. The economist reads off a list of figures. Does Vasya know where they came from? The director says that they have to do such and such because there is some sort of resolution and some law. Can Vasya really check if this is correct? You need a permanent control organ. The work-collective councils over the past five years have not really proven themselves. So you need a body that will defend our fundamental interests, a trade union that will monitor all these things. And where our workers' trade unions exist, they do exert effective control over the administration.

The work-collective councils in the big auto plants were the most militant supporters of the transfer of enterprises to the workers. And although the councils included many people with higher eduction, they were still deceived—the workers ended up with a minority share of stocks. Management always has more information, and information is power. The STKs are the organ of the entire collective, including the administration. Besides, there are many conflicting interests among the workers themselves, and these relations have to be sorted out.

In my opinion, until there are trade unions to put the relations within the enterprise in order, all the ideas about collective and joint-stock property are empty talk in our country, except perhaps in small enterprises where the collective can directly monitor its hired administration. In general, you can't ask a worker to answer for everything—he has to be responsible for his own work. But he should have elected representatives who can demand an accounting from management and from politicians.

A final question: Is nationalism among Russian miners on the rise, and how do you view that?

There is a growth of national consciousness, but it's healthy, not chauvinistic. The miners in the Donbass, who are mainly Russian and Russian-speaking, struck in the spring for Ukrainian sovereignty. They were applauded by the nationalist parties. But when the Donbass miners said they wanted to stay in a single organization with the Russian, Byelorussian and Kazakhstan miners, the nationalists turned against them. The problems will be serious there. We have a couple of organizations in western Ukraine, but it's harder to work there, because the nationalists say that the IMU in Moscow is dominated by *Moskali* [a pejorative Ukrainian term for Russians; Western Ukraine, which was annexed in 1940, is predominantly Ukrainian-speaking and the center of Ukrainian nationalism].

Aleksandr Sergeev
[July 1992]

I spoke again with Aleksandr Sergeev in the new offices of the Russian IMU in the skyscraper of the Russian Coal Ministry. This was a sharp contrast to the IMU's shabby old one-room office. Sergeev explained that they had been evicted by cooperators. Meanwhile, the former state union of coalminers was still sitting comfortably in the Federation of Independent Trade Unions' (FITR) vast complex on Leninski Prospekt.

The Russian IMU had been among the strongest supporters of Yeltsin. I was curious to hear what Sergeev thought of Yeltsin's government seven months into "shock therapy." My young anarchist friends at the *Information Bulletin of the Labor Movement* who had initially been sympathetic to the IMU now dismissed the Russian branch as a new state union.

I began by asking Aleksandr about the conflict in the Kuzbass coalfields that coincided with the launching of "shock therapy" at the start of the year.

You know that we have two coal unions: our Independent Union of Miners and what is now called the Independent Union of Employees of the Coal Industry [IUECI] which belongs to the FITR. It changed its name but didn't conduct a new registration of its members or elect new officers. They just threw away their party cards and announced, "We're independent now."

They signed a collective agreement on December 3, 1991, when we were only in the process of founding our Russian IMU and preparing to present the government with our own draft collective agreement. That's normal competition between unions. Well, even at that time, it was clear that the wage levels fixed in the IUECI's agreement didn't suit anyone, because prices were rising rapidly. Their agreement had a clause on indexation, but it was so vague that it was left completely unclear how it should be applied. So naturally, people were getting upset.

Another source of tension was that prices on metal and equipment were freed, while the price of coal remained fixed. Mines weren't earning enough to cover costs, and I think it was the directors who put pressure on the government to increase wages and subsidies.

Finally, at our congress in December, we decided that we would strike if the government refused to negotiate a collective agreement with us. The government decided to talk to both unions at once solely on the issue of wages. For two days, we refused to participate. Prices were rising everywhere and every enterprise was suffering losses. If the other union concluded a bad agreement, then it should have admitted it rather than shout that sausage was expensive. But naturally, they blamed it all on the government and demanded a 600 percent increase in wages. The government offered an increase of 280 percent and we proposed a compromise of 300 percent for underground workers and 200 percent for surface workers, as well as a moratorium on strikes for the next quarter while we watched how things went. We doubted that the other union could organize anything, except on a local scale. In the end, wages were raised threefold.

But the other union insisted that this increase cover all employees in the branch. And that's what provoked all the tension in the country. There are only 200,000 to 300,000 underground miners in Russia, and a threefold increase in their wages wouldn't have been felt strongly in the economy. Instead, 1.5 million people got a threefold increase. Naturally, workers in other branches, who were doing the exact same work—teachers, medical workers, railroad workers—were upset. Of course, the old, sluggish local unions, which express the group egoism of their members, played a role in whipping this up.

So there were local strikes by the "budget employees" that eventually won wage raises and a review of the official minimum wage. Of course, their wages needed to be increased, but this could have been done without strikes. And I blame the parliament, not the government, since the parliament sets the minimum wage. Its inaction helped to undermine not only the economy but also the political situation, giving a boost to the Communists [the opposition that arose out of the recently banned Communist Party of the Soviet Union], who created all the hysteria about the "impossible" material situation of the people. You saw what happened at Ostankino. [In June 1992 several hundred demonstrators, many elderly, camped in front of the Ostankino television station to demand air time for the opposition. In the early morning of June 22, they were dispersed by club-wielding police. The liberal press and politicians, including Yeltsin, began warning of a "brown-red" threat, that is, a union of communist and "patriotic" or fascistic elements.] You saw their ugly, distorted faces. You can see that they're ready to take to the barricades and beat up anyone who disagrees with them.

My conclusion is that these old unions are a brake, that they want to take us backward. Despite their declarations about defending the working people, they don't defend them but exploit group egoism to grab yet another piece of the rapidly disappearing state budget. You can see the connection between the brown-red opposition and the FITR. So in January, the government simply made a mistake. Otherwise, there would have been no strikes. We have democracy now. This is a really democratic government that tries to talk to everyone. And the opposition groupings are exploiting that to intensify the pressure.

The Kuzbass workers' committees, which are closely linked to your union, publicly condemned the teachers' strike, after the miners themselves had won hefty wage increases by threatening to strike. They teach the miners' kids, but live below subsistence level.

The workers' committee had every right to condemn the strike. We made clear that we had participated in the negotiations but that we had demanded something very different from what the government finally granted. The other union accused us of being conciliatory toward the government. Yet the public blamed us, called us rip-off artists, thinking that it was really the doing of the miners. The only thing we did wrong was to go along with the 300 percent across-the-board increase. But the government didn't understand us.

It's obvious that you believe in this government. Why are you so sure these reforms will lead to anything good?

No, I'm not sure that these reforms will lead to good. They won't. But our life of the past seventy years didn't lead to anything good either. A person has to have hope, but I don't believe everyone will live happily. Not everyone should, but everyone should have equal opportunities. Of course, that's still ahead, but some things are happening already. The enterprises are now free. That is, the gates have been opened, but we simply haven't yet learned how to use the new freedom. Now is the time simply to realize oneself, to create a normal trade union, to redistribute surplus value within the enterprises, to review the production cycle, to see what the price consists of. These are all the concerns of the union. Unions should be busy in the enterprises and not organizing demonstrations to grab another bit of the state budget, as the FITR does.

Of course, there will be problems, and big ones, unemployment and all the rest. But you have to remember that 80 percent of our industry makes producers' goods and only 20 percent makes consumer goods. So there has to be restructuring, and that includes the work force. This can only happen by restructuring some enterprises, closing down others, and then opening new ones.

How to do that is another question. Should I resist being unemployed or demand that I be paid full wages until the state creates another job for me? We are used to the state taking care of us. But it isn't obliged to take care of everyone—only the poor and those who can't feed themselves. For the others, the state has to create conditions that allow them to earn a living. That's all.

You say "that's all." But in countries like Canada, which your politicians take as their ultimate model, the state doesn't create those conditions, even though the labor movement has always demanded that it do so.

Look, I don't deny that Russia has big problems. But I don't believe that we're heading for the abyss either. You can't go around yelling, like the opposition does, that we're all reduced to misery. Sure, there are strata of the population that are poor. They have to be taken care of.

Aren't you risking a lot in supporting this government without any real of guarantees?

Why shouldn't we risk? For two years we tried to change the

political order in the country. You remember our political strikes. We have to move forward, but we still have to defend ourselves. We know we're not a political party; we're a union. Anyway, what's the alternative? Some propose a return to the reds, to the Communists. Who else can offer an alternative? The Socialist Party of Workers? The Party of Labor? [These "democratic left" parties arose in the fall of 1991. The Party of Labor was founded mainly by former socialist and anarcho-syndicalist dissidents and is seeking support in the former state unions; the Socialist Party of Workers was formed mainly by former members of the CPSU.] They're still small, and they include the whole gamut, from decent people to rabble.

Let's look at the concrete issue of jobs. What's the situation you're faced with?

We foresee unemployment. The whole industry is being reorganized. Coal prices are being raised and gradually brought to world levels. That will allow us to know how much coal we really need to produce. If the cost of production in a mine is too high, there's no reason to keep workers buried down there: either change the technology or shut down the mines. That's a normal, realistic approach, something we've been demanding since 1989. Of course, there are employment problems that we have to work out with the government. There's the issue of resettlement, especially for the miners in the far north. We've already created a joint-stock company to help with that.

So things are going in the right direction. We just have to sit down with the government and see what solutions are best and insist that our views be considered, not simply shout that we won't allow any closures. Why should the state maintain mines working at a loss that hurt the whole society? In general, we had a corrupt economy; now we have to create a normal one.

But who will decide what "normal" is?
Life will decide.

You mean the market?
No, life. Imagine the following situation. A ton of coal costs seventy rubles to extract. The state buys it for fifty rubles—though on the world market it sells for thirty dollars—and pays the mine twenty rubles [a tiny fraction] in subsidies. Then the state turns

around and sells that ton, pocketing the difference. In a normally functioning system the enterprise would sell the coal at a normal price, distribute the earnings within the enterprises, and pay taxes to the state. That's why I say we had a corrupt economy, and it is still corrupt. I don't say it was a planned economy. There was some attempt at planning in the first years after the revolution. After that, it was pure corruption: you scratch my back, and I'll scratch yours. I told you last time that there is no such thing as communist or capitalist economics—only general economic laws that we must respect.

Haven't you wondered, for example, why the British miners fought so hard against the closure of their mines?

I agree that in the West your main problem is employment. If we had mines equipped like those in England and with English wages, I'd also fight against their closure. Those miners won't find other jobs like those in England, so they want to protect their mines.

Even in the West, coal mining isn't exactly heaven. We just lost forty-six miners in an accident in eastern Canada.

I know that. But all the same, Western miners are satisfied with their conditions. Your situation is different. In your economy, all the sectors are saturated. That's not true here. We have sectors that need to be expanded and developed. So you can't automatically transfer union experience from one country to the next. It's curious that the FITR argues that you can't copy the capitalist economic model, but then shouts, "We're just acting like normal trade unions." Nothing can be achieved without a transitional period.

So you don't mind it when people accuse your union of being loyal to the government in the tripartite commission [a commission made up of union, government, and management representatives]?

Not at all. The crooks from the FITR, who are in opposition, are also sitting on that commission. The FITR still controls social security, and we have evidence that shows they have siphoned off billions of rubles. Yet they shout, "People are perishing. You have to support everyone." What's the sense of this demagoguery? Sure you can make demands now and go on strike. But who was it that struck before the coup? Only we did. Where was the FITR when we defeated the Communist plague, when we really got freedom?

During our strikes, I got called in every day by the KGB—not for questioning, but for "chats." We were slandered and threatened with prosecution. Now we are free to strike, but in the name of what? The government is ready to talk to anyone. And now, you can see how the directors and the FITR unions are closing ranks. Excuse me, my dears, but when the political situation is somewhat more stable, then we can talk about demands and protests.

Some German trade unionists have already condemned me for having this "grand" office. But they've seen the FITR complex on Leninski Prospekt and all their cars. That wasn't built on union dues but on money diverted from the workers' social security payments.

But sure, we have our complaints about this government, and we might even strike over the issue of social security.

Isn't the government supposed to take over its administration from the FITR next year?

That's not what bothers us. We don't want the union employees simply to become state employees. We want the whole corrupt system reformed. This was one of the reasons why we decided in June to remove our signature from the general agreement with the government. Incidentally, we're the only union to do that, even though the government hasn't carried out a whole series of its provisions. The remaining signatories—the FITR, Sotsprof [a small confederation of alternative unions], the pilots unions—agree not to strike. Of course, we're not about to strike now. We're offering to work out a compromise with the government. But we have set a time limit.

You seem to reject not only the FITR but all the unions affiliated with it. Are there any exceptions?

No one is making a blanket rejection of those unions. But it's taking too long to reform them. The leaders don't want reform. They want to keep their monopoly by any means, by tossing out sops, by demagoguery. They want to be the leaders of the labor movement. What do the local unions do? They distribute goods. They're not with the workers. That's why I don't believe they can be reformed. I'm not calling for their forcible disbandment, as was done with the Communist Party. But people have to be given the freedom to choose whether or not to join them. The automatic dues check-off has to be ended. It's like in Brazil—everyone has to pay dues, whether they want to or not. In Russia, most people don't even know they pay union dues. Secondly, we want the administration of social security taken out of union hands. And finally, we want them to stop speaking in the name of all working people.

When the process of turning the enterprises into joint-stock companies gets going, when the workers really start to get squeezed, they'll realize that it isn't the ration of food and consumer goods distributed by the unions that will save them, but their own struggle for survival. But the existing union structures won't permit that struggle to develop, and that's when the workers will start to explode them from below. Maybe some of these structures can be cleaned out from top to bottom. But others will be destroyed and replaced. However, that will only occur when there is real property—private, joint-stock companies.

If those unions really wanted to reform themselves, they would fight for private property—I mean for the existence of different forms of property, including private. But they don't need that. And let me add this: at their plenary session, the other miners' union declared, "The IMU is our political opponent." Notice that they didn't say "ideological" but "political." From that I conclude that they are still defending our Communist past, despite their change of name. They just stopped talking about communism and now talk about patriotism and nationalism. So things are clear; the mask is off. We were the only union to strike on August 19 against the coup. The other union limited itself to a declaration.

Postscript: Five months after this interview, at the Second Congress of the Russian IMU in Vorkuta on December 8, 1992, Aleksandr Sergeev was re-elected president. The congress also affirmed its support for Yeltsin and his economic reforms. Its "Appeal to Work Collectives in the Mining Industry and to All Citizens" [*Informatsionnyi byuleten* 50:3 (1992)] stated: "While we are aware of and criticize all the errors of the President and of the government he heads, we are sure that progressive transformations will be realized in Russia through our common efforts." The Russian IMU has also supported Yeltsin in his struggle against the parliament's opposition to his policies.

V

THE COUP AND AFTER

Kolya Naumov
[October 1991]

On August 19, 1991, most of Gorbachev's cabinet declared a state of emergency. Their stated goal was to restore order, and they did not renounce the market reforms. Gorbachev himself was reported "sick" and apparently kept under armed guard at his vacation place in Crimea. This state coup collapsed on August 21, mostly out of its own internal weaknesses.

Kolya, who sympathized with the workers' movement, was always apologizing for not being an activist. So I was surprised to hear that he had been among the few workers who went to defend the White House (the seat of the Russian government at the time) at what he certainly must have felt to be a considerable personal risk. I began by asking him how he felt now about Yeltsin.

I used to think that there were people up there who knew what they were doing. Now I see that there will be economic ruin, wild privatization, and that young capitalists will win and install their own president. But I don't blame Yeltsin. The same would happen no matter who was up there, even one of your friends.

Maybe you're right, so long as the workers don't become an independent political force.

You keep talking about the people. Let me tell you how the people got me a television set.

After I bought the car last year, they began allocating videocassette players at the factory. I didn't put in any requests, and anyway I had no money. The distribution is done by the shop's trade union committee; don't ask me how. One day, the committee got furniture—kitchen sets, sofas and armchairs, wall modules. Our section was given one set of each. You remember that little guy Oleg, the sly fellow who's always sucking up to me? He asked me what I needed. The women who runs the storeroom had just got her new apartment so she asked for the kitchen set. Then there was Nikolai, who was injured while climbing for parts in the storeroom. It's several floors high, and when he was five meters up one of the metal trays fell on him. It tore up his stomach and smashed his heel. The wound constantly reopens and the doctors can't do anything. So it was agreed that he'd get the soft furniture and I would get the wall module.

But when the time came, it turned out Nikolai didn't get the furniture. And I didn't have enough conscience to offer him the wall module, because we only have one room and a kitchen for the three of us, and we always dreamt of a wall module as a divider for the room. The price of modules had risen 200 to 300 percent, but we were to get it at the old price.

After a while, I was called over by my adjuster, who is chairman of the trade-union committee. He gets paid as if he works for us, while he's busy allocating goods. He gives me a coupon and says, "Mum's the word. I'm giving you a good module, because there are good ones and bad ones." I thanked him, of course. I simply want to say that our committee has the power to give you something of good quality or not. You see what kind of power they have?

Then there was talk of freezers. Everybody was saying how in the West people all have freezers. But I didn't fill out a request form. One day I bumped into the adjuster again. He mentioned the freezers. I told him I hadn't put in for one. He said that didn't matter—when they came, he'd give me one anyway. But when they came and I reminded him, he just said: "What do you need a freezer for?" Well, as the time passed, many people got refrigerators, sewing and washing machines, freezers. They fought and bickered over them. But I kept away from that business. It was a question of pride. That adjuster doesn't do any work in the shop. You saw how I work for the others; I do the repairs myself, because my mechanics can't manage. I have the feeling that I deserve these things (laughs).

About a month and a half ago, the adjuster went on vacation and was replaced by Valera, a worker from the assembly line. He says to me, "Kolya, do you have a mechanical screwdriver for me?" They're in very short supply, so I told him to ask the Komsomol organizer for his—he had recently left his job on the line—and to bring me the old one. But the Komsomol organizer refused. So I gave him one that I had, and not "for a glass"; usually when someone does something for you, you offer him some vodka or promise something else.

Sometime later, he comes to me and says: "We have televisions. Do you want one?" I suspect that part of what they get is not accounted for and they buy it themselves or else sell it to others in return for bribes, because not long after that, someone else asked me if I needed a television. He said that for a hundred rubles or a bottle of cognac, I could get a coupon. Anyway, I told Valera that I wouldn't mind one. When I came for the coupon, he said not to say anything to anyone. I thanked him and said I owed him one. He said, "I didn't give it to you for that; I just respect you."

After that, I got a coupon for the perfume shop. They opened up an Estée Lauder store in the factory. Everything is sold at a third of what it costs at the market or in the private stores. So I bought a set: perfume, eau de cologne, men's toilet water, lipstick. Part of it I sold to the private store, but I kept the toilet water for Valera. Who knows, I thought, one day he might be useful (laughs). At first he refused but he finally accepted it.

You can't find aspirin or antibiotics in the drugstores, but they keep you supplied with imported perfume?

I can't understand it either. Obviously, someone is making a lot of money on that. Anyway, I quietly bought the television in the hope of selling it too. But my wife and I decided to keep it, since it can be hooked up to a videocassette player and my son dreams of getting one.

About three weeks went by when I overheard a woman, a supervisor, saying to Valera, "I hear refrigerators arrived." Again, no one knew about this. I thought that a refrigerator wouldn't be bad. We could use it ourselves—my wife had been complaining how small ours was—or else I could resell it and make good my promise to donate money to the poor. When I bought the car, I promised I would give part of the money to the poor. My cousin was supposed to take it to a woman in my home town who knows who to give it to, but he didn't do it and we spent the money. So I asked Valera about the refrigerators. He said, "We have to decide at the meeting of the shop committee, and it's very hard." He asked if I had put in a request. Again, I hadn't. So he said, "Take a crumpled piece of paper, write a request, and backdate it a year." I did, on one of the old forms for "socialist commitments" (laughs).

Before the shop committee met, the department head asked them who was to get the various goods. He himself has bought many things—several televisions, washing machines, videocassette players, and so on. But he needs more. He's building himself a *dacha* and needs the money. One of my mechanics is always working on his *dacha*. When Valera mentioned my name, the department head told them to give the refrigerator to someone else. Apparently, he also has friends who buy the goods for him. So they crossed me off. But Valera defended me, and they ended up allotting me a freezer instead. At the committee meeting, however, there was a terrible uproar. People accused each other of being speculators.

I paid 3,000 rubles for the freezer. In the commercial store is costs 11,000. It's hard to understand why they spend foreign currency on Italian freezers. I can only think that our mafia has international links.

Does everyone in the shop end up getting something good? Or are some people totally passed over?

Nikolai, the worker that fell—we've been trying to get him a car. But they won't give him one. He's not energetic enough, and of course he's sick. He isn't able to get himself a fake document saying he's learning to drive, and without that you can't buy a car. But almost all workers, even if they've worked only five years, have bought a car.

Is the situation different in Novopolskii's [final assembly] shop?

Yes, the collective there is solidly behind him and has taken the allocation under its control. Everything is transparent, while in our shop it's all secret. Of course, I suspect that Novopolskii has to do some manoeuvering now and then, to give some favors, otherwise the crooks in his shop would devour him. There are workers there who steal together with the bosses. But on the whole, he distributes things fairly.

What about people in smaller, less important enterprises or in institutions like schools and libraries?

They don't get much at all. Even if their organizations are allocated something, it probably disappears before it reaches them.

I was saying that I had been allotted a freezer. I was waiting for it to arrive, when I bumped into Valera again. He had a bunch of Estée Lauder coupons. He gave me four. I said: "Thanks, I owe you one." Again, he wouldn't hear of it. I offered the coupons to my workers, but only one of them took one. I guess they are more or less honest. So I had three left and I went and bought a load of that crap and again gave Valera a bottle of toilet water. I bought that junk because, after buying the freezer, we were out of money, although my wife did buy a leather jacket for herself, and we still have 10,000 rubles in our savings account, but we didn't want to touch it.

Why am I telling you all of this? I know that it's all wrong and ugly, but I've given in. You can see how my own psychology has changed. I saw others who have spent a lot fewer years at the plant getting all sorts of things and I felt I had to join in, even though I knew how corrupting that whole mess is. Up until a year and a half ago, this allocation didn't exist. Not many years ago, you could get many of these things without any trouble in the state stores. This is my answer to your idea about workers controlling the people who are in power. I'm trying to explain how even on the plant level management keeps a leash on the workers.

You wonder why I passively accept the introduction of capitalism? I'm sick of all this. You wouldn't believe the time that's lost at work with people running around the factory to get these goods. I would like it all to be sold openly on the free market.

Okay, tell me now about the coup.

I came to work on August 19, late again (laughs), without having heard the radio. I was in the changing room, and Sasha, a worker who used to be head of our shop's party committee, says to me, "So, it's finally happened." I asked what he was talking about. He said, "Martial law." I still didn't understand. He explained that Gorbachev had been removed. I thought it was a joke. Then the news came on at eight and they read the declaration of the Committee for the State of Emergency. I couldn't stop laughing; I just couldn't take it seriously. A granny, a cleaning woman, piped up: "Good, they finally got rid of Gorbachev."

And Sasha was also inspired. I remember when Yeltsin was just appointed head of the Moscow party committee, we had a closed meeting at the factory with party veterans from Sverdlovsk, where Yeltsin had previously been party boss. They praised Yeltsin as a real Communist who had put things in order and asked us to support him. At that time, Sasha was strongly pro-Yeltsin. Now he said that it was good that Gorbachev was removed—he had ruined the country; now there would be order. I said, "Sasha, don't ever repeat those words, because after a while you'll be very ashamed of them. These people are clowns and have nothing serious to propose."

I went to work, and at 11:30 the supervisors and the head of the shop met for our usual operational meeting. Tolya from the assembly line ran in, slamming the door, "Well, now we'll put things in order!" He was overwrought. A normal person would have understood that this was delirium. I don't really think he believed what he was saying, but he was in a dead end. He's a real Bolshevik, a sincere communist. And with the coup, his torment was over. Everything in which he believed had been crumbling and now he would be spared having to think about what direction to take, what to do. The shop director said: "You've heard about the state of emergency. It turns out that democracy couldn't solve anything and that harsh measures are needed." He was probably repeating what he had heard from above. "We'll probably have to go out to the countryside to help with the harvest, and they will demand that we fulfill the plan. But what else can we do? We have to get out of the crisis." [It had been usual for urban workers and employees to help with the harvest, but by 1990 this practice had been undermined as a consequence of the weakening of central control over the enterprises and the localities.] Tolya gets up and announces, "The latest report is that the committee has promised to take inventory of all food supplies, to fight against the mafia." All nice things, but how could they do that? It was ridiculous; it was like a dream.

My own sense was that the coup had been prepared, that they had food stocks that would keep people quiet for a few months, and then it would collapse. So I was calm. I felt that we would have a few quiet months and that I could catch up on my reading. Still, though

I wanted to go home, I decided to go downtown after work. Pushkin Square [near the Moscow soviet, the site of numerous demonstrations over the last years] is on our subway line. I was sure that the police would block off access to it. But there were no police to be seen. So I rode farther, to Red Square [next to the Kremlin]. The square was closed off by police barriers, and I could see KGB agents in the cars. People were standing around, drunken fools, excited people arguing with the police. I asked where the tanks were. A policemen pointed somewhere, but I couldn't see anything.

So I decided to go to Manège Square [next to Red Square, scene of many mass meetings over the past years] where I saw a chain of buses closing off Red Square and rather unattractive soldiers in black berets and uniforms standing in front of them. People were shouting, "What are you laughing at? You're children. How can you shoot at us!" And others yelled back, "Leave them alone! The soldiers aren't to blame!" There were small groups of people standing around and some Moscow soviet deputies carrying a megaphone, whom I knew from the early perestroika clubs. These are not very serious people, loudmouths who only know how to criticize and call demonstrations. I listened a bit, but it was boring and I began to walk back toward Pushkin Square.

At the exit from Manège Square, I saw a car and pretty girls smoking cigarettes standing next to it (laughs). You can usually see these girls hanging around the democrat-revolutionaries. These are guys who like to run around with flags and are usually surrounded by rather freewheeling girls with cigarettes who like to drink and talk politics and aren't opposed to jumping into bed with them (laughs). In Tolstoy's *Resurrection* he writes of a similar phenomenon around the political convicts.

So being a revolutionary has its rewards?
No, I'm serious. There are girls who like that kind of thing. Anyway, one of those guys shouts, "People! All to the White House to organize resistance! They're building barricades there. Equipment is arriving. Food will be supplied. Our car has been arrested" (laughs).

As I approached Pushkin Square, I saw armored personnel carriers. On the carriers had been pasted Yeltsin's decree calling on the people not to obey the putschists, traitors of the fatherland. The soldiers did nothing. There was traffic on Gorky Street [main shopping street in central Moscow]. People tried to walk on the roadway and block traffic, but the police wouldn't let them. Otherwise it looked normal. There were lines of handsome people in jeans in front of the foreign perfume stores, Dior, Nina Ricci, and nearby people who had already got their perfume were speculating with it. So life went on.

Then we saw a column of tanks, and we began to move into the street. Someone climbed up on a fence and yelled, "People! You are sheep! Let's move against the tanks! Why are you walking on the sidewalk?" Fortunately, the tanks obeyed the traffic signals and stopped at a red light. So we ran up and crowded around them. A young soldier stuck out his frightened face. We stood there and shouted, "Yeltsin! Yeltsin!" Everyone was yelling it, so I did too. You had to yell something. We showed the soldiers that we supported Yeltsin who was in the White House.

Still, I'd like to know what exactly that meant to you.
Well, we wanted to show the soldiers that we weren't some mob acting against the interests of the country. At the last elections, Yeltsin was a symbol of the fight against corruption.

And when people at the White House shouted "Russia! Russia!"?
Independent Russia meant separation from the old party-run central power, from the empire.

Against the party's rule, and for what?
For some people, it means a strong Russia. For me, it means a Christian Russia, that is, a Russia that aspires not to domination but to religion, to self-limitation.

I had some apples that, incidentally, had been sold at the factory along with other food (laughs). I decided to give them to the soldiers. But they were afraid to take them, until finally the commander of one tank ordered them to take the apples. People sat on the tanks. I felt very sorry for the soldiers. They had tears in their eyes, they were afraid.

After that, I took the subway home, ate, and told my wife that I was going to the White House. I got out of the subway at about eleven p.m. and saw a broad stream of people moving toward the White House. There were also girls, but not with cigarettes; normal, honest

Russian girls. But people were also moving in the other direction, from the White House.

Why do you say Russian girls? How do you know they weren't Ukrainians or Jews?

It's just an expression. The Jewish girls consider themselves Russian.

When I got to the White House, I saw barricades being built. Underground passages were under construction nearby, and people were taking building materials from there. I heard tanks and people cheering. I understood that they were ours. Someone shouted, "Form a chain!" Then other tanks came. It wasn't clear on whose side they were. People came up and talked to the soldiers. But the barricades were puny.

Do you have any idea how many people were there?

That first night, maybe 16,000. It was mostly young people, students, intelligentsia. Only in the morning did I meet a girl from our shop. I spent the night sleeping on a board under my umbrella. In the morning at work, a supervisor from our shop asked me if it was me sleeping under the umbrella. He had been there too.

What was happening at the plant?

It was perfectly calm. Everybody warmly greeted the GKChP (State Committee for the State of Emergency). Everyone was glad Gorbachev had been overthrown. They didn't give a damn about Yeltsin. But to tell the truth, I didn't speak to people. I came to the factory, did a few things, slept a little on the table, went to an operational meeting with the head of the shop, and then went home to eat and sleep a bit before returning to the White House.

At nine o'clock, my wife woke me up to see the news about the resistance at the White House that was being organized by Yeltsin.

Didn't it strike you as odd that under martial law the main news program was informing people about the resistance?

Not really. I simply understood that they were incompetents. They announced a curfew in Moscow. I went anyway. I had stolen a bunch of work gloves from the factory to give to people building the barricades, and I bought some sunflower seeds to give to the soldiers. The crowd was giving them all sorts of food. I didn't know if

I'd be able to reach the barricades because of the curfew, but there were no police or soldiers when I got out of the subway. People were just strolling around. They had just come down out of curiosity to see what was happening—all kinds of people. I heard one girl telling another about a conversation between two prostitutes, "You know, I worked all night in the tanks" (laughs).

About midnight, we heard a machine-gun volley and the crash of metal on metal. We thought the tanks were moving, and people began to shout frightfully. We moved toward the noise. There were a lot of people. I figured that if they opened fire, I'd run for it. I wouldn't have thrown myself under the tank. But if Yeltsin was beside me, I would have jumped on his back.

Do you mean you would or wouldn't have taken a bullet for him?
I wouldn't have. But that evening I saw people, including nurses, formed into lines. They were supposed to stand up before tanks. They would have taken bullets for Boris Nikolaevich [Yeltsin]. But I didn't join them. Maybe if I had come during the day, I would have. Still, I felt it was my duty to be there because there were defenseless women. They loved Yeltsin, stupidly and fanatically, without any valid basis in reality—but I couldn't leave them.

We were walking, and another volley went off. The bullets whistled over our heads, though they were probably quite high over the White House. We couldn't find out what had happened, so I went back and lay down to sleep.

Did you really think they would storm the White House?
No. Personally, I nurtured the hope that it wouldn't happen. Of course, the gunfire frightened me. I thought that if there was an attack, it wouldn't occur before dawn. But I couldn't get much sleep, as the loudspeaker had been hooked up and someone kept telling the news, though he really had nothing interesting to say. So I got up to walk around. Two people were shouting, "Why are you gathered here? Are you crazy!? Don't you know two people have been crushed? What are you doing!?" The crowd yelled back, "Provocateurs! Kill them!" but the leaders stopped them. Then the radio announced that a tragedy had occurred. [That night three young men were killed in incidents with tanks.]

At dawn, we were told to line up, since there could be an attack.

We were told to move fifty meters in front of the White House, since if the attack came, there would be shooting from the building. I couldn't understand that at all—if they opened fire, they would hit us in the back. But we stood there anyway. There were a few alarms, but nothing materialized, and I left.

I entered Smolensk Square and saw the fenced off area where the men had been killed. There were burned-out trolleys, but we had heard nothing.

Do you think the tanks intentionally crushed them?

No, it was an accident. There were orders not to allow bloodshed.

I returned to the factory, but soon left again, since I heard that Yeltsin had called a demonstration. I came and left a few times, since I was still worried there would be an attack, and I also wanted to feed the soldiers. I bought some corn (laughs).

The third night was calm. There was a concert. I didn't want to go home. I felt good.

How many people had been there the second night?

More than the first. Many people. Maybe three or four times as many.

Did you see many workers?

Well, it's hard to say who was a worker. But there were many from the intelligentsia, students, housewives, pensioners, some old couples holding hands.

Were you at the mass funeral demonstration with the huge Russian flag?

Yes, I left work for that, though I didn't see that flag. But I felt very proud for our Russian flag. I felt that now I could hang that flag out on holidays.

On the fourth day after work, I couldn't hold back and again went downtown. I walked through the streets in a triumphal mood. At Red Square, everything was as usual. On Manège Square some democrats were making speeches—total garbage, idiocy. Suddenly, someone ran up to the microphone and said, "Comrades! Who knows how to smash monuments? They are smashing Dzerzhinskii's monument but they don't know how." So I hurried over there. [Felix Dzerzhinskii headed the Cheka, the political police force set up after the October Revolution. It was eventually transformed by Stalin into his terror apparatus.]

When I arrived, a young guy was sitting on the statue's head, and another was at its waist. One end of a rope was tied around its head and the other was attached to a bus. Someone was yelling not to do it, so I gathered a group of people around the monument so that the work would not be halted. In the end, it was done professionally with a crane.

Didn't anyone call to storm the Lubyanka? [The Lubyanka, behind the Dzerzhinskii statue, is headquarters of the KGB.]

That's a good question. Not one window was broken. But even before that I had understood that despite the arrest of the putschists nothing had really changed. After a few days, the euphoria completely disappeared and was replaced by a terribly oppressive feeling.

Volodya Fedorov and
Aleksandr Safronov:
Locomotive Engineers
[July 1992]

I met Volodya Fedorov at a reception thrown by a "trade union" to mark the launching of its publishing house. I had received the invitation from the secretary of the Independent Miners' Union. This trade union turned out to be a union of cooperators, that is, a business organization. Despite the general collapse of living standards, there was no austerity here. Volodya, an activist of the new Union of Locomotive Brigades, had just come from his shift. He spoke with passion about his work, and seemed oblivious to the contrast he presented to the fashionably dressed *nouveaux riches* who filled the hall. We agreed to do an interview, and I met a few weeks later with Volodya and his friend Aleksandr Safronov.

[ALEKSANDR] I was elected chairman of the union committee [at his rail depot] in 1988 and quit after seven months to go back to being an engineer. The basic reason was that the union really existed only on paper; in practice, it was busy allocating various benefits. They weren't even thinking about defending the workers. My predecessor, Chibisova, had been chair for ten years, and the entire work collective was fed up with her. She allocated refrigerators, cars, and plots of land but did nothing to defend us against administrative arbitrariness. The workers were getting ready to kick her out in disgrace at the union election conference two months away, so higher levels of the union quickly promoted her out of the depot into the district council.

I told Olga Vakulenko, the chairwoman of the district union council, that the work we were doing wasn't suitable for a union. She agreed but said there was no one else to do it. I asked when we were supposed to do our union work, but she claimed we were doing it. What was I doing? I was allocating one food mixer, one refrigerator, one vacuum cleaner for 600 people. We'd get one car in six months or a year, and it was a tough job figuring out what to do with it: veterans who had served at the front had priority, but so did workers with long seniority, and people who had been in line a long time.

The other thing I was doing was giving union consent to dismissals for disciplinary violations, mostly drunkenness. If it was a first offense, we usually sent the worker for a cure. But if the person was caught several times, the union committee would consent to the dismissal.

And another thing. I was elected by the workers of the depot and I should have been working in the depot, going around to the workplaces to keep abreast of the situation, to know what was going on. But they didn't let me do this. Chibisova once phoned me from the district council: "Aleksandr Dmitrievich, you have to go to some seminar or other." I said, "Lidiya Vasilevna, I'm up to my ears in work here at the depot." She said, "I told you to go." So I went. I figured maybe I'd learn something. After all, I'm not a lawyer, or a teacher, or an accountant, but I need all those skills at work. So I go, and they're giving a lecture on Marxist-Leninist philosophy. I told her, "I'm wasting my time there," and she said, "I have a quota to fill for attendance."

The next time I went, I signed up and immediately returned to the depot. But they got wind of this. They saw that there were only a few people in the hall. I guess I wasn't the only one who got that idea. Maybe the others went to the movies, but I was at work. So they started to re-register the people after the lunch break. I had a serious talk with the district council, but I couldn't convince them. I threatened to quit. They tried to dissuade me. But what was I really doing at the depot anyway? I was putting together a financial report, allocating subsidized vacation trips.

The system in the depot leaves the engineers without any social protection at all, without any rights. I don't know when it began, but I think it was a long time ago. If anything goes wrong, like a train was late, the line engineer, the car engineer, the traffic engineer, the traction engineer, and even your own superior—they all try to foist the blame for the delay and any related delays on you. And you have to fight this attack all on your own. The union, whose consent is formally needed for the punishment, is there only for show.

Back in 1972, when I was at the depot for practical training, I decided then that if I was to work in transport, I'd have to raise my skills, become a technically literate person, an engineer. After my military service, my late father also made me promise to study. I studied for a long time, eight years, two more than is usually allowed, because of my family situation. And what's the result of all this study? I'm a person without rights. The problem may result from the careless work of the other services, but we are told, "The engineer is the last person who can prevent a crash." He's the only skilled person—and he is made to pay. It's curious that a station duty chief will always defend his subordinates, but I've never heard of the director of a depot defending an engineer. And that's why I quit my union job after seven months, and then in February of this year we formed a new union of locomotive brigades.

At the time there was also the wage issue. Before perestroika, an ordinary factory wage was 200 rubles a month, and we earned about 220. But the difference was in the hours we put in. An ordinary worker put in 173 hours a month on average. We worked 220 to 230 hours. We practically had no days off. They paid us time and a half, but this is calculated only on the basis of our basic wage. The bonus is up to 50 percent of our take-home pay.

People were afraid to complain, because it was easy to get rid of them. They'd begin by calling you in for some infraction. You have to know a mass of rules about the technical operation of the locomotive, rules on traffic, signals, safety, and so on. But some of these rules contradict each other, and if you're right according to one rule, you can be violating another.

There are three warning cards. Say you didn't raise up the platform. They call you in to write up an explanation, and they take away your green warning card and give you a yellow one. Next time they can take the yellow one away and give you a red one. After that, you have to take the exams again. Even the director of the depot, who knows the locomotives well, can easily fail them.

On the other hand, people who are compliant, who don't ask any questions, are able to get away with all sorts of infractions. After all, the bosses can be punished too, and it isn't hard to catch them on something. People aren't textbooks; they can't remember everything, and there are so many rules and charts. It's not enough that you can open a book and find out what you need to know. You have to know it by heart, and they can get you on that.

Do you know what it takes to become an engineer? First you have to work six months on the machinery. Then, it's up to the administration if they want to send you to engineers' school, though you can get there on your own. So you get your license to drive, but you're still not an engineer. The administration has to see how you work. That used to take a year or more; now it's much faster. Then they have to give you the go-ahead to take the exam. If you pass, you work a year to get your third class, another two for second class, and more for the first class rating.

From one point of view, it's good. But it takes ten, twelve, fifteen years to get your first class, and then in half a year you can be demoted to assistant.

[VOLODYA] The thing is, they themselves admit that the engineers who were demoted—those who fought for their rights—are technically more literate than those now driving in their place.

[ALEKSANDR] It increases the chance of an accident. I have twelve years of work experience, five as an engineer. We're both active in the new union—I'm chair of the local committee—and we've both been demoted to assistant.

We ask, for example, why locomotive brigades have so little time to rest at home with their families. Why do they work on their days off? Why aren't there enough people to cope with the existing volume of work, so people have to work two and even three weeks without a day off? Why is there an order from above to cut personnel?

They began with the elimination of the conductors in the last car. Their job was to watch the passengers getting in and out. Now it's the job of the engineer's assistant. Many passengers have died as a result. But it was really after the creation of our trade union last January and after we struck that documents specifying the number and the individual people to cut in the locomotive brigades started to arrive.

Here's another issue: for the third month in a row, they haven't paid our wages on time. Our union committee sent an official inquiry to the administration. We got no explanation. That was in April. You can see how much worse the situation in the country has become since. Our lads are mostly young, only a few are over forty. It's because of the war. They have a lot of children—I don't know why they've had so many kids—and we barely scrape through from pay to pay.

I was born in 1954, and Volodya here in 1961. When we were apprentices, the bulk of the engineers were only six or seven years from their pensions. Between them and us, a whole generation was missing.

Anyway, last month one of our engineers, Maksimov, refused to work because he hadn't been paid his wages. It was his right, wouldn't you say? The Russian Labor Code clearly states that a person who doesn't get paid can refuse work. He gave management thirteen hours warning, since he finished work at 1 a.m. and was to go back on at 2:35 p.m.

Was the union involved in this?

No, it was a purely individual act. He called me after he had given the warning. The guy was hungry; he had nothing to live on. Myself, I somehow get by. My family left Moscow for Anapa for what was supposed to be a rest, and I gave them all the money we had, leaving only 1,000 rubles for myself. I thought we'd get paid any day now and I'd manage. Then my wife calls me to send her 2,000 rubles: she says she's leaving Anapa, since it has become too expensive. I was lucky that Volodya here bailed me out. So believe me when I say that Maksimov was hungry.

How long have they held up your wages?

Sometimes two weeks, sometimes a week. They say the situation in the country is serious, there's a currency shortage. But when the other railroad services get paid, and we don't, that's not because of the general situation. Either it's the fault of the administration, or else it's trying to provoke us. They say directly, "They aren't giving us money to pay your wages. Now's when you should have been striking."

So one man lost patience. Of course if he had consulted us, we would have tried to dissuade him from individual actions, especially on the issue of wages. It's completely obvious that this was a provocation to get us to strike and use us to force the government to raise prices again, to sneak into the people's pockets again.

The administration could have easily found a replacement and let Maksimov have his day off. But they waited on purpose. He refused because management had not carried out its contractual obligations. No one is supposed to work for free. He was demoted to assistant. The next day, we were paid our wages.

Doesn't the union have to consent to demotions?

In principle, yes, though I'm not sure what the case is right now. First of all, they don't recognize our union committee. According to the law, all transfers require the consent of the union committee, and the transfer of elected union officials requires the consent of higher union authorities. And we've just heard that last Friday the Russian Supreme Soviet adopted amendments to the Labor Code that deprive unions of any rights vis-à-vis the administration in the area of punishing workers.

But we have some ideas. For example, we've thought of having all fifty of our union members at the depot elected to some union body or another. If Maksimov had been an elected union official, we could have defended him; as a rank-and-file member, it is much easier to fire him. But one of the things we've heard is that the new amendments have eliminated demotions as a punishment. Now it's notice, reprimand, severe reprimand, and out the door. Management has been waiting a long time for this. Now they'll be able to say, "I don't like you. Get out!"

Before, the union had the right to demand the dismissal of the director, but the amendments have apparently also taken that away. We've tried to use that right. We sent a letter to our boss's superior in which we laid out all his violations of the labor legislation and demanded his removal. There is also an article of the criminal code on hindering trade union activity. But they replied that we were just a few young engineers trying to promote our own ambitions, that the Labor Code is above ambitions, and that they won't allow us to fire a young, capable depot director. He was born in 1960. He began his career when his dad was depot director. His dad did the same thing for his other son, Misha. It's the most ordinary nepotism. That's how people get ahead in our country.

Volodya, why did you decide to become an engineer?

[VOLODYA] I was attracted to the work and dreamt of it since I was a kid. I grew up alongside the railroad, and today I can't imagine working at anything else. The work itself forces you to be disciplined. And when you're driving, you're alone with your assistant and have to make decisions. There's no one above you. It's responsible work, and I suppose there's a certain prestige involved. They say it was prestigious in tsarist times too.

How many kilometers is your route?

[ALEKSANDR] At our depot it's 260. We rest and then drive back. It depends on the arm that the depot services. Some arms are 360 kilometers. It depends on the type of current. Ours is direct current. Farther down, it's alternating.

So once you're moving, you have no boss looking over your shoulder?

Well, of course, we have a traffic controller. But no one with direct executive power. We watch the situation. And they're right to say we're highly skilled. What does that mean? When we're moving, it's not just that we feel what the locomotive is doing; we feel the road, the tension of the load. Nowadays, there are a lot of warnings, and it's very hard to drive a train. Limited speed warnings because of faulty roadbed. Each train gets a sheet that says that on such-and-such kilometer the speed is so much for such-and-such a reason. We drive the train guided by our schedule and these warnings. Some warnings are permanent because the cause can't be removed. There are places on the main line where the speed is twenty-five kilometers.

It's absurd. They say that in Stalin's time people would have been shot for allowing that. It was never that slow before. So besides the mass of information that we have to juggle, we have to watch ahead and consider all the possibilities. And we still have to think about economy. We have a meter on the locomotive. Each train has a specific norm, a coefficient of the engine. It's to encourage us to make better use of the train's kinetic energy. It's very complicated, and I'm not an economist. I consider it my job to run the train according to schedule. Economy is my last consideration.

I gather you've totally given up on the old unions. Why do you feel they can't be reformed?

That's the position of the Russian Federation of Independent Trade Unions: force the old structures to work. The FITR unites these same state branch unions. I read an article by its chairman, Klochkov, where he argues that we don't need new unions. All we need to do is change the people in the old ones. But we consider that it isn't a question of people but of a system that has to be changed so that people can and are obliged to do the work they are supposed to: defend workers rights' so that they are able to work in a normal way, so that relations between workers and management are normal. What sort of union is it where management and workers are together? It's clear that the trade unions leaders will defend the positions of the administration, because they are dependent on the administration.

How did you come to the decision to form a new trade union of locomotive brigades?

[VOLODYA] It began in February 1991, when the locomotive brigades of the Ilich depot held a conference of the Moscow locomotives brigades. Forty-four depots sent delegates and I was one of them. I'm not really sure where it came from. Apparently, the leadership of the Moscow railroad union, and probably the railroad administration itself, wanted to control the workers' growing dissatisfaction. A number of grievances had accumulated. The miners had already struck for wage demands, and the Moscow public transport workers were starting.

There were a lot of people at the conference. We adopted a list of fifteen demands. The engineers and assistants formed a Moscow Coordinating Council for the Social Defense of Railroad Workers; representatives of the administration were not included.

But the head of the Moscow railroad and the chairman of the branch union central committee did take the floor. They spoke of the tense situation on the railroad and expressed their support for the workers. And they sent off telegrams supporting our demands, which remain unchanged to this day. Afterward, however, for some reason, they began to fight against us.

The Coordinating Council was mandated to negotiate these demands with the authorities. There were several meetings with the branch union central committee, the ministry, and the railroad administration, but in the end they applied the brakes. They started saying, "You don't legally represent anyone, and we won't negotiate with you." So we began to think about forming a union, one that the law would require them to negotiate with. We began the preparatory work in the depots. Normally, planning sessions with the locomotive brigades and the administration are held every week. So at the end of the meetings we would ask for a few minutes to talk about the coordinating council and our organizing work. But after a month of this, the administration purposely began to drag out the meeting, and it refused to give us any other place to meet in an effort to stop us.

We set January 27, 1992, as the date for our founding congress. In accordance with the December 18 resolution of the Russian Supreme Soviet, we held organizational meetings in those depots where we were strong. But we had already lost some of the people who had begun to work on the union. Some had been fired, others were stuck in conditions that were impossible to work in, and others just dropped out on their own. In our depot, thirty-five people met on January 22, decided to create a local union, and elected delegates to the founding congress. At the congress we adopted a constitution and elected a Russian committee that included representatives of eleven depots. We transferred the negotiating mandate of the Coordinating Committee to it. According to the law, unions no longer have to be registered. Their constitution and other documents merely have to be notarized and deposited with the Ministry of Justice, which puts your name on its list and gives you a number.

The first demand was a wage increase. However, we've removed this demand for now, since after the freeing of prices, the administration itself began raising wages, and we're way past what we demanded then. Of course, those are nominal wages that have been eaten up by inflation. But we decided that in the given conditions this demand shouldn't have priority.

There is also the demand for special wage supplements for people working in areas affected by the Chernobyl disaster. We also demanded payment at base rates for the time we spend in the depots at the end of our run. We want a reduced, six-hour workday. It's a question of health and of saving families. Half of our engineers are divorced because their wives couldn't stand the burden their husbands' work regime places on them. It's also a means of defense against unemployment: we know that passenger and shipping volume will decline because of price increases.

We also wanted the pension calculated on the basis of each year worked as an engineer or assistant. At present, we can take our pension at age fifty-five; if we win this demand, we could retire at age forty-eight after twenty-five years' continuous work. Another demand was around work-related illnesses: ulcers, gastritis, cardiovascular disease, rheumatism. At present, only two illnesses are recognized as work-related: hearing loss—the noise is especially loud when the windows are banged at the crossings—and vibration disease. We want preventive checkups, as provided by the Labor Code, two weeks before vacation every year and again once every three years before going to the medical commission.

Finally, we demanded the abolition of the Railroad Disciplinary Code, which is like a military code. At present, it's suspended but not abolished. Among other things, it has an article that allows punishment of a worker without the union's consent. The worker can only appeal to his boss's superior, just like in the army. If the director of the depot decides on a reprimand, you can only go to the director of the branch.

The Moscow Coordinating Council had made these and other demands long ago to Gorbachev, to Yeltsin, and to the Supreme

Soviet. The only result was that they immediately began to attack our activists.

Did you get an answer?

No. So the Coordinating Council called a strike for December 27, 1991, since they refused to negotiate with us. The Law on Labor Conflicts makes it very hard to strike. You have to assemble at least two-thirds of the collective, and to do that in our depot is impossible. Actually, the law forbids strikes on the railroad, but what are we to do if they refuse even to answer us? We met all the requirements of the Law on Labor Conflicts. At the final stage, we sent all the documents to the Supreme Soviet, and waited the required month. Still no sign of life, so our only recourse was to strike. If they don't observe the law, why should we?

On December 25, representatives of the Russian ministry and the central committee of the union branch finally brought answers to our demands, so we decided to suspend the strike. But communications are very bad, and the Moscow-2 union didn't get the order, so they struck for two hours. Actually, they received the documents, but the one with the decision to suspend the strike was missing. We can't help wondering if this was a set-up.

Sergei Stankevich, adviser to Yeltsin, came, and we worked out an agreement to form a tripartite commission: representatives of the Moscow Council, the Moscow government, and the Ministry of Means of Communication. In the first two weeks of January, we reached an agreement on all fifteen points. Dates were set for their fulfillment, and the demands that couldn't be met were set aside for a future industrywide settlement.

However, none of the demands were carried out on schedule. And for some reason, all the people who signed the agreement with us went on to other jobs. Then we founded our union and began the whole process all over again.

On February 17, we held a plenary meeting of locomotive brigades. We invited the government and the branch union, but no one came. Representatives of eight depots voted for a strike on March 2, but again we had problems with communication. At Moscow-Kursk, the whole depot struck, but they changed the schedule at our depot. I was supposed to leave Moscow at 11:18 p.m. on March 1, and we had agreed that trains leaving before the midnight deadline would continue to their destinations. All my guys were at Sukhenichi [the terminal station of their route], and it was impossible to contact them. As a result, nothing happened at our depot. On March 3, however, two brigades refused to take their trains out.

At that time, representatives of the Moscow-Kursk line were negotiating but couldn't reach an agreement. When the administration heard that the Moscow-Kiev line was striking in support, they signed at once. But that agreement is also not being carried out.

The next day, our administration removed the two brigades. We charged them with violating the Labor Code and exceeding their legal authority, and we demanded that the matter be discussed at a general assembly of the depot's work collective. They flatly refused. So the next day, we struck to get our comrades' jobs back. Fifty-three people struck during those twenty-four hours. So the administration reinstated the two brigades but took the union and our committee to court, charging us with violating the Soviet Law on Resolution of Labor Conflicts, an antilabor, antistrike law.

The court claimed our strike was illegal. We appealed to the Supreme Court, arguing that there had been a huge number of procedural irregularities and that the decision violated both the Russian Declaration of Human Rights and the Russian constitution. We lost the appeal. We learned that the Declaration was only words, nothing to be taken seriously. But in February 1991, when Yeltsin told the press that the miners had every right to call a strike, since "that's the right of every person," it was apparently a different matter! It seems that a right is not always a right. [The 1991 miners' strike, which demanded Gorbachev's resignation and the transfer of the mines to Russian jurisdiction, was an important element in Yeltsin's struggle for power.]

How many members do you have now?

In our depot, there are forty-nine people who left the branch union and came over to us. A percentage of the workers are wavering, waiting to see the outcome of the struggle. If we win, they'll join. In all, there are 315 engineers and assistants at the depot. We have locals in over sixteen depots in Moscow. I don't know how many there are in the rest of Russia: they exist in Petersburg, Kaliningrad, Rostov, Magnitogorsk, Ekaterininburg, and other towns.

Four engineers, including myself, have been demoted to assistants. Three assistants have been demoted to mechanics. The other forty-odd people received severe reprimands, reprimands, or just notices. Yet, even the Law on Labor Conflicts states in article 15 that strikers who end their strike before it is declared illegal bear no material or legal responsibility. Our strike was declared illegal by the court two months after it ended. And I said, "Even if you had the legal right to do it, you have to get the union committee's consent to punishments." But the director just answered: "I don't recognize your union." Even so, half of the strikers were members of the branch union.

So now we are working on restoring these people through the civil courts, but we are coming up against all sort of judicial irregularities. The prosecutor even told us that the Labor Code applied only to the branch unions, not the new unions, which were formed after the code was adopted. In other words, they pick and choose the laws according to what suits them. The administration has now gone to court to claim that our union wasn't formed in accordance with the law. That's absurd, and yet the court agreed to hear the case. But in all these cases, there won't be a decision for a long time, since there's almost no one working now in the civil courts. We are also involved with other independent unions in a case before the Constitutional Court to strike down parts of the law.

Did you ever turn to the Moscow Federation of Trade Unions [the regional federation of former branch unions] for help?

We went to them for legal advice when the administration sued us. We spoke with a very intelligent woman lawyer, who told us: "You guys are fantastic. You've really stirred things up, but you're going to have a very hard time winning with the legal approach you're taking." She gave us some good advice.

One of our big problems is the lack of information, even among the locomotive brigades. And the public has been told that we're asking for huge wage increases at their expense. The government raises prices, and the public blames us. An *Izvestiya* journalist interviewed me, but when I called back to ask when the article would come out, she said, "Well, you see, it's a very delicate question...." This is the kind of censorship that exists.

That's why its hard to ask for a wage increase now. People link our demands with the price increase of railroad tickets. At my wife's job, for example, all the women are saying, "Oh, your husband earns a lot and now they are getting another raise. And look what's happening on the railroads—they don't serve tea anymore, they take so much money for bedding, and they're all torn," and so on. They don't realize that I have nothing to do with it; that's the ministry's doing. My job is to deliver the passengers to their destination safe and on time.

[ALEKSANDR] A week after they increase our wages, the ministry will go on television to announce it, and the very next day they'll raise the price of tickets. And prices of other goods that go by rail will go up. My parents are pensioners—will they raise their pensions? So I'm not interested in getting a wage increase at their expense. All the same, railroad transportation is still the cheapest kind in Russia.

In light of all this, how do you view the present regime? Has anything changed for you since the defeat of the coup last summer?

[VOLODYA] In my opinion, nothing. [Nevertheless, their union supported Yeltsin in his spring 1993 referendum.]

Do the people carrying out the economic reform want trade unions?

[ALEKSANDR] No way! Let me tell you about the mafia. Our railroad needs money. So what do they do? They say, let's allow a cooperative on our territory, and it will pay us part of its profits as rent. Well, the cooperative worked there for a couple of years, and now it's moving on, taking even the boards with it. So then they set up a small [private] enterprise to repair locomotives and cars. At the depot's expense, they supply it with fuel, electricity, lubricants, cranes. No one gets anything from it except the mechanics who work for it. No one knows where all the rest goes. When I was in the chief engineer's office, I accidentally learned that this small enterprise was getting work that normally went to the depot. Everything is done secretly.

Who runs this enterprise?

In practice, it's the chief engineer.

Well, do you support this economic reform?

Is there any question here? The *nomenklatura* sat on our necks and still sit on our necks. They stole and continue to steal. Who do you think the reform is for? The pensioners who have to stand in line for their pensions? A set of living-room chairs and sofa costs 42,000 rubles now. Is that for me? I'll never earn enough to afford it.

What do you think about Yeltsin, then?
[VOLODYA] If he wanted to, he could take measures to put a stop to the attacks on the labor movement.

Do you think some kind of workers' party is the answer?
We need to start with strong unions and a strong federation. The Independent Miners' Union held a rally the other week to mark the anniversary of their founding. I liked how the lads from Donetsk asked the Russians not to load any coal for Ukraine after July 20, when their strike was to start. You see their solidarity, how they've managed to organize themselves?

Many people are now criticizing the Russian IMU, saying they have become a new official union in return for high wages.
When our comrades went to [IMU chairman Aleksandr] Sergeev to ask his union's support against the repression following our strike, I didn't much like his answer: "Why should we defend you? Didn't you break the law?" But they have given us some technical support. Time will tell.

Of course, we need a party. But I don't think that can work now, because the workers aren't prepared to support parties. But unions are another matter.

What about the other railroad workers? Is anything happening there?
The mechanics? Well, the administration is feeding them through these small enterprises. These businesses exist not just in our depot but all over the railroad. This is beyond a doubt theft of state resources. And to tell the truth, many of the mechanics are scared. But there are comrade mechanics who have left the branch union. For the time being, they aren't joining any other. And if they form their own union, we are ready to work with them.

I wanted to say also that our union is not only there to look after the narrow interests of our members. We made many proposals on how to improve things generally at the depot, but they don't want to listen. We've got a lot of people with higher education, people whose heads are working.

[ALEKSANDR] When I was chairman of the union branch committee a computer arrived. The chief engineer got hold of a computer poker game and during work hours he was playing strip poker with two women. I totally forgot about that until one day he said to me, "Sasha, why are you going to court? There's no time left for work." This is a guy who boasts that he has thrown away his copy of the labor code.

You said that they were laying off workers. What about management?

[VOLODYA] No way! It's frightening how their numbers have grown. And now they've set up a computing center. What do they have to compute there? But they go ahead and announce that they're laying off locomotive brigades.

[ALEKSANDR] We're financed from the state budget, but they are trying to force us to be financially self-supporting, at least in part. So I'm not indifferent when I see management doing nothing or issuing ridiculous orders that I still have to carry out. It gets me mad.

[VOLODYA] All I know is that our comrades are no longer capable of working under the old conditions. They won't stop fighting, even under the threat of being laid off. We know what lies ahead.

[ALEKSANDR] They know we are trying to create a real union and they want to crush us to discourage the others. Take yesterday. The instructor said, "Sasha, don't go to court. Forget all this business, and tomorrow you'll be working again as an engineer." I said "I know perfectly well that that's all it would take, but do you want me to give up everything I've fought for? I can't do that." I didn't want to say to him that he was asking me to become a traitor.

[VOLODYA] And last December, the boss said to me, "We'll be allocating six apartments soon. What's your housing situation?" I said, "But I'm not in the line." "Well," he said, "that problem can be resolved."

And this instructor tells me yesterday, "Why are you going after the boss? He's already made big contacts. Stop making all this noise, and they'll restore you. After all, he's the boss. Okay, so the boss is wrong, you can swallow it." I said, "Georgievich, excuse me, but that's the psychology of a person who isn't right in his mind, the psychology of a slave. If I do what you propose, I'll simply stop respecting myself. And if I don't respect myself, why should I bother doing any of what I'm doing? Let the administration do what it likes, but we have principles."

So, we know what we're up against, and we are going ahead with our eyes open. They've given us warning.

Natalya Kuzental
Union Chairwoman in a Leased Factory
[August 1992]

Natalya Kuzental is another of those activists who seems to have a limitless store of energy and tenacity. She has been active in Leningrad from the early days of perestroika and has suffered the repeated disappointments of seeing movements created to defend the people hijacked by interests foreign to them.

When I first met Natalya, in the fall of 1991, she was working as an engineer at the scientific-production institute of the Krasnaya Zarya electronics factory and was active in the work-collective council movement. Since then, she had quit the Leningrad Union of Work Collectives and had been elected chairwoman of a former state trade union. We had this conversation after her work, sitting on a bench in a courtyard near her factory in the Vyborg district (known as "red Vyborg" in 1917).

Last summer, a conflict arose over wages at the Pargolov factory. The workers in the main production shop wanted to strike, but the Law on the Resolution of Labor Conflicts requires that they go through a lengthy series of preliminary stages. When they reached the conciliation stage, they asked the Leningrad Union of Work Collectives for help, and it delegated me to represent the workers in the conciliation commission.

The Pargolov factory was leased from the state by the work collective two years ago. And the lawyer who chaired the conciliation commission ruled that the proposed strike was illegal, since the workers' demands were wrongly addressed to the director instead of to the leaseholders' council, which makes decisions on the wage system. Of course, I refused to sign that decision and wrote my own opinion, which, naturally, was ignored. They pressured me to endorse the majority decision, phoning me at my factory, even trying through party channels, but by that time the party wasn't working.

When the workers were finally able to strike legally in the fall, they called me again. They struck and removed the director, whom they accused of shady dealings and outright theft. In a leased enterprise, it's the work collective that hires the director. And this guy was already their second appointment. But the law says that an elected official who loses his job by decision of the collective is subject to the rules governing layoffs; that is, he has to be offered a series of vacant positions in the enterprise. So he took the collective to court over this, and I acted as a witness for the collective.

Well, I ask you, what kind of job can you offer a director who has been fired for financial scheming and theft?! No one would trust him with a managerial post, and he's certainly not going to work as a janitor. But the court found in his favor. In the end, we persuaded him to leave of his own accord.

About that time, the workers also decided to get rid of the head of the trade-union committee. You see, when the director went to court to have the strike declared illegal, the head of the union testified on the side of the director! So they were looking for a new chairman, and the leaseholders' council asked me to run. The work collective elected me on December 17, 1991, from among four candidates.

It's a relatively small plant by Soviet standards—1,200 people. But the building is in good shape, and the equipment is relatively modern. It's a good factory. I've heard there are people interested in buying it.

Why did you decide to leave the work-collective council movement, whose main goals are self-management and worker ownership, to head a trade union?

Actually, when the head of the leaseholders' council asked me to run, I said, "Why do they need a trade union in a leased enterprise?" But he insisted that I put forth my candidacy. So I began reading up on the subject and saw that our Soviet literature says that trade unions are necessary under *any* form of ownership. It made no sense to me. As leaseholders, the collective was, in practice, the boss at the enterprise; yet the workers worked as hired labor. But I was drawn to the job by my interest in self management and collective ownership. I thought that I might be able to do something useful there.

How does this leasing arrangement work?

The collective goes to the state authorities and asks them to lease the enterprise to the collective. But this is generally a fiction, since clever directors, through various tricks, end up paying only kopecks in rent. That's the way it is at Pargolov. I'd say the collective was lucky to get the plant practically for free. The fixed assets still formally belong to the state, but the profits, the materials, and all the product belong to the workers.

But we have such a clever state! The situation I've described is virtually the same at state plants that aren't leased. There, too, the profits belong to the collective. You probably can't understand that. I certainly can't.

So the status of state property is totally unclear?

I see you've caught on! But the government has got a hold of itself and now claims it wants to restore order. They're forcing us all into open joint-stock companies. [In open joint-stock companies, the stocks can be bought and sold freely. In closed companies, they can be owned only by people working at the enterprise and cannot be sold.] When I read the new decree on this, I felt sick. On all counts it's the very opposite of everything we were fighting for. I won't bore you with the details, but all state plants by the start of 1993 must become open joint-stock companies. In the model company charter, the general director becomes the head of the board of directors. That means the power of management is strengthened ten, 100 times.

The work collective has only one right: to choose one of three ways to privatize their plant. The first method gives the collective a certain percentage of the stocks, but these stocks don't come with voting rights. Under the second method, the workers can buy a majority of the stock, but there's little chance of their being able to do that, especially in view of the total lawlessness governing the evaluation process. Under the third method, the administration runs the plant for a year, and if it is successful, it gets 20 percent of the stock.

But to this day, the resolutions of the Supreme Soviet on privatization and the amendments to the Law on Privatization, as well as the program of privatization itself, have not been published. It makes you only wonder: laws and resolutions are adopted, months go by, and nowhere can you read what's in them. We hope there may be some special provision for leased enterprises, but who can say?

I left the Leningrad Union of Work Collectives because I felt that Sergei Andreev, its leader, was saying one thing while the union was busy doing something quite different: it was making propaganda for the creation of joint-stock companies. I thought we should have leased and collective enterprises. We are Soviet people, after all; we tend to think in social terms, people's property. Of course, were never really owners, but now they want to make that part of the constitution. It used to proclaim "state property" with "of the whole people" in brackets. Now the phrase "of the whole people" has disappeared, and no one knows where it has gone. We are now informed that we can buy this property from the state.

You were at the Congress of Work Collectives last fall when we decided that before any privatization occurs, the enterprise should be transferred to the full economic management of the collectives. ["Full economic management" signifies that the work collective runs the enterprise autonomously in a leasing arrangement with the state.] But you know how completely illiterate we were. We are only now beginning to understand what "ownership" and "full economic management" mean, and what the difference between them is. And those who have the power can easily get around us in this question. In the old days, they tortured us with all sorts of damned economics courses. No one wanted to study, but they forced us. That gradually ended under perestroika.

Take me, for example. I'm a radioelectronics engineer, and I didn't feel any need for economics until perestroika. Then, since I was active, I took the two-year course offered at the House of Scientific-Technical Propaganda. This was at the start of perestroika, and the courses were still free and taught by professors with decent orientations. It all began with "economic cost-accounting" [a regime under which enterprises enjoyed various degrees of economic autonomy in return for fixed payments to the state]. It might not seem like much to you, but to us at the time it was practically miraculous.

Anyway, here I am agitating for leasing, and the Union of Work Collectives is calling for the creation of joint-stock companies. I said to them, "What are you telling people?! Don't you know that stocks are capital? Capital always ends up in the hands of the same people. We need to look to other models, like the Mondragon workers' cooperatives in Spain, where the workers themselves run things in their own interests. Didn't our movement begin with the idea of self-management? How is that possible if the enterprise is divided into shares that can be bought and sold on the market?"

Intellectuals who used to support leasing now point to Yugoslavia to show that the original ideas of the movement can't work. But Yugoslavia never had real people's enterprises—there was no self-management, no democracy, nothing. On television we are constantly being told that open-stock companies are best because they attract investment. But we need to go our own way. I've read everything that I can get my hands on about collective enterprises around the world and I think that they are much closer to us than any open stock companies.

I saw that no one in the Leningrad Union of Collectives was interested in leasing or collective enterprises, so I left in protest. Besides that, I found that Andreev's aides were organizing some sort of business center.

To train businesspeople?

No, to do business. And people in the union's leadership were going to enterprises to ask for money for the business center. Not a kopeck went to the union itself. When the union elected a new council, Andreev attacked me viciously and asked that I not be elected so that there wouldn't be an opposition within the council.

So I left. Many people expressed their regret. I still get phone calls, but I tell them that these are differences of principle. I can't work in an organization that won't tolerate any opposition and that refuses to do real work with the enterprises and to give the collectives concrete help. I used to spend my time in the enterprises, but Andreev only made speeches.

In practice, he has formed a party. The new constitution of the Leningrad Union of Work Collectives even has a clause on individual membership. They're getting ready for new parliamentary elections. Together with businesspeople, they've created a school to train future members of parliament: the businesspeople give the money, and Andreev selects and trains suitable candidates. Need I say any more?

Andreev was a nobody who wanted a public career, so he latched onto the work-collective movement. He became head of the Leningrad Union of Work Collectives, though he himself represented no collective. He was director of some private institute in Leningrad and he even had the nerve to make his post as head of the union a paid one. I couldn't stomach that. You know, I'm a Soviet person, and to me everything should be done for free. It's hard to become non-Soviet. You've got to act in a way that suits your soul. Anyway, he succeeded in making a career, and as a result, nothing is left of that movement. Lashch [see her May 1991 interview in Part III] and Andreev always worked together. They're members of Supreme Economic Council of the Russian Supreme Soviet. She worked out of its offices, and it gave them money. Soon after I spoke out publicly about the dealings, I got a phone call from the Leningrad Union: they were giving me a bonus for my work. I refused it, but they insisted that they had already signed for the money and received it. I still refused and I asked where such big money came from.

In my old enterprise, where I chaired the work-collective council, our charter stated that "the right of full economic management is transferred to the collective"—not to the administration, but to the collective. That was the original demand of the Union of Work Collectives. But what good is that when the collective doesn't know what it means and when the work-collective council itself is in the pocket of the administration? Even at Pargolov, a leased enterprise, the administration has managed to subordinate the leaseholders' council to itself and unilaterally assigns the workers their wage coefficients and bonuses.

The Krasnaya Zarya Production Association fell apart in the same stupid way as the Soviet Union—with everyone at each other's throats. This allowed management to grab all it needed. To this day, the association's property hasn't been legally divided up, and yet the various enterprises exist autonomously. You can grab a room, grab property, do anything you want—except make the enterprise run normally. There are no orders. Some of the biggest layoffs in the city are happening there.

But the head of the trade union committee at my institute [that belongs to the association] is a very good woman. And it was probably her example that helped decide me to take my present union job. Previously, I had scarcely taken any notice of the unions. They could never really function in this country. The Central Committee of the Communist Party, the Council of Ministers, and the All-Union Council of Trade Unions all jointly signed resolutions—so what was there left for the unions to do? They paid sick leave. They administered social security. Now the government has been declared that they will administer social security for another year, but after that no one knows what will happen.

In brief, I came to trade-union work with a significant baggage of legal knowledge and experience about work collectives and work relations, things that traditional union activists never had to know. Since I began this job, I've carefully gone over all the union documents and the labor code, and I've been able to organize the union work in a completely new way.

I began working in December. Sometime in January they elected the new director. Now the comrades at the factory are saying that the third revolution is in progress, because this is the third time they've replaced the director and a certain part of the collective feels that the new one doesn't suit the job either, that there is more anarchy and lawlessness in the enterprise than ever.

Actually, he had already been director there and was kicked out, with the help of the party. Maybe that made him attractive to the workers. He became some kind of private cultural entrepreneur, with an art school and workshops. I don't know if he was kicked out for real violations or not, but he's definitely a tough, ruthless man. The workers tried to find some organization that had a data bank on potential directors and other specialists. At the time there was none, though now there is. You see the progress?

He was hired by the leaseholders' council, which is elected by the work collective. But we still can't find out what his program is, on what basis the council decided to hire him. The council's head himself went over the papers and just scratched his head: "How could we have done this? How could he turn our heads to that extent?" Well, it's true that the workshops he'd been managing had made a good profit. He showed that he had been given a million rubles and turned them into ten million, and so forth.

But he immediately started to issue orders, for example, that the people had to work on Saturday. The law requires the union's consent for overtime. So I asked him if the plant was going to be running on Saturday. He said it wasn't, but when I came to work on Monday, I learned that the main shop had worked. So not only had he not got the union's consent, he lied to me as well.

I wrote to the leaseholders' council that management was violating the labor code. The director accused me of merely wanting to assert my power. But this was no mere formality. It was a question of overtime pay. I wanted to ask why there had to be Saturday work, why this extra expense for the plant? After all, the money came out of the pockets of the other workers.

That's when the director said to me, "Why do I need your agreement? I'll get the Independence trade union to sign." So I figured I'd better look into this new union. It had no committee, no regular presence at the factory. After the strike in the fall, some workers here formed a branch of this Independence union. In my opinion, it's really a "dictatorship of the proletariat"-type party, rather than a union. They consider that the manual workers should hire engineering-technical personnel and kick out those they consider not up to the mark. It's good at leading strikes. In fact, it does little else. Its demands are all political, and it has no individual membership. Anyone who took part in the strike is considered a member.

At any rate, when I began to prepare a draft collective agreement, I included two members of Independence in the drafting committee. Well, these two guys come to me and say, "We've decided that we don't need a collective agreement. We need a system of individual contracts." So I said, "First, you show me a law on that contract system. Give me an example of a contract and explain how it will benefit the workers. Or, if you like, come to the factory conference and tell it to the workers. We'll see what they say."

I knew I'd have a hard time with them. It isn't a union that takes up grievances, deals with wages, layoffs, and dismissals. But when the director needs a signature on some order, he knows where to get it.

Trade unions are springing up like mushrooms. Ten people get together and form a new union.

I understand now that we need trade unions like we need oxygen itself. Unity makes unions strong. Of course, there can be different unions, but they should put forth similar, concrete demands: against unemployment, for higher wages, etc. But individual enterprises or groups of workers can't act on their own. Even if they win a wage increase, what about the others? That's what's happening—public transport workers, miners, teachers, medical workers, one after the other and all separately.

Lately, out of the blue, articles have started appearing in the press saying that trade unions are nonsense, we don't need them, they're not doing what trade unions are supposed to do. In the past they were forced to distribute scarce consumer goods among their members—three cars among 1,000 workers—but I firmly declared at the factory that we would distribute nothing. Our union concerns are wages, employment, collective agreements, layoffs. We won't distribute anything because it's always a source of conflict and division among the workers. Besides, there's nothing more to distribute. And in the future, everything will be on open sale.

Maybe it's easier for me, since I have no past in the trade unions. I don't know how it is for the old-time leaders, but I want to speak on the radio—I have some connections with a small station—and say that union members should not leave their unions. Instead, they should hold new elections, because everything depends on what kind of people are in the union committee. The laws exist. A federation of trade unions exists that has good economists and lawyers. Everything exists that makes it possible for the unions to function properly, but the basic work has to be done in the factories. Look at my union. No one controls us, no one tells us what to do. I sometimes even think that's bad; it might be good if we got some direction.

What union federation are you referring to?

The Leningrad Federation of Trade Unions. I've got no use whatsoever for my branch union [the Union of Workers of Automobile and Agricultural Implement Construction]. I'm a member of its council of representatives *ex officio*. I find absolutely no help there. It's bad, and I want to take my union out of it, although some of the other branch unions are strong organizations. But I do need the Leningrad federation. It has certain structures that one can't find anywhere else; it gives help to union activists. You know, over the past years I've been a member of the Perestroika Club [a democratic group from the early perestroika period], the Popular Front, Democratic Russia. No one defends workers' interests, at least not in Leningrad. The unions are my last hope.

When I told the branch union that my director violated article 85 of the Labor Code by making the plant work on Saturday without the union's consent, they answered: "You can't do anything. The law only provides for a ten ruble fine." Ten rubles is next to nothing now, but they haven't gotten around to modifying the Labor Code.

Listen, I wouldn't take that sort of union leader even if they gave me them for free. I can think up better things myself. I started to work on article 37: "Punishment of a Manager on the Initiative of a Trade Union Organization." I had already come across it at my old factory. The situation at Pargolov became clear to me when the director said, "We don't need a union" and "I don't need a trade union chairwoman who thinks systematically." In brief, he didn't like my militancy and he began actively to come out against me. He doesn't know the law, and when I showed him the Law on Collective Agreements, he just said: "I've grown used to skirting the law, and I'll go around this one too."

I told you that the old director took the Independence union to court over the strike last fall. Well, the court found in the director's favor. Luckily, that director is gone and the matter has been forgotten. But these Independence guys might have had to pay a fortune. When I asked them where they would have gotten the money, all they did was shrug their shoulders. Or take the case of the October Railroad, which struck for only a few hours causing the trains from Finland to be late. The Finns are now demanding several million dollars in compensation. When I heard that on the radio, my hair stood on end.

So they've made it very hard and dangerous for us to strike. Knowing all this, I said to the director, "Look, I understand that we can't strike. The factory has no money. So let's sign a collective agreement in a civilized manner, like they do all over the world. We'll see what we can produce and sell, and on that basis, we'll set the highest wage the plant can afford." But he wouldn't have anything to do with it. To this day we still don't have a collective agreement.

Incidentally, the Law on Collective Agreements was adopted on March 12, but it was published only in May. That's how it is with all the basic legislation. In all likelihood, they didn't want the law. You remember the terrible battle over the law on trade unions in the Supreme Soviet. Only Gorbachev's intervention got it passed. That law allowed the unions to continue to exist.

And now, as I was saying, articles are appearing on the harmfulness of the unions, the need to disperse them. Back in May, Democratic Russia organized a sort of civic forum where Yeltsin spoke. Someone goes up to the podium and says, "Boris Nikolaevich, you've dispersed the party. Now it's time to disperse the unions. You should issue a decree forcing unions to prove their membership claims." I said to myself: "That's all we need! As if we didn't already have total lawlessness in the enterprises."

The leaseholders' council appoints the director. It is elected by the work collective, as is your own union committee. How is it, then, that the director, who is the employee of the work collective, is able to push you around? You were elected by his employers to defend their interests.

To explain that, I have to first explain the new wage system. At the start of the year, when I first began to work there, the leaseholders' council was putting together a new wage system. Prices had just been freed, and they decided not only to raise wages but to introduce a new system of coefficients. All the workers are divided into skill grades, and each grade is assigned a coefficient, from the cleaning women who have the lowest to the director with the highest, a difference of, say, 1 to 4.5. Well, it was this new wage system that made possible the total arbitrariness of the new director, who, along with his department head, decides everything and lets the collective discuss nothing. He sets the coefficients and decides when to raise the grade of a worker or to lower it. It's total lawlessness.

The union committee came out against this system from the start. But we were forced to give our temporary approval for a three-month period because of a legal technicality—otherwise the workers wouldn't have been paid in January. The workers asked us to sign, because they would no longer be getting 200 rubles like last year, but 2,000, 3,000, 5,000 rubles. But as the weeks went by we saw that the director was completely ignoring the union. And we sounded the alarm. We wanted clear criteria for raising and lowering the workers' grades, we wanted the initial coefficients to be established by a commission made up not only representatives of the administration but also of representatives of the union and the leaseholders' council.

But we're Soviet people, we're used to fictitious workers' participation, and the administration just said, "Nowhere in the West do workers participate in matters regarding the distribution of profits." But we're quite a long way from the West, and I answered, "You know, I don't have any data on what goes on in the West, but the Labor Code says that the rules governing wages must be agreed upon by the trade union committee."

In our factory, it's the leaseholders' council that adopts rules governing wages. I kept writing to them, but the director is very palsy-walsy with the members of the council. He attends all its meetings and can see how they vote. And since he sets their wage coefficients, he's got them under his control. And what did I discover? The entire council votes for whatever the director proposes. Only the chairman, whom the council itself elected, has refused to play the director's game.

Why don't the workers recall their representatives in the leaseholders' council?

Council members are elected by sectors of sixty to seventy workers each, and only the sector can recall its representative. The general conference of workers decides only the total number of council members and elects its chairman. I have no trouble with the chairman, who is a strong person.

The director likes to tell me, "You're the union. You represent the workers as hired labor. The main power is the leaseholders' council." I answer: "Wrong. Not the leaseholders' council, but the work collective as a whole." He keeps getting it wrong. In short, I have a whole pile of complaints from the workers, and the confrontation is growing. He even tried to lay workers off, but the chairman and I told him that we won't allow it. Strange as it sounds, the leaseholders' council itself is demanding these layoffs, saying that it will allow the remaining workers to earn more. We told them that if they wanted to raise wages, they should do it by increasing production and sales, not by laying off their comrades.

You can only fire a leaseholder for violation of the Labor Code. But our laws contradict each other. You tell me—how can a government issue a decree that allows for layoffs of up to 30 percent of the work force when the form of ownership of an enterprise changes, when there is no unemployment insurance fund or program to create new jobs? Do you think they register the unemployed in this country? No, they do everything they *cannot* to register the person. So the statistics don't reflect the real situation.

But even our imperfect laws are being violated right and left by the director. He hasn't even read the collective agreement, which he also constantly violates.

If this is happening in a leased enterprise, I hate to think what's happening in the state and private enterprises. The power of management seems as if it will soon surpass what it was under Brezhnev.

Before perestroika, if I had a problem with the administration, I could go to the party committee, and if it didn't bother the district party committee, I could get help. So the party was a small recourse. On the other hand, if my activity bothered them, I might get sent to a mental hospital if I persisted. But the main thing was that the administration was constrained within a framework. Today, there is total lawlessness, no framework at all. The managers are involved in all sorts of shady operations, but the workers aren't even let close to management. There are only a handful of people like me, who take firm positions against their administration, and it's very hard.

The biggest problem is that our workers lack knowledge. Last March I spoke on the radio about the procedure for "liberating" workers—that's what they now call layoffs. I explained that the union committees and the work-collective councils, together with the administration, have to work out a set of rules and explain them to each worker. I had model rules written by the head of our union at Krasnaya Zarya. It's magnificent, full of traps for management. They've been trying for months to lay off workers there but they haven't yet succeeded thanks to these rules that give the final word to the union. After that radio broadcast, I got a flood of phone calls from the factories. People don't know what to do, and they want advice.

Of course, the issue of layoffs is a very tough one for union committees. The plants often really don't have orders or money to pay wages, and the people who aren't being laid off ask the union to sign the layoff order. You tell them that these people won't be able to feed their families, that they aren't to blame for the director's failure to get new orders. It's especially important to defend people who have some knowledge, who have opened their mouths against management. When they began a campaign against the chief engineer, I told them straight off, "You'll lay him off over my dead body." Of course, as a member of the administration, the chief engineer's dismissal doesn't require union consent, but I still have the right to take the case to court in my own name. People from other factories who have been laid off call me, and I ask them: "What about your union?" But they say the union okayed the layoff. So I tell them to go to court. This is a country of extremes—the courts restore practically everyone to their jobs.

Some people say it's impossible to reform the old unions, even through democratic elections.

I know people say that. But I think it depends on us. I'm able to do everything that the new trade unions say they are trying to do, and within the framework of the former state union. Much depends on the individuals in the union committee.

What sort of support do you get from your collective?

I have their confidence. Except for a few members of the administration, almost no one has left the union. One of the administrators who quit the union said he was opposed to the head of the union coming from outside, not being a member of the work collective. Personally, I say that my having been hired from the outside makes my work much easier, since when my time is up, I won't go back to working at this factory—and anyway, my skills aren't needed there. That makes me absolutely independent of the administration. But when you know in the back of your mind that you'll have to return to your former job, even if the law protects you for two years, it makes you cautious. I think union officials should be elected from outside the enterprise. It's a profession, like any other. Anyway, that's my experience.

But to return to the question of reforming the old unions, you know what our Soviet people are like. Nowadays they say, "Oh, we don't believe in anything. We're tired." And I say to them, "What are you tired from? What have you done? You spent your whole life looking in the bosses' mouths." The most we ever did was to curse Brezhnev at home in front of our televisions. And under Gorbachev we marched in neat columns to the elections and voted without knowing what the candidates stood for.

We couldn't even get the workers to come to the union conference on housing. The enterprise built a new apartment building that was to be completed at the end of the year, but, as usual, it was delayed. We were supposed to pay the builders a final installment of 700,000 rubles, for a total of five million. But in January, we got a new bill: the 700,000 had suddenly grown into 30 million! Of course, we were able to beat down that sum but we still ended up paying 13 million instead of five. And that isn't all. The building began as a state building, then it became a leased building, and now we have the market. Even if we only pay the book value, thirteen million, where are people going to find that money? Their wages barely cover the cost of food. Savings are now worth a tenth of their original value.

We called this conference to discuss the problem and to decide who should get the apartments. How can you understand leaseholders who don't show up to such a conference? It took three tries to get a quorum. Only those who were in line for an apartment and who were mad because they weren't in line came—and there were twice as many of the latter. Of course, you can understand them; their work helped pay for the building. So I ask the workers, "And you people complain that you are tired?!"

What other conflicts have you had with the director?

Over privatization. The law was changed, but the changes haven't all been published. I learned through channels that for leased enterprises there are special rights: if the collective decides to buy the plant, then no other buyers are considered. The council chairman and I quickly proposed that we privatize the plant as a collective. The workers supported this at once. You should have seen the fuss the director raised against this. So it was decided to form a commission on privatization with two representatives from the union, two from the leaseholders' council, and two from management. This commission was to report to the next conference.

But the conference twice failed to meet. We know that this was the director's doing. When it finally met, he complained that the idea was all my invention, that there's no need to rush to form any commission on privatization, that we should leave well enough alone. I took the floor and said, "Comrades, you're going to have to make a decision on privatization, and you'll need materials, documents, figures. How will you be in a position to decide if some official comes here to privatize the plant?" People understood me. They know the lawlessness that prevails in this area. We have information that already there have been offers to buy the plant. But when we ask for details, they answer, "Commercial secret!"

What does the law say about someone from the outside buying an enterprise?
Until the law is changed, all potential buyers are equal. All you have to do is show that your money is from a legitimate source. But, as you well know, the mafia has no trouble laundering its money.

So the government can sell the plant out from under the workers?
Yes. The government committee on property makes its proposal twice to the collective. If the collective rejects both proposals, the government committee can go ahead without the collective's approval. It seems that leaseholders are an exception, but since nothing is published, we don't really know. So we took precautions, just in case.

Do you think that workers support the idea of collective ownership?
They do, although they often don't realize it or fully understand its meaning. After all, we've lived with the idea for seventy years, and before that there was Russian peasant collectivism. They know for sure that they don't want to be hired labor. They're only now realizing that they were hired labor all their lives.

But the government has other ideas. There was a huge article in *Rossiiskaya Gazeta* on how well off we would all be if the enterprises were turned into joint-stock companies. And a little later, we got

Yeltsin's decree ordering the enterprises to do this. Why must all enterprises do this? In all other countries there are different forms of ownership, state enterprises, leased and collective enterprises, all sorts. But we're to have only open joint-stock companies. What happens next is clear: any plant that's worth anything will be bought up by those with money and connections.

Take my factory, Krasnaya Zarya. I suspect it was sold long ago to Italians. There is really no work-collective council there, and people are totally in the dark. Krasnaya Zarya was a member of the Telekom concern, which included over 150 enterprises of Union significance. [Under the old command economy, virtually all important enterprises were subordinated to a Union ministry in Moscow.] In fact, this concern was only the old Ministry of the Industry of Means of Communication that changed its name and became independent of the state. All of the ministry's officials crossed over to the concern. Then the concern became a non-state, joint-stock company, even though the state had invested millions in foreign currency in it.

So I asked the director of Krasnaya Zarya, "We are members of that joint-stock company. Where are our stocks now that it has been split up? The concern is no longer a state company. Who is the owner?" He only mumbled something. You see, they're silent when we ask these inconvenient questions. Of course, all the enterprise managers are on the board of directors. In practice, it has become theirs.

What's the position of the Leningrad Federation of Trade Unions on privatization?

We had a plenary meeting of the Leningrad federation two months ago to adopt our conception of the economic reform. A few people took the floor; the rest sat and slept. I fought for collective property, and somehow, with difficulty, it got through.

Were people opposed to it?

They didn't want it because they don't know what it is. Even at the federation's commission on privatization they didn't have a clue about what I was saying. The union head of the Kirov factory, Vladimir Yudin, a very clever man, is a member of the commission [see interview with Aleksandr Kalachev]. I specially called him to come. He's a member, but he usually stays away from it. When I saw that they were ready to kill me, I turned to him: "Vladimir Ivanovich, why are you silent? You know what I am talking about." But he doesn't open his mouth. Meanwhile, his factory is literally seething over this very issue. He finally mumbled a few words in my support.

But who else is there to work with? There's only the federation. We'll see what happens on the issue of privatization. The federation has also decided to conduct a poll among the union members on what sort of collective actions they are ready to support. In the fall, we hope to hold a conference on the question of privatization. Maybe afterward we'll come out with some general political action. True, the federation leadership is afraid of that; they aren't sure workers will support a political action. But maybe by then something will have ripened below.

I read an article on this yesterday in a Leningrad paper. It accused the unions of preparing to overthrow the government.

You see, as soon as the unions begin to behave like unions, the press turns against them. But, in fact, they aren't implacably opposed to the government. You can't come out directly against the government now; you can only demand that it change its course.

But you know as well as I do that there are many good, competent people in Russia. You'd make a much better president than Yeltsin. Is he supposed to be some sort of genius? Isn't it above all a question of whose interests the president defends?

I really don't see anyone better than Yeltsin. Don't forget our psychology: "There must be a tsar." You don't understand how he works on people. I saw him at the Kirov factory [see Aleksandr Kalachev interview below]. The auditorium was pure working class. He cracked jokes. It was a miracle to see how he worked on the crowd!

You see what we lack, why we are going wrong? I read that in the West when a party presents its program and gets elected, the people follow its activity to make sure the program is being carried out. But we don't understand anything. Anyway, workers today react negatively to parties. They aren't ready to support them.

What about the leadership of the Leningrad Federation of Trade Unions?

I know the vice president, Lisyuk, pretty well, since he created the commission on privatization that has come out for collective property. Of course, he has a past too. A former classmate of mine worked in the plant where he was union head, and it wasn't such a pretty picture. But he's doing what I want now, and I can work with him. These people can easily change their skins. As for the federation's president, Makarov, he doesn't recognize collectively-owned property. He says he was in the United States, where he learned it isn't efficient. Can you talk with a person like that?

But I've cast my lot with the unions. I can tell you that the work I do in my former state union is much better than anything the new unions are doing. It's concrete work in a concrete enterprise. And it's better work than the work-collective councils are doing. In general, although I was active in those councils from their inception, I now have a great mistrust of them. Management is able to lure these people over to its side. I know of no independent work-collective councils. And so I tell people: "You have a bad union? Hold new elections. Because if you destroy these unions, you'll be left with nothing. It takes a long time to build a new structure."

Postscript: On December 25, 1992, the leaseholders' council fired the director of the Pargolov factory, claiming that the director had turned a blossoming factory into a candidate for bankruptcy. The force behind the dismissal was the union committee.

Aleksandr Kalachev
Chairman of the
Kirov Factory Workers' Committee
[August 1992]

Politically, the Kirov factory is one of the most important factories in Russia. This has been so since the beginning of the century, when it was called the Putilov factory. It was the Putilov workers who marched to the Winter Palace on Bloody Sunday, January 9, 1905, to demand a decent wage, an eight-hour workday, and democracy, only to be massacred by the tsar's troops. This was the start of the first Russian Revolution. The Putilov factory was also in the van-

guard of the renewed labor militancy preceding World War I, striking for 102 days in 1913 and 145 days in the first half of 1914, mostly over political issues. On June 18, 1917, its 36,000 workers led a demonstration against the liberal provisional government, marching behind a banner that read: "Comrades, we have been deceived! Prepare for battle!"

Aleksandr Kalachev works in the tractor assembly shop, the militant core of the Kirov factory. Things were quiet when we spoke. Along with most Kirov workers, he was on forced leave until September.

Our enterprise has about 30,000 workers in Leningrad, and if you include the branch in Tikhvino, there are 45,000 workers in all. We had military, metallurgical, turbine, and tractor production. In brief, we had overproduction.

I'm a mechanic in the tractor assembly shop and—modesty aside—one of the founders of the workers' committee. I was a member of the Communist Party since 1980. That year I enrolled in the journalism faculty of the university. I edited the factory's wall newspaper and tried to be an active Communist. I struggled, I tried to do things, took photographs. I had the idea of showing a portrait of the contemporary worker. In 1988, I was elected head of the shop's work-collective council.

How many people are there in that shop?

At the time we had 1,500. Now we are down to 800, and the cutbacks continue.

My election wasn't at all to the administration's liking. Its plan had been to hold the elections on March 8, so there would be only a few people around. [March 8, International Women's Day, was an official holiday in the former Soviet Union, but is no longer observed by the Russian government.] It was announced as a holiday assembly, and then they intended to pull out the elections. Well, I had some pretty tough friends there, all young people—my brigade was a young one—who came to that meeting and said, "This one won't pass!" We immediately gathered material for the press on this maneuver, and, in short, real elections were held two weeks later. And I was elected chairman.

I continued to study. I stopped after the second year for family reasons. I returned a year later but dropped out again after another third. Three years later, I went back again, and so forth. I finally graduated in 1990.

Being an active Communist I considered that having been elected, I could begin to inculcate a communist attitude to work. So I started reorganizing things. Thanks to the work-collective council, we were able to introduce a contract brigade system, including coefficients of labor participation. [Under this system, the brigade concluded a contract with management to deliver a specific quantity and quality of finished goods by a specific date in return for the parts, raw materials and a total wage. The elected brigade council assigned wage coefficients according to the worker's contribution to the final outcome, including skill level, work discipline, etc.] In other words, the brigade itself decided what to do with the total wage it had earned. This was self-management on the brigade level, and management didn't like it one bit.

They didn't want the participation coefficient. We had one assembly line with two shifts, but the output wasn't calculated separately for each shift. So the day shift might make, say, fifty tractors, while the night shift made none because there were no parts. The fifty tractors were merely divided into two groups of twenty-five, one group for each shift. It was a radical leveling system that let management do as it liked. And that got me mad. So through the work-collective council, we first got the output of the two shifts separated and then, in turn, split the shifts into brigades and introduced individual participation coefficients.

And things changed dramatically. In the old days, the evening shift might come and find there were no parts. So a few hundred workers would go running to the director's office and yell, "Let us go home!" He'd say, "By all means, go!" And everyone was happy. Now they began demanding work, since it wasn't in their interest to go home.

How does this participation coefficient work? What criteria go into it?

Even though it was assembly-line work, the jobs varied. A young guy might come, work three months, know next to nothing, and earn the same as an ace who can handle two jobs at once. The contribution is different, but the earnings were the same. There was no justice. With the coefficient, two people doing the same job could earn different amounts, say ten and twenty rubles. A real incentive appeared.

We managed to introduce this in our brigade, while the others sat around scratching themselves. But when they saw that a person could earn twice as much by applying his skills, the other brigades also started to introduce the new system. This process took about two years.

How big could the differences in wages be as a result of the coefficients?

On the order of 1-to-1.5 or 1-to-2.

Maybe I'm not very modest, but I have to say that I'm idealistic when it comes to these issues. I always wanted things to be just, and it drove me nuts that a young guy who doesn't know how to really work could earn the same as me.

Why didn't the administration like the changes?

We had to use all sorts of intrigues to introduce the new system, even though we had the support of the work-collective council. So we began as an experimental brigade, for a three-month period only. I twice got anonymous threatening phone calls: "With all your public activism, don't you think you're a bit too healthy?" I left the evening shift because of the danger.

You see, the new system changed the workers' attitudes. They were no longer interested in going home. They wanted to work, and this put pressure on management to completely reorganize the assembly line, and the factory in general. As soon as the shifts were separated for accounting purposes, we stopped working on days off. Before that, one shift would work, the next would be idle, and then everyone had to come out on Saturday to work like crazy. And can you imagine, they were happy. "Oh, how great that we are going to work on our day off!" You sit a whole week and do nothing, then they herd you out to work on the weekend for practically the same money.

With the new system, not only did work on days off stop, but wages rose almost 50 percent. I said, "You see how they made fools of you?" And of course, that's what enraged the entire administration: they had to reorganize things to provide regular work for everyone.

They also had a positive interest. You see, the administrators also got paid extra for coming out on their days off. They have different interests than us, corporate interests. They get medals for it; it was considered an act of heroism to organize work on days off.

What happened to your work-collective council?

It just died. I was elected for three years, but I took three months' leave to finish my degree and gave notice to hold new elections. No one moved; no one needed them. I don't know why.

In December 1989, we became acquainted with the Leningrad Union of Workers' Committees. It seemed to me that representatives of all the big factories were there, and I liked the idea of working together. I became a member of its executive, and two months later, in February 1990, we created a workers' committee in my shop.

The workers' committee includes only workers. Even though we had a majority in the work-collective council, the administration, with its 30 percent, could find ways to block any decision.

We put up a notice that elections would take place during the shift change. About seventy people came. I gave a short speech. Fourteen candidates were put forward, and everyone approved. The enterprise work-collective council, of course, immediately got up in arms. The party officials came running too. "Why do such a thing?" they said. I was a party member at that time, and I answered, "Why not? The Communists always say that the working class is the principal force, and so forth. But where are its defenders? Who defends the working class?" Well, they hissed a lot, but we created it.

Immediately, the committee began to make demands backed up by strike threats. The shop workers' committee had a mandate, signed by 100 workers, to negotiate these demands. When we showed this to the administration, it had to talk to us, and we did reach certain compromise solutions. This was in February 1990. There were five of us in the committee.

Then we made the proposal to the enterprise work-collective council to organize the election of an enterprise-wide workers' committee. But they objected, saying there would be too many organizations and that we should work together with them. We realized it was no use, and the five of us decided to create such a workers' committee on our own. It was elected at a conference on December 15, 1990. But there were only a few people—some sixty delegates, representing about fifty workers each. The press reported that we represented 1,200 workers.

We immediately came under attack from the Communists. That's because we issued a declaration that the party committee should be removed from the factory. They claimed we didn't represent anybody but ourselves.

As I recall, Yeltsin came to the factory on the invitation of your workers' committee.

That visit made us very famous—and I don't consider that a good thing. We invited Yeltsin in January 1991, offered him our support. At that time, he was a pariah—he was being attacked—so he agreed to come in February. And everyone was saying, "My God, the head of the Supreme Soviet himself is coming!" And the administration immediately sought us out. "Listen, lads, let's live peacefully together." They were insulted that we didn't allot them any tickets.

That's when our notoriety began to grow. We were almost officially recognized by the administration. They began to consult us, to invite us to conferences. But all this went to the head of some of our members, and as a result, two of them became interested exclusively in politics. You see, they were members of the People's Front and much of their activity was oriented to that movement's political goals. I thought that the main task was to create shop committees that would eventually evolve into independent trade unions. But when we started to get involved in politics, running here and there, making television appearances, and so on, we lost touch with our real tasks. These guys were constantly asking the workers to endorse telegrams of support for this or that political figure, and they practically forgot about factory affairs.

Well, since we had become famous, the miners came to us in the spring for support in their strike. They went through the different shops and held a meeting in the tractor assembly shop. "Support us," they said, "we'll overthrow the Union government, and we'll live well under Russian jurisdiction." We ourselves didn't have the kind of force at the factory to back up those demands. It was only on May 6 that we finally put forth our demands, backed by a strike threat.

So your factory supported Yeltsin in his struggle for power with the Soviet Union?

Did we ever! And when he came, the reception was tremendous. It was the first time I'd seen how the administration greets a political leader. The assembly line was shut down for two hours. Everyone stood at the gates waiting. He came early, at 7 a.m., and we walked through the shops with him. Then he came to our assembly line. You should have seen it—people pushing to get a look, as if he were a god.

First of all, everyone knew that he was in the opposition, a pariah being squeezed from above by the Soviet government, by Gorbachev, and so forth. So he was the symbol of the unflinching fighter for us. And when he came to the assembly line after walking around the factory and meeting with the administration, he spoke into the megaphone: "Citizens of Russia, do you support me?" And they answered, "Yes, we support you! Don't give up!" Well, it was in that spirit.

Then Pavlov [Gorbachev's prime minister] decided to come?

After Yeltsin's visit, they all started to bargain with the Kirov factory. Exactly three days later, Pavlov flew in and began whispering with the administration, offering it privileged conditions, throwing us some crumbs. And it was all thanks to the workers' committee. Our administration didn't know what to take: the silver, the gold, or the diamonds.

The one-day strike planned for May 6 didn't come off, except for our shop and one other, where it lasted an hour. The work-collective council officially opposed it. It was right after that we lost one of the two members I mentioned before. Either he was lured away by a good salary or maybe he felt the strike was harmful to Yeltsin and would create political complications for him. [On April 26, Yeltsin and Gorbachev signed an agreement that would have given most of the Soviet Union's governing powers to the republics.]

Then came the presidential election campaign in the summer of 1991. It was widely known that Yeltsin had been endorsed by the Kirov workers and that had a certain impact on worker opinion elsewhere: "If the Kirov workers support him, he must be a good man. You can't fool them." And we did vote for him, organized rallies to explain why he should be elected. In brief, he became president. And then came the so-called coup.

Why "so-called"?

Because it was phoney. A real coup, of course, isn't carried out in that way. It would have been enough to show one battalion—say, the Lithuanian—and the coup would have been a fact in fifteen minutes. Instead, they put on this comedy. Well, there was a demonstration on the Palace Square, and our workers were in the first rows. Sobachak, the mayor of Leningrad, came to the factory and spent the night there speaking on the phone with Yeltsin. We have a direct line to the government.

There's one version that says that when Sobachak flew in from Moscow, he was met by Samsonov and Kurkov [military commanders in the Leningrad region who refused to support the coup] who told him, "Whatever you do, make sure there are no strikes in Leningrad." But he said, "At least let me hold a rally." You see, it was a question of honor for him, a question of his own prestige to show that he was organizing the defense of democracy and that he had the support of the Kirov workers.

Anyway, we got a call on the evening of the nineteenth telling us to mobilize the workers the next day. There wasn't exactly tremendous enthusiasm, but we brought the people out and marched to the Palace Square, with slogans like, "We will defend democracy!"

Sobachak appeared in the morning, made a speech, we made some speeches, we defended democracy, and so forth. Now, personally, I am deeply disappointed. That Belovezhskii conspiracy can in no way be justified. [The reference is to the agreement between Yeltsin and the leaders of Ukraine and Belarus (formerly Byelorussia) in December 1991 to dissolve the Soviet Union and create the Commonwealth of Independent States. That agreement was negotiated in total secrecy and disregarded the March referendum that gave overwhelming support to a renewed Union.]

You mean the dismantling of the USSR?

Yes, and the so-called reforms—"shock therapy"—that began on January 2. And now our workers' committee has split between supporters of Yeltsin and his reforms and those who don't consider them reforms. I'm in the latter group.

On April 16, the workers' committee organized a round table with representatives of various political parties, since we realized that we were alone in the city—there are no other workers' committees.

We needed allies, especially political allies. So the main function of the round table was to give us a chance to see who our allies were, who we could maintain contact with.

The press was there but they apparently didn't find it newsworthy. Anyway, after it was over, we declared publicly that these reforms are anti-people, robbery, and so on. We said that our allies are the movement of free trade unions and parties with a socialist and worker orientation. That declaration sparked the final departure of two of our members. Now only four of us remain in the committee; two of us are also members of the enterprise work-collective council, and a third is also the head of our shop workers' committee.

After the round table, Kondrashev, one of the two who split, accused us of having degenerated. In his opinion, the workers' committee had been founded on different principles. I showed him that this was untrue, that he started to oppose our positions only after we started to oppose "Borya," our precious Yeltsin. And he says, "You're liars. I will personally inform Yeltsin that this declaration was not adopted by the workers' committee."

He's linked with the Americans. They even shot a television film about him here last year. He feels that these are good reforms, that this is the victory of democracy. The fact of the matter is he puts in twenty-four hours at the plant for pennies and then takes three days off to make big money in a cooperative. That's why he can say, "Things are fine now. I can buy whatever I like. The stores have everything." And I said to that journalist, "Yes, he can buy anything, because he works in the cooperative. Even under Gorbachev, when I was earning 400 rubles a month, he was making 200 a day at the cooperative."

All these people, the activists of the first hour, they've come to power or close to those in power, they've become comfortable, and they say, "What the hell are you whining about? Everything's as it should be." They have it good. Incidentally, they've tried to buy the rest of us many times with offers of apartments, cars, and the like.

What are your relations like with the union committee?

I can't say they're great. We have a common interest in defending the workers. We're doing what we can to reform the union. But it's impossible to reform the people who are in the union structure now since they are the products of particular conditions.

You mean they used to be party functionaries?

Yes, for the most part. And even now the union head says, "I will never give up my party card, because I'm a defender of the workers." But they're really sons of bitches. They've used the union to form a business called Zolushka ["Cinderella"] which buys and sells, that is, speculates.

But why can't you just hold new elections and put some decent people in the union, at least in your shop?

We've given that a lot of thought. In principle, it's possible, but any person who gets elected will soon forget about the workers. He'll be tied to the enterprise union committee and to the administration in some way. His basic wage will be 85 percent of the department head's salary. In the old days, he would also get various bonuses. That's why, when the administration wanted us to work on a day off, the union committee was expected to give its consent automatically—the union head's bonus depended on the shop's performance. Besides that, the union committees are also involved in distribution of goods, the sale of food. That's also a clever thing, since a worker who leaves the union deprives himself of this food supplement.

Then, the allocation of consumer goods continues even after the prices have been freed?

Yes, the plant is forced to conclude barter deals.

Besides food, what is distributed?

Anything and everything, from noodles to salt, if salt can't be got in the stores. The rest is sold through a kiosk that they've set up directly in the shop. Before New Year's Eve, for example, they allowed each worker to buy 1.5 kilos of meat. There are also durable goods, like cars and furniture. As soon as we formed our workers' committee, this distribution came under careful scrutiny, and they had to become honest. We had the union head surrounded: on his left, sat the work-collective council, and on his right, the workers' committee.

Before Yeltsin came, Pavlov was here and said, "By way of exception, I can let you become a joint-stock company." He even signed some papers. Then Yeltsin came and signed even more papers. Management was tending toward this joint-stock form of property.

At that time, two members of our workers' committee were taking an economics courses at the Leningrad Union of Work Collectives. We invited Sergei Andreev to the factory several times, and he explained that joint-stock companies are a nightmare, since there are no laws governing them. He said we'd best avoid that or we'd be cheated.

I've heard the exact opposite thing about Andreev from the chairwoman of the Pargolov factory union: that he has been calling for the formation of joint-stock companies. That's one of the reasons she said she left the Leningrad Union of Work Collectives.

Who the hell knows! I was at several meetings of the union, and as far as I can tell, Andreev is an intelligent person and he has been of some use to us. He even drafted a counterproposal to management's privatization program, but the administration rejected it.

Why did the movement peter out?

First of all, it's an obvious fact that rank-and-file workers have only a weak grasp of this issue. And there is absolutely no support from above. I know that Andreev tried very hard to persuade the government to change the discounted 25 percent of shares that are supposed to go to the workers into ordinary voting shares that the workers should get for free. He failed, of course, so maybe he just gave up.

After all, how much can you do? I'm also tired of the struggle at this factory. There are really only four of us left, and we've been going on like this for six years. You put so much of your time in it and get only hostility in return. And now they're trying to lure us into business. We're getting offers to join some firm to sell eggs, salami, or tractors for the factory. That's how they want to draw the activists away from the factories, so there will be no organizing force to unite the workers.

We spent most of 1991 preventing management from moving ahead on its privatization plan. The general director met with us several times and told us we had to hurry because the government was on our side and conditions were favorable. He needed our support because we were really the only independent workers organization and we had the potential to stop him. He also remembered that Yeltsin had come on our invitation. Well, we refused. We brought in experts who said that the company charter was no good, that it had to be changed. We also brought in the factory's deputies in the city soviet.

On February 15, 1992, Yeltsin flew into Piter [the name used by locals for Leningrad/St. Petersburg] and we drove out to the airport to see him. He said, "I'll make an exception for you. Draw up your own program, come to see me, and I'll sign it." He said this before the press. So we worked out our program, but then they published the laws on privatization, and it seemed that our program was no good. The authorities wouldn't approve it. And we couldn't get a meeting with Yeltsin either. We did meet Gaidar [Yeltsin's minister in charge of the economic reform, forced out by the parliament in the fall of 1992 and returned by Yeltsin in the fall of 1993]. Our documents are still lying somewhere in his offices.

So how do I see things? When Yeltsin needed our support to become president, he came to the factory and said, "Lads, whatever your problems, just come to me. The door will always be open." He became president, and we went with our privatization program many times, but we couldn't get in to see him.

What was your program?

Our original idea was that the workers should have a controlling share. But there was tremendous resistance to that idea, and we were forced to change our program several times in the face of new laws and other pressures. In the end, we asked that the discounted 25 percent of non-voting shares that the law allots to the workers should be given to us for free and as voting shares. We also wanted all the shares to remain within the collective, a closed joint-stock company. But management objected; they said, "We need to attract foreign investment."

Two members of the work-collective council, who are also members of our workers' committee, are in the working group on privatization. So you can't say the workers are being excluded. At the end of May, there was a factory conference that adopted a resolution on the transition to a joint-stock company. The adopted program differs a bit from the government's in that the employees are to get 40 percent of the shares. The government keeps the rest. But we don't get control.

I spoke out against adopting this. It would be ruinous for us: the enterprise could well find itself bankrupt within year, and we'll be told, "You're bankrupt and no one is to responsible but yourselves. You've got to close the factory."

Our general director is a sly fox. One thing I can say—and I'm not afraid to repeat it publicly—our administration is involved in various private businesses, joint ventures, and joint-stock companies, that they've created using the Kirov factory as a base. As a rule, our administrators are also top officers of these private companies.

I remember that already in 1990 the workers at a Novosibirsk factory revolted against this corruption and forced their administrators to cut all links with private enterprises.

That's exactly what we tried to do too. A joint commission of our shop's work-collective council, union committee, and workers' committee demanded in the factory paper that the administration make public the list of all the private businesses that it's involved in. We got a note back from the assistant director: "Lads, don't increase the tension at the enterprise." And they raised wages a bit.

Over the past two and a half years they've raked in a lot of money, and now they're in a rush to buy up the enterprise. It's the easiest way to launder the money that they've been stealing from the enterprise.

Are the rank-and-file workers disillusioned with Yeltsin?

Let me give you an example. Before the coup, when the Communist reaction was on the rise, an acquaintance of mine said, "I'll shoot all the Communists. I've got all the bullets I need." The coup is history, and now he says: "I'd wipe out every goddamn democrat. They're worse than the Communists." That's how much views have changed. Personally, I feel that the democrats are waging war against the people.

I began keeping accounts of my family's income and expenses since prices were freed. In January, my wife and I brought home 2,835 rubles and spent 2,625 on food alone. The vice chairman of our work-collective took a ten-day course on market economics—he calculated the movement of living standards roughly as follows: under socialism, with my ten rubles, I could buy five kilos of beef. In January, I earned eighty rubles a day, and a kilo of meat cost roughly 100 rubles. So my living standards have declined over 500 percent.

What would be the difference in how many months' wages it takes to buy a car?

You've got to be joking. Look at my shoes. Before, under social-ism, these would have been in the garbage long ago. Now we're constantly patching.

Why is it that the assembly line always seems to be the most militant section?

Well, we have the advantage in that if we push the button and our brigade of seventy workers stops, the whole shop stops. Management comes running and starts to negotiate. We just have to yell, "Tomor-row, we strike!" and they know we can carry it off.

So in February our earnings were 6,000 rubles, and our expendi-tures were 3,000. March: wages, 5,000; expenditures, 4,677. April: wages, again 5,000; expenditures, 5,180. May: wages, 8,550—there was a special supplement of 1,300 rubles, and we got 800 rubles more because of a modification in the assembly line that meant extra work—expenditures, 5,932. June: 5,165 and 6,750. All this is just for food.

What about clothes and other dry goods?

Well, if you can't eat it, you don't buy it.

Do you have kids?

Two. One is going into grade two and the other is in pre-school. Now it's summer and we should be preparing for the fall, buying clothes and other things, but I don't know what with. I calculated that over the past six months we earned on the average 1,300 rubles per person, while the poverty level is 2,900 to 3,000. In other words, I'm living somewhere near the subsistence level.

The papers wrote about a demonstration of Kirov workers on April 2.

In February, our workers' committee made demands and called for a political protest. It originated in the tractor assembly shop and others took it up. We discussed the question in the work-collective council and decided to wait, as the mood wasn't yet ripe. Then around April, spontaneous local protests began: "We've got to do something. They're robbing us!" So the union, fearing the outbreak of political strikes, had to move.

Actually, it was the union together with management. Management had its own reasons. They wanted to hold back the increase of fuel and energy prices at least until June, when they were planning to send us on involuntary leave. They knew that if the prices were raised in April, as the government had promised in its memorandum to the International Monetary Fund, the factory would go down the tube then and there.

I have to say right off that anyone who wanted to could go, except for workers in continuous-cycle production. We worked through lunch and then gathered outside. To tell the truth, there weren't that many—about 7,000, it seemed to me. That's not a lot for the day shift. But as we moved along the streets, small streams of people flowed into the demonstration. And a lot of people took the subway from the factory to the Palace Square, because it's too far to walk, especially for older workers.

Now most of the workers are on involuntary leave. Did the union agree to this?

Well, what do you think? Together with management, they explained to the workers that there was no work. We had 1,500 unfinished tractors waiting for parts. There was no more storage space to go on producing. So at the end of May, they said, "Let's take a couple of months' rest, and maybe in the meantime the parts will arrive and we'll be able to sell the tractors." And the director declared in the factory paper that anyone who manages to sell a tractor will get 3,000 rubles commission.

The next day, five us in the work-collective council went to the union head and asked how he could give his consent without consulting anyone. We forced him to agree to call a union conference. The next day, the department head calls us over. "You know, we have a management group in charge of selling tractors. It's going on a trip around Russia. Would you like to join?" I said, "This smells like the director's way of getting rid of us and avoiding the conference. Anyway, we're workers, not merchants." He replies: "Don't worry. It's only for two weeks, and you'll pick it up. The pay's good and there's also commission." We walked out laughing. They might as well have offered to send us to the United States or Canada and told us not to return before New Year's. That would have been more honest.

So the conference took place, and we strongly criticized what was happening in the factory. I gave a political speech. I said that what is happening now in this country is like a bomb with a slow fuse. Transformation of property relations means revolution. It happened in 1917; this time, the *nomenklatura* way, the people's property is being transformed into private property. Sooner or later it will cause an explosion. I said that we shouldn't allow it, we shouldn't agree to the joint-stock company. Later, it will be too late to correct the mistake. As for Yeltsin, I called him an evil person.

None of this got into the press. For the first time in seven years of speaking publicly at the factory, I got whistled down.

Who was at that conference?
The same official delegates as always. A miracle if there were even 5 percent workers taking part. I sent a written question about this to the presidium but got no answer.

Officially, it was the emergency situation at the factory and the administration's proposals on getting us out of it. They showed us the huge sums our creditors owed us—every factory today owes and is owed huge sums—that we are, in fact, bankrupt, and that if we don't get a breathing space and reduce expenses through this two-month leave, we might as well prepare the enterprise for burial. We had to agree with this assessment.

Are you on leave now?
June was my regular vacation, and I had to stay out in July too. The assembly line really isn't working. When we get parts, we finish up the tractors that are standing in the yard.

These reforms, logically, will provoke a protest from the mass of people, since their immiseration will continue. I don't believe the promises that stability will be achieved by the fall and inflation brought under control. In the Communist spirit, "Borya" will once again hang noodles from his ears in order to calm people down. You recall that he first promised stabilization by March, then by the fall, and so forth.

Gaidar has now said it will happen at the end of 1993.
Soon they'll be saying the first decade of the twenty-first century.

They're capable of that. I think that continued decline will lead to a cataclysm—civil war or national conflicts. In principle, only a military overthrow could stop it—there's no other force. Or else a right-wing nationalist party like Zhirinovskii's will come to power. [Zhirinovskii is the leader of a nationalist party calling for strong government, viewed by many as a potentially fascist-type leader.] The people want a firm, authoritarian regime, since what they have now is pure lawlessness in all areas of life.

And what would be the economic policy of such a regime?
The market. It would be a 100-percent Chilean model. Representatives of Zhirinovskii's party came to our round table. To tell the truth, I don't like that party's ideas, but they had this army captain who offered a curious analysis: every time Russia is about to become a great economic and military power, the big capitalists who control the course of world events intervene to put an end to it. This, in his view, is was what lay behind perestroika. Of course, it's overblown, but I can agree at least in part with the idea that no capitalist country wants so powerful a competitor as was the USSR. And we were strong, at least in the area of military production and some high technology sectors.

In May, a Western television crew came to our assembly shop, and the journalist asked me: "Who profits from your perestroika?" I said, "You, first of all." I explained that we were first or second in arms production. Now this is all gone. We're squeezed out of the world market. They've destroyed our heavy industry, our scientific and technological potential.

Then he asked, "Your Russian government is buying tear gas from us. What would you do if you are brought to a state of rebellion and they disperse you with this gas?" You know, the question shocked me. I thought to myself, "Well, that's interesting!" Personally, if I'm brought to that situation, I'll reach for a gun, because I have nothing to lose.

Do you think the army would go against workers?
The army is worse off than the people. How could it go against us? I'll tell you one thing. If the army overthrows this government, no one is going to go to defend the White House this time. I've already said this publicly.

Isn't there any mass political organization of workers?

They trust people like me and my comrades, and they say to us, "Just say the word, and we'll come out. Just tell us what to do." They have activists that they are prepared to support, but they aren't willing to join any party. They don't seem to want that.

I've been active in the workers' committee and the work-collective council. I showed the workers whose side I was on and how I could help them. But the workers just reacted with apathy: "We elected you, so you tell us what has to be done." They're willing to lend a hand, of course. But if it's a question of coming to a meeting with workers from another plant, of a union meeting, or a meeting with a political party that would require them to use their brains politically, they say, "You go. You're the elected one. Tell us after what happened."

The workers' movement in Piter is weak now. In general, it was based upon strike committees, nothing more. These were groups of activists who called themselves strike committees. But the Kirov workers' committee was the only really solid one, and they naturally turned to us. We were famous. And that's about how it remained.

You know, until around 1990, if they dared to reduce piece rates or if output fell so that take home pay fell by 20 percent, there would immediately have been a strike. Our former department head said to me, "When I was in charge, if I took off one kopeck, there'd be a strike right off. Now your wages aren't rising, but prices go up almost each day. You're five times worse off and you're silent." I can't understand it either. It doesn't make sense.

People need to start thinking in a totally new way. I'm not even necessarily talking about a party or political programs, but simply a sobering of minds so people say, "We can't live like this." You can't live with this deception. And this stupid market—to tell the truth, I don't know if it's a market or what. It seems to me only that mafia, criminal capital has been legalized.

I consider a reform acceptable if it doesn't cause a deterioration in the existing standard of living. And if it provokes evil emotions then we know it isn't a popular reform, but a reform based upon evil.

You can draw a balance sheet—what was and what is now. And people are thinking: when the Communists were in power, at least

I didn't think about my stomach, I had enough to eat and I could live on the miserable salary. Even a vagabond could live by collecting and redeeming empty bottles. Just try to do that now. The opposition in Piter had to fight just to get a half hour of air time on television. And they call this democracy!

Postscript: Three months later, the tractor-assembly shop struck for a day and a half to demand wages equal to four "minimum consumer baskets." But the strike also had a political goal: to incite the workers in other factories to join in the formation of a regional strike committee. The strike, which went unreported by the media except for an article in the weekly paper of the Moscow Federation of Trade Unions, ended in a partial wage raise. But the following letter, authored by Kalachev and signed by 2,500 workers, was sent to the Seventh Congress of People's Deputies that was about to convene in Russia. It too went unpublished in the mass media.

We turn to you, the deputies of the Seventh Congress of Russia, as representatives of the people. We, the workers of the Kirov Factory, are a part of that same people thanks to whom, until now, ours has remained an independent country. We are therefore in our rights to ask you why the peoples of Russia are today suffering from your actions, why moans fill the air and blood is flowing. Who is in charge of the dismal affairs of the Russian state in which arbitrary power and illegality reign even more than before? Why is a powerful economy perishing? Why are factories and mills closing, agriculture being destroyed and hundreds of thousands of unemployed appearing? Why have terror on the part of criminals and economic genocide on the part of the government become the norm for the people of labor? Who gave you the right to observe in silence the misdeeds of the new rulers? We workers have had our fill of anti-popular propaganda that interprets as a good this ruinous restructuring (perestroika), reforms that are devastating for the people. Whoever loves his motherland—Russia— will never cause her pain and suffering. Leaders that respect their people will find the correct direction for needed reforms and reject the path along which we are now being taken.

At the Seventh Congress of Russia you have to decide the issue of confidence in a president and government who do not express the interests of the majority of citizens of Russia. Our patience has come to an end. A social explosion is inevitable. If the congress does not change the anti-popular character of the Yeltsin-Gaidar government's reforms, the only way out for us will be a political strike. Your duty is not to allow another civil war in Russia. We remember our bloody history and we will not allow it to repeat itself. History will call to strict account each individual politicians for all the victims of the peaceful "restructuring" period. The congress must resolve all these contradictions in a peaceful fashion. Otherwise, the irreparable may occur. (*Informatsionnyi byuleten*, no. 48, 1992.)

This, and similar events that went unreported, no doubt played a role in bolstering the hitherto rather malleable congress's resolve to stand up to Yeltsin and oppose his "shock therapy." In contrast to the Kirov Factory letter, miners' committees from Vorkuta and Kuzbass sent a delegation to the congress in Moscow to support the president "elected by all the people and the course of reform he is carrying out" against the "*nomenklatura revanche.*" The Moscow Federation paper published the following note by Kalachev:

There wasn't a single strikebreaker in the entire shop, despite the fact that from the very first day they tried to scare the strikers with jail sentences for "insulting the president." The director said that the factory's economic situation is such that it will have to close and the workers will be sent on involuntary leave. (*Solidarnost*, no. 30, 1992.)

Grigorii Artemenko
[July 1993]

It had been over a year and half since I last saw Grigorii, and I readily accepted his invitation to come to Odessa. There was no mistaking that Ukraine had become an independent republic. I wasted close to a week trying to get a visa. My train arrived at the Ukrainian border at two a.m. A border guard briefly examined my documents by match-light and then shyly apologized for the inconvenience.

It was a bone-crushing bus ride from Odessa (the fuel shortage had forced schedule cuts) to Nerubaiskoe, a town of 10,000. Here I gained more insight into the conditions that had fostered (or perhaps reflected) Grigorii's independent spirit. He and his wife, who also worked for the railroad, had built a comfortable home entirely with their own labor and wages. (According to Grigorii, that would be impossible today.) They kept a small truck-garden, fruit trees, vines, a goat, and chickens, which somewhat sheltered them from the drastic decline in real wages. At the depot, I saw the huge container-crane that Grigorii not only operates, but also maintains and repairs. He is a worker who knows his value, and it was clear that management, with whom he spoke as an equal, knows it too.

I asked him how things stood in the year and a half since the Ukrainian government declared independence.

The situation hasn't improved. There is still no democracy. Individual freedom without economic well-being is a deception. And since independence, our economic situation has continued to deteriorate in connection with the breakdown of economic relations and the government's willingness to cut itself off from Russian sources of raw materials, especially oil. Industry is simply being destroyed. If we didn't live too well before, now it's much worse.

The proclaimed independence is empty of content. Our government and President Kravchuk are still celebrating sovereignty, but you won't find in their sovereignty any measures for economic stabilization, especially as long as that precludes the repairing of economic relations with Russia.

Ukraine, much more than the other republics, went in for a break in economic ties. This was a political decision, not an inevitable process. The dismantling of the Soviet Union was a conscious political act, and it was followed by the erection of barriers to the movement of goods and especially to the movement of payments between republics. Of course, the process was partially spontaneous, but all the same, the lead belonged to Ukraine.

When people voted for Kravchuk, they saw him as a leader whose orientation was socialist. He was a former secretary of the Ukrainian Communist Party. His electoral campaign was based upon socialism, at least in the sense of preserving and building upon the rights that the people had already won. The nationalist candidate, Vyacheslav Chernovil, stated openly that the soviets had outlived their usefulness and that society had been moving in the wrong direction—it had to shift to capitalism. And the people dealt him a crushing defeat. Out of five candidates, Kravchuk won on the first round with over 66 percent of the vote and a turnout of about 87 percent. That shows a high level of mass activism at the time.

But when he returned from the meeting at Belovezhskoe pushche, Kravchuk shifted. [In the fall of 1991, the leaders of the Ukrainian, Russian and Byelorussian republics, without any popular mandate, declared the Soviet Union defunct.] He saw that the Communist fraction in the Supreme Soviet had fallen apart. It had always been an artificial grouping of people with very disparate interests. They voted together not out of conviction, but out of party discipline. But now the party was banned. However, the parliament had a homogeneous group of intellectuals linked to the Rukh, the nationalist party led by Chernovil.

So Kravchuk lost his old political base and was looking for a new one?

Yes. Not only was the CPSU banned, but it was—and still is—the object of slander and persecution, not unlike McCarthyism in the United States. The nationalists, of course, claimed the campaign wasn't aimed at honest Communists, only those who had worked in party structures. But this wasn't true. Several times, even I was reminded that, as a conscientious worker, I was also responsible for the old system, which would not have survived so long had I worked less well. According to the nationalists' logic, the good workers are guilty of their good work.

But if Ukraine is to get itself out of this hole, it will be thanks to the efforts of workers who know how and want to work. Any social system depends for its prosperity on the labor of its citizens. But people have stopped working because their work doesn't even give them the minimum necessary for survival. Everything is now directed toward speculation. Especially since the collapse of the Union, the government's goal has been to foster a new bourgeois stratum that would serve as its social base. In agriculture, workers make 6,000 to 9,000 coupons [Ukrainian currency] a month. A kilo of meat costs 10,000. So the more you work, the poorer you get. And it's all the more demoralizing when you see the new bourgeois raking in millions through speculation.

Earlier you said that Kravchuk's nationalist turn was a political mistake.

Yes, at Rukh's congress he declared: "We are a European state and we will orient ourselves toward Europe." Only his total ignorance of economics explains that statement. Yes, we're in Europe. But we were very tightly integrated into the Union of fifteen republics. Kravchuk has publicly admitted his error. But the majority of workers have absolutely no confidence in this man. He has constantly deceived us. His electoral platform turned into its opposite.

Why was it a mistake to make Rukh his political base? Rukh is not a very large movement, but neither were the Bolsheviks in 1917. The difference is that the Bolsheviks' ideas were close to the people, while Rukh's ideas were not accepted by the majority of the population. Yes, it's true that in western Ukraine [separated by religious, cultural, and linguistic differences from the central and eastern regions] the majority did adhere to these ideas. But in the central, and even more in the southern and eastern parts, they were not accepted at all. In our district, Rukh's activists are not stable, conscientious workers but total layabouts. It was obvious that Rukh was being well financed from somewhere, even when the Communist Party still existed. Otherwise it could never have afforded its wonderful equipment, the computers, xeroxes, faxes. It got this money, which attracted people who hoped to cash in on it.

I repeat, except for Kiev—the city, not the region—in our central, southern, and eastern regions, Rukh had no real strength. In the Odessa region, its most successful demonstrations attracted 200 to 300 people, and many of them were curious onlookers.

It still isn't clear to me why Kravchuk decided to throw in his lot with the nationalists, if most people wanted to maintain close economic ties with Russia.

Unfortunately, the situation became much more complicated. By the time he shifted to Rukh's positions, much had changed, including the Supreme Soviet itself. Many elements of the intelligentsia who were close to the elite embraced Rukh's ideas. They publicly condemned their Communist past. And they had access to the mass media, something denied to workers.

But, anyway, workers had no desire or reason to recant. Their labor had built one of the most powerful states in the world. Those intellectuals weren't acting out of conviction—they were merely replacing the Communist feed-trough with a nationalist one. They betrayed the workers, and not just the workers, but all toilers—collective farm members, factory technicians and engineers. The latter are the technical intelligentsia, who always worked closely with us and live in the same tragic conditions. You won't find many of them in the president's inner circle.

The nationalists in the Supreme Soviet are writers, poets, journalists, university teachers who, one might say, are unfamiliar with real life. This was obvious when they introduced the draft constitution, written together with the president, at the end of the spring of 1992, a nationalist constitution.

First it was presented in the press for "national discussion," as our Communist leaders used to say. But this discussion was to take place exclusively in the press, where the political leadership could control which opinions would find expression. Afterwards, they would proclaim: "This is the people's will." But matters took an unexpected turn when the soviets and the work collectives got involved. The Law on Privatization had already taught the work collectives the real value of the government's fine words about democracy. They had learnt to read between the lines.

What was the essence of the draft constitution?

It gave unlimited powers to the president. It was oriented toward construction of nationalist state with absolutely no consideration for the aspirations and thoughts of the various nationalities that live in Ukraine. We have 11 to 12 million Russians. And how many Russian-speakers are there? I don't know if anyone has counted, but they say 30 million. In reality, the entire population of the larger cities, and much of the smaller, converses in Russian. This is absolutely the case in eastern and central Ukraine. Even in Western Ukraine, there are very significant numbers of Russian speakers. This constitution would have allowed their forced Ukrainization. Of course, it didn't say so openly, but that clearly flowed from it.

Besides, it practically liquidated the representative organs of power, the soviets, giving the president a free hand during his five-year term, since there was no recall mechanism. Parliament itself was to consist of two houses, both of which, in practice, could decide nothing—they would have been mere screens for presidential power. But by that time, the soviets had already experienced the true meaning of presidential power—power that was responsible to no one. The administrative officials appointed by the president in the regions and localities answer only to the president, and, in fact, to no one, since the president is a long way off. Most are corrupt.

We discussed the draft in the Odessa regional soviet, which categorically rejected it. We were the first. To tell the truth, we didn't expect such unanimity. Then the president declared that the soviets are obstructing reform. The soviets, on their part, called a conference in Kiev. The conference was a stormy affair, and afterwards, the president began to shift policy.

He respected the results of the conference?
I have to say that he did. It was a very serious discussion with the participation of experts in legal and constitutional questions. The criticism of the section on human rights and regional self-government was particularly strong.

With the support of the Supreme Soviet—strange as it seems—the president liquidated the executive committees of the regional and district soviets. He proceeded to appoint his personal representatives in the regions, governors, and they in turn appointed administrative heads in the districts. This structure is not accountable to the soviets at any level, nor to the Supreme Soviets, nor even to the cabinet. It answers only to the president.

There arose a kind of dual power, since the soviets retained some powers, in particular the power to form and dispose of the budget. The tension between the two structures continues to grow, since the soviet deputies, after all, were elected locally, they are thus closer to their electorate and so they have to be responsive to them at least to some degree.

We have a paradoxical situation where the deputies are aware of all the abuses in the administration but can do nothing about them. In theory, the cabinet of ministers runs the economy, but in practice it's the president. His representatives run everything in the localities—industry, agriculture, the legal institutions, the National Guard. In fact, you could say there is triple power: the presidential structure, the cabinet of ministers, and the soviets. We have a saying: "A child with seven nannies is without supervision."

The president finally retreated and agreed to a real discussion. A congress of soviets was set for February 1993. Everything was worked out, but it hasn't taken place. Of course, the situation has changed over the year. Not only the president but the Supreme Soviet are afraid of this congress, all the more so after the latest strike in the Donbass, in which the miners and metallurgical workers forced the Supreme Soviet to accept referenda on confidence in the Supreme Soviet and president in September. [According to the agreement, the referenda were to take place in September; the parliament has yet to set a date.] Many seem to fear that it could be a repeat of the Congress of Soviets of October 1917 that received power from the Petrograd Soviet that had overthrown the Provisional Government.

The nationalists fear the soviets, since they know nationalism lacks a political base in central, southern and eastern Ukraine and that new soviet elections would show that. In essence, it's a conflict between nationalists and internationalists. The former claim the latter are destructive forces that reject Ukrainian sovereignty.

In reality, almost everyone understands that the Union, in its old form that totally denied autonomy to republics on economic and political questions, is gone forever. But people do want a close economic and political union with the other republics, one that would respect the sovereignty of the republican governments but with a superstructure capable of coordinating the interests and activity of the republics. They also want a state policy for the development of the economy of the entire region that was once the Soviet Union. They feel that this is a necessity for the survival of all. There is no doubt in my mind that the majority of the population of Russia, Ukraine, Belarus, and Kazakhstan, republics with 90 percent of the population of the former USSR, now understand that without close cooperation, not only will there be no economic, but also no political, independence. Moreover, few people today believe the declarations that the integrity of the current borders will be respected, if we continue along the current path.

You support Ukrainian sovereignty. What, in your view, are the rational, the just elements of the nationalist movement?
A main problem in the old system was that the center imposed economic programs that didn't correspond to the interests, and especially the ecological interests, of the population of the republics. But I want to emphasize that that wasn't a Russian center, as the nationalists contend. Russia had nothing to do with it. It suffered from the incompetent center along with the others.

What about language?
That problem existed but it's much more complicated than the nationalists would have it. The basic problem was that there was one Union, and the language of international communication was Russian. Specialists who graduated from institutes of higher education, wherever they were located, were sent to places where they were most needed. Imagine a graduate of the Odessa Institute of Low-Temperature Technology who was sent to Uzbekistan knowing only Ukrainian. This, in my opinion, was one of the main reasons why higher educated was conducted in Russian.

No one prevented the studying of Ukrainian. I can say that with authority, since I was chairman of the parents' committee of our secondary school, which has over 1,000 students, for more than ten years. I witnessed the process by which Russian classes arose. Parents went to the principal and asked for them. These were often people who had moved here from Russia, just as people from our region moved to other republics, like the Baltics, in search of a better life, better earnings. But there were also local people who knew that after high school their kids would go on to higher education where, for the reason I already indicated, the language of teaching was Russian.

And so they opened Russian classes. But Ukrainian classes continued to exist in parallel. The paradox was that the Russian classes attracted the best students and came to be seen as elite classes. But no one stopped anyone from going to Ukrainian classes, though to tell the truth, by the time the nationalist movement arose, not a single Ukrainian high school remained in the city of Odessa.

Do you mean things had been better before from the point of view of the Ukrainian language?

Yes, and by the way, in Stalin's time there were many Ukrainian schools in Odessa and other regions, and there were specific instructions that those classes could not shift to Russian. But after Stalin, a certain democratization, or at least decentralization, occurred. I can't talk with authority about the situation in Western Ukraine, though I've spoken to people and visited the region many times for work. But at least in this southern region nothing was imposed.

Nor was anything forced when the original decision to return to Ukrainian was taken in the early perestroika period. It was to be a complex, lengthy and entirely voluntary process, not some five-year plan. There are also purely practical reasons why this can't be done overnight. We lack a base for teaching in Ukrainian in higher education. For example, there aren't any dictionaries. Today, when they translate from English to Ukrainian, they have to go through Russian.

Moreover, in this vast republic there are different versions and different interpreters of the Ukrainian language. We still haven't decided which version is official and which are dialects. So what should we teach in our universities and institutes? Besides, Ukraine produces no paper; it doesn't have the printing capacity to publish the necessary textbooks in a short period. It also lacks the teaching personnel. It's impossible to teach a huge number of people in so short a time. Many world-class specialists would simply leave Ukraine. Fortunately, the process was relaxed following a wave of protest.

You have to understand the nature of nationalism in western Ukraine that once belonged to Austro-Hungary, Poland, and even in part to Czechoslovakia. It was never in the same state as the rest of Ukraine. National oppression under Poland was probably the worst. I have a hard time pronouncing the phrase: "National oppression under Russia," though no one can suspect me of sympathies to Russia. My family has been Ukrainian at least as far back as the seventeenth century, and I openly expressed my pro-Ukrainian attitudes at a time when they weren't politically acceptable.

In my view, what we did in Malinovksii district of Odessa could serve a model of how to proceed. It was back in 1987, when I joined the party during the process of democratization. Until then the party had been closed to me, and, besides, I hadn't had the slightest desire to join it. I joined in 1987 because I felt I could have some influence on what was happening in society.

I was one of the initiators of the movement for the renaissance of the Ukrainian language and culture. It's true that a vast number of Ukrainians had migrated to the cities and forgot their language and culture. But we decided to proceed on a strictly voluntary basis.

We started Ukrainian classes in kindergarten, leaving the choice to the parents. These classes had artistic circles for the children— theater, dances, singing. They dressed in bright national costumes, put on performances, held competitions. The teachers earned a bit more, as an incentive.

Within a year, the classes were overflowing, and we had to create new ones. With the graduates, we created the first Ukrainian classes in the district's elementary schools. Within fifteen years, we would have had our first high school graduates, and with them we could have shifted higher education to Ukrainian, though I am very wary of that. It will be a long and very complicated process.

Thank God that, for now at least, common sense prevails. During our May Day demonstration, representatives of the Ukrainian communities in Moldavia and the Baltic republics told about the discriminatory practices that they were being subjected to over there—the same that they tried to apply here to the Russian-speaking population.

The soviets blocked Kravchuk's constitution. And I know that at least the Odessa and Donetsk regional soviets have voted resolutions of no confidence in him. Does this mark a shift in the soviets' positions since independence?

In our regional soviet, there has been a definite and significant shift to the left, not only on the constitutional issue but on economic policy too. Here's a small personal example. There was a vacant spot on the commission studying the proposal to build an oil complex in the Odessa harbor. That, incidentally, is an ecologically disastrous idea being pushed by the nationalists who want to be free of dependence on Russian oil. The chairman of the commission proposed me, saying specifically that I am a worker, co-chairman of the Union of Work Collectives. Of course, he also said that I was a serious, disciplined person who had been very active in the soviet. But a year ago, I would never have received such support.

If there is a referendum on confidence in the president, will he lose?

I think so, though you shouldn't forget that he controls the television and the radio, and now he has shifted policy somewhat. He's a crafty character with a good political instinct, more flexible than Yeltsin.

The social stratum that supports privatization is not that strong. And after the Lvov Congress of Work Collectives, the president really couldn't push it through. He understood that our movement had the potential of uniting large masses of people behind its demands. This was a very real possibility on the background of the deteriorating economic situation. Workers get nothing for their work, or worse—there is no work. They have no money, and it's clear that privatization will be carried out by the moneybags.

Why, then, has your self-management movement failed to take off?

First the Communist authorities got frightened by the processes they had unleashed and by the power that the work-collective councils wielded. True, this power wasn't always used conscientiously, much was done on pure emotion and for immediate gain. All kinds of people got elected to the councils. But the main problem was that the councils bore no legal responsibility for their decisions—only the administration. If the councils, that is the workers themselves, really had to answer economically for their decisions, the loudmouths and demagogues wouldn't have lasted long. Of course, there are many reasons, but that is an important one. Many competent managers were fired, and those who remained were frightened and became very cautious.

Had the councils been able to hold on to their powers, there could be no question today of wild privatization, of the theft of the enterprises. The workers would be able to recall their delegates if they failed to prevent management from violating their rights.

Weren't the work-collective councils often "pocket" councils, subservient to management?

Yes, we discussed that problem often. The administration had many means for taming the councils. It was and remains a problem. Of course, now the councils have been liquidated in many enterprises. That's why our constitution recognizes any elected organization that is mandated with self-management functions, be it a union or an enterprise council.

Many directors used the work-collective councils to defend themselves from their administrative superiors. They had their decisions adopted by the councils, and the state functionaries couldn't force them to change them. The director would say he was only carrying out the will of the collective. Nor was this always a bad thing. In some cases much good was done for the workers and for the enterprise.

It was mainly in big enterprises, and in particular in the military-industrial complex that one could find effective STKs. Maybe it was easier to find leaders in such huge masses of workers. The picture in the small ones was depressing. But even there there were exceptions, like the furniture factory in Cherkassy, where one person, Aleksandr Kauk, made a revolution. They fired the director and hired a new one who is very competent. Now the plant is flourishing. Kauk won the support of the collective. But to become such a leader you almost have to be Jesus Christ—honest, principled, without any sins that can leave you vulnerable to attack. Where there was such a person, then things moved.

But given the hostility of the state authorities, especially after 1988, did the movement really have much of a chance?

Alas, you're right. When new laws were adopted that favored management, the correlation of forces in the enterprises shifted. But we met with Kravchuk before the presidential elections, and he assured us of his support. He said that he was seeking to build his political base especially on the work collectives. Moreover, his program had a socialist orientation. And, unfortunately, we played a role in his getting elected. Once elected, he did an about-face.

Of course, the work-collective councils had many shortcomings. But the law that created them was itself flawed. This might have been done consciously, since it was written by the *nomenklatura* that certainly foresaw the probable consequences. But the law could have been improved. Representatives of the work-collective councils themselves proposed to put an end to the possibility of arbitrary intervention into managerial decisions.

In our program, the administration has no representatives in the self-management body. It works on contract for the work collective. At the same time, however, its rights are strictly guaranteed. The self-management body does not intervene into the day-to-day management of the enterprise. Rather, the work collective and its council set the basic policy of the enterprise.

What about the claim that self-managed enterprises "eat" their profits in the form of wages and benefits and don't invest in modernization and expansion?

That can't be ruled out. But I can cite cases where the opposite occurred. Take our own depot. In 1991, we had the possibility of constructing apartments, giving ourselves the "thirteenth month" [annual bonus]—that is, stealing from ourselves. But our director, a respected, capable person whom we had incidentally elected, explained to the work-collective council that if we consume this money without creating a basis for the future, if we stick uniquely to our loading and unloading activities, then given the very real prospect of economic collapse, we'd soon be forced to dismiss a large part of our work force. He convinced us to build oil-storage facilities, even though it was a type of activity that was quite foreign to us. And to be honest, it's only thanks to that that we now exist, because our depot is now handling only 20 percent of its former volume. Now we can at least look to tomorrow and we have other plans for expansion into construction materials. And we are not building apartments now, but cottages for our workers.

So I'm not too worried about self-managed enterprises not investing. After all, who is an enemy unto himself? Besides, everyone wants to work on good machines. At a time when we had trouble paying wages, we decided to buy Japanese equipment to mechanize small operations.

What is the position of the Union of Work Collectives on privatization?

We strongly opposed the draft law on privatization, demanding that the Supreme Soviet suspend debate on it until it consulted our Union. We want the enterprises transferred without payment to the work collectives, either in full ownership or at least with a controlling share.

There was a lot of debate about what kind of property the enterprise should become. I was for collective property, along the lines of the Mondragon cooperatives in Spain. This position had a lot of support at the congress. They even wanted me to be full-time chairman. But I insisted that there be one co-chairman from each region.

Besides, I have my job and am also a deputy to the regional soviet. Maybe this was a mistake—it's hard to do serious work in only your free time. But I couldn't leave the soviet since it offers a forum for our ideas and gives me some access to the media. The sessions are broadcast locally on television, and, strange as it may seem, people still show interest in what is going on there. A part of the population still has confidence in the soviets, perhaps not a large part, but a part, and they listen when something important is being discussed.

I sometimes meet strangers on the train or streetcar who comment on what I said in the soviet, who congratulate for speaking out strongly. Others say: "You're a representative of the workers; we want to hear something good from you." But I answer: "How can I say anything good, when so far I see nothing good?" People really want someone to give them hope. But what should I do? Lie, when I really see no light ahead?

The mood among most workers is depressed. People are in shock; they can't recover. You know, people somehow grew attached to the state. At least that is how they were trained under the Soviet regime. That was especially true in the last thirty years when living standards constantly rose and a certain democratization was occurring, in the sense that workers were getting more of a chance to influence the administration, to influence processes and quality. They were even given the right to put their own personal stamp of quality on goods. Of course, I'm talking about the best workers. They worked without a work-collective council and, to a degree, felt themselves the owners of their enterprise. Of course, that was largely an illusion, but it did exist.

And the property, legally and formally, belonged to all the people. They also introduced the thirteenth month wage, which gave the workers something, at least when it was honestly earned. People somehow started to have trust in the state. And here we have our president saying that the decline is ending, that things are about to improve, that he can see the light at the end of the tunnel. It's all a lie. But people so want to believe that the state is taking care of them.

Unfortunately, worker leaders, like myself, bear some of the responsibility. We haven't been up to the task. Of course, there are reasons for that. For one thing, we have no access to the mass media—they are all working for business. Even the astrological predictions they print are written for businessmen. We can't inform people of our demands, we can't inform them of what we think. We have no printing or copying equipment; we don't even have money for glue to put up posters.

But now many workers are shifting positions. Many are opposing privatization. They aren't necessarily opposed to privatization of small shops, restaurants, laundries, rental outlets, though the watch repairman on the train told us he was against that too since it gave the workers absolutely nothing. People wouldn't oppose this "small privatization," if the shops went to the people who worked in them. But they know that workers can't compete with the new bourgeois at public auctions. The law in Ukraine gives no priority to the collectives in privatization.

So for the majority of workers, if that is privatization, then better the enterprises remain state property. Besides, who will buy our giant factories? In Canada, a factory with 10,000 employees is considered huge. Here it is medium-size. A large enterprise has from 25,000 to 100,000 and more.

You said that you are for collective ownership by the work collective. What would be the role of the state in such a system?

I think that the role of the state would be very large, especially in the present period of restructuring of industry. The state has to support enterprises trying to change their profile. But in any case, not all collectives would want to own their plants. For example, I can't understand why the miners are demanding privatization of the mines. That would be fatal. All over the world coalmines are subsidized. Someone has seriously misled the miners. In many branches privatization is not in the workers' interests.

But even in state-owned plants, there would be self-management, and the collective should have the right to dispose independently of a part of the production. That probably would give them much more than actual ownership of the enterprise.

You know, I can easily imagine a situation in which the work collective owns the plant but the state bureaucracy or the new bourgeoisie disposes of its production, leaving the workers worse off than they were before they became owners. In fact, this is already happening—the private commercial structures are raking in the profits, grossly inflating prices, while efficient, hardworking producer collectives drag out a miserable existence.

So the enterprises can well remain state property, but give the workers self-management rights and the right to at least the added value they produce. The state doesn't have to directly intervene.

I always explain that it isn't enough to own or to run your factory. Many factories couldn't survive on their own. You also need regional self-management, you need inter-enterprise and inter-branch investment funds. Maybe the fact that I'm a regional soviet deputy has made me more sensitive to this. But as a railroad worker, I also know that there are planning and investment decisions that have to be taken on the republican and inter-republican levels. But for that, we'll have to put an end to the demagoguery that constantly tries to scare people that their sovereignty is under attack.

The problem is that the people have no instrument. There is still no organized force to express their discontent. But you have only to look at the recent strike in the Donbass to see that workers have the potential to control the state. After all, that strike was led by a small detachment of workers, the miners, and in only one region; yet it was able to force the hand of the president and the parliament, who now have to hold referenda of confidence in themselves. If they lose, elections should logically follow.

Personally, I think that if our Union of Work Collectives can get on its feet, obtain some resources and explain its alternative in an attractive form, it can become one of the main democratic forces in the country. We are actively seeking supporters among the political parties. We've found little sympathy among the nationalists; however, there are individual leaders, like Stepan Khmara, who for all his anti-Communism seems to have understood where this *nomenklatura* privatization is leading. He expresses ideas that are not far from our own.

Then there is the Socialist Party which broadly supports us, and also the other newly-organized left movements. But so far, only the Socialist Party is a serious force. In practice, it is the most serious political force in Ukraine, having arisen on the ruins of the Communist Party. If that party were really to show itself in concrete actions, to show that it really wants to carry out our program, it could become very popular. At present, it still bears the stigma of the old Communist Party, the target of the slander campaign conducted by the propaganda machine.

What about the trade unions?

Unfortunately, we haven't yet found practical support there. Verbal support, yes—but not in practice. They fear that we are competitors, a new kind of union. They consider that they alone have the right to defend the workers and that they are in competition with us for the minds of the workers. They don't understand that today you can't defend the workers' conditions and living standards if you can't defend the enterprise, the collective as a whole.

And the unions themselves are viewed with hostility by the Supreme Soviet and the president. The last thing they need is strong unions. The unions still have a well-oiled structure and material base. But they aren't yet capable of using it to create a strong labor movement.

Do the unions have a position on privatization?

They call for it to be carried out "in the interests of the work collectives." But what that means and how to do it—so far they haven't said. Even if the workers are guaranteed 15 or 25 percent of the shares, they will own them individually—that won't give them control. Besides, in Russia the shares reserved for the workers are nonvoting. The distribution of shares to workers is a propaganda ploy to neutralize their opposition to privatization. And so far it's working, though less here than in Russia. There is also strong opposition to this privatization on the part of a section of the Supreme Soviet that feels the hot breath of the masses below them.

So there is a chance that our movement will gain force, but to be frank, not a big one. In particular, we lack a material base—newspapers, journals. When they wanted to make me full-time chairman, they were counting on funds from the enterprises. But now a government decree has suspended the self-management rights of the work collectives.

You spoke about the need to restore economic ties between the former Soviet republics and even for some interrepublican planning. What about relations with the rest of the world, especially the developed capitalist countries?

Of course, it's a very good thing that the military confrontation between East and West is over. But I'm worried by the United States assuming the role of world gendarme. So far, it seems to me, the world hasn't profited from the fact that instead of two superpowers there is now only one.

We need closer cooperation among the workers of all countries, and I don't give a damn if that sounds like a communist slogan. Without worker internationalism, without worker solidarity, things will only get worse. Our new-found capitalists are exporting our raw materials even though our factories stand idle. They sell them abroad for cheap and workers elsewhere in the resource sector are without jobs. But our resources can be sold for cheap because our workers are paid nothing; we are turning into paupers. Of course, we need international solidarity.

Oleg Rybakov: Electrical Worker
[July 1993]

A largely Russian-speaking city of about 1 million in eastern Ukraine, Donetsk is a center of coalmining and heavy industry. On June 7 through 17, 1993, a near-general strike broke out in the Donbass and part of eastern Ukraine against the government's economic policies. The strike forced the government and parliament in Kiev to agree to hold referenda of confidence in those two bodies.

Oleg Rybakov had been very active in that strike. I spoke with him in the Center for Political Education, adjacent to the regional soviet next to the square where the miners congregated during their strikes.

I'm a member of the political council of the Socialist Party of Ukraine [successor to the banned Communist Party of Ukraine]. During the strike, I was a member of the Donetsk coordinating council of the strike. I work as assistant to the head of the electrical power department of the Donetsk Metallurgical Factory. I've been there a long time, almost twenty-eight years.

How did the strike begin?

The initiators, of course, were the miners. A part of the miners is organized in the Independent Miners' Union, the IMU, which, at least in Donetsk, is practically indistinguishable from the miners' strike committee, which immediately assumed leadership of the strike.

It broke out as an economic protest against the government's decision to raise prices, although a Donbass miners' conference on May 28 adopted demands that were not economic but political. That conference had set a strike date for later in June, but when the strike broke out in response to the government's action on June 7, it naturally bore an economic character. As such, the strikers could have obtained satisfaction of all their demands literally in a couple of days. In fact, the mine directors got busy with that aim in mind. At first, it was a velvet strike, very calm. The miners' issued declarations, the questions were quickly resolved, particularly the wage issues.

But on June 8 and 9, when enterprises from other industrial sectors joined the miners here on the square, the miners saw they weren't alone, support was coming. Management also realized that they wouldn't be able to wrap it up in only a couple of days.

In the Socialist Party, we also saw what was unfolding and we got busy from the first days. When the Zasyadko mine struck and went to the Kiev district soviet, our people came with leaflets and addressed the crowd, trying to give the strike some direction. It's easy to satisfy economic demands: all the government has to do is print more money, fuelling the already runaway inflation. But there will still be no production. That much we had learned from past experience. Incidentally, in the Donetsk mining region, prices are 20 percent higher than in the rest of Ukraine.

I keep hearing that it was a "directors' strike." Did they support the strike?

More than that. To some degree they set it off. After all, their problems and those of the miners' have many common sources, in particular the undermining of the established economic relations with Russia. The present breakdown has cruelly hit not only the miners but all sectors. Take our cotton mill here—the workers are idle because they can't get cotton from Central Asia; 80 percent of the electrical power equipment comes from Russia. At our factory, most of the additives for steel alloys come from there.

The directors are suffering from the breakdown of ties and from government restrictions on their freedom to sell the coal. The mines are subsidized, and the directors need money from the government. So the directors just have to say to the workers: We can't pay your wages and buy equipment because we have no profits. And that's the push. Many points in the agreement signed with the government didn't originate with the miners but with the directors. But we didn't cross them out because we know they are also important for us.

So the directors at first looked favorably on the strike. We don't deny that. But after a week, they started to get fidgety. The vice-prime minister called them in for a meeting. They began to promise everything in order to end the strike quickly. So did the vice-prime minister. But we held out. We wanted to raise up all the workers. There was a terrible media blackout of the strike in the first days. Kiev television first reported it only on the third day.

Still, the miners' leaders say the strike was spontaneous.

Without doubt, the miners were reacting to the price rise. But the administration probably also played a role.

By the way, the [former official] Federation of Independent Trade Unions of the Ukraine also planned a strike for June 15. I have to say that we're very dissatisfied with that federation, even though our union belongs to it. The federation and the branch union leaders have to radically change their ways and stop letting the president play around with them.

The unions have to guard the interests of the working person. There has to be respect for the law, and the unions must make sure the laws are observed. To this day, the general tariff agreement [between the federation and the government setting minimal standards for wages, social security and benefits] hasn't been concluded. It was only after the strike that they at least somewhat corrected the problem of interrepublican ties. The presidents of the republics have now signed a document on an economic union.

The government would have liked to end the strike by giving only the miners a raise. That would have allowed it to accuse the miners again of "pulling the blanket over to their side" at the expense of the rest of the workers. Thanks to our efforts and the fact that the other sectors joined the strike, a wage raise limited to the miners, that would have done nothing but boost inflation, was avoided. The government has now promised that the basis for all future wage increases will be the 1990 correlation of wages among the different branches. That means that in metallurgy, for example, our wages will be four-fifths that of mining wages.

You said that you are dissatisfied with the federation.

Unfortunately, we didn't find the support we hoped for there. They wanted to take a more peaceful path. In reality, they were awaiting orders from Kiev. But the regional committees of the unions supported us. For example, Shendrik, chairman of the regional committee of the Union of Machine-construction Workers, was a member of the coordinating council of the strike. But we needed the support of workers from all over Ukraine.

I'm saying that the federation should have raised the entire working class and not simply declare that on June 15 there should be warning actions that could take the form of strikes, demonstrations, blowing factory horns, or whatever. That's not serious. If we had all come out as a single fist, then we really could have resolved our problems. The disunity, the lack of solidarity, did irreparable damage to the movement. Stoyan's [chairman of the federation and former advisor to Kravchuk] position was sort of: "It doesn't really concern me."

How did your own plant decide to join the strike?

First of all, you have to understand the specific conditions in metallurgy. You can stop work at a mine if you keep up basic maintenance. But in metallurgy or in the coke-chemical industry, if the batteries and furnaces go out, there's nothing left but to dismantle them and build new ones. So we had to maintain a minimum of production.

Nevertheless, our people went out to the square. If you exclude the people who were on vacation and not in town, 90 percent passed through the square. And almost everyone took part in the protest march. There were always at least 10,000 people on the square and over 50,000 during each of the two protest demonstrations. People stood under the blazing sun for three hours.

In our plant, the decision to strike was taken in the following way. The plant union contacted its regional committee, which sent some people over. Workers from the different shops, including myself, met with them, and we decided to call a conference of shop representatives, which elected a strike committee. It included four people from the plant's union committee.

How was the city coordinating committee formed?

It was important that for the first time a strike committee was formed with representatives from all branches. I said that the miners' strike committee assumed leadership almost from the start. But the strike would have led to nothing had it remained a miners' strike. We told them: "Dear miners, after the strike they'll line you up against the wall, if you remain alone." They reacted positively to our suggestion to form an interbranch coordinating committee.

I'd say that in 80 percent of the cases it was the unions that led the strike. And that was good. The unions have finally to show their teeth. It's time to stop being the plaything of the authorities and the administration.

The IMU leadership has generally been anti-Communist. How did they get along with you as a member of the Socialist Party?

We had been trying to enter into contact with them since last year when I went with a comrade and offered to work together. But they claimed that we wanted to dominate them politically, and nothing

I said would change their mind. That's different now. They've begun to understand our common interests.

On the other hand, the disunity in the trade-union movement can have disastrous results for the labor movement. The IMU, of course, argues that unions have to be independent, and, unfortunately, it doesn't find a common language with the federation and its relations with the Independent Union of Workers of the Coal Industry [the former state union] are bad. The IMU opposes the presence of management in the federation's unions. They also say that they want a union just for miners and not for everyone working in the coal industry. But I don't see why we need separate unions in my factory. In metallurgy, besides the people at the furnaces, you have construction workers, power workers, even railroad workers. If they have particular interests, let them form sections within the same union. After all, it's one plant, one sector. Otherwise, there's a great risk of division and isolation.

Did you get active support from outside of the Donetsk region?
Yes, Lugansk, Dnepropetrvosk, Kirovograd, Krasnodon [mining regions adjacent to the Donetsk region]—they all struck after a couple of days, as soon as they got the information. Kharkov [a major industrial city of the Ukraine outside of the Donbass region] woke up on June 24 to a big demonstration. But that should have happened during our strike.

The end was rather painful. Again, it was largely because of our disunity. The IMU is a good union, they're good lads, but unfortunately they're alone. They don't have ties with the other unions. That's bad. We need very close ties. In some mines, half the workers belong to the IMU and the other half to the federation union. The IMU people at first didn't even want the federation unions to be the coordinating committee. But 80 percent of the people who came to work in it were from those unions, and they worked together. This was something new. We'll see if it continues.

If the referenda lead to the resignation of Kravchuk and the parliament, does the IMU have its own program for reform? They speak of regional autonomy, but that doesn't seem like much of an answer to the terrible economic crisis.
Of course, it isn't an answer. The Socialist Party has an anticrisis

program. But to a degree, regional self-management can help solve our problems, since our region is first in the country in industry and fifth in agriculture, but we are not allowed by Kiev to keep our fair share.

In Russia, the IMU leaders still seem strongly pro-capitalist. Is the same true here?

I wouldn't say that. Their sense is that it doesn't matter what you call the system, as long as we live well. But among the leaders, some are still strongly anti-Communist. The Communist Party, which is being resurrected now, held its congress here two days after the strike ended. During the strike, the miners' leaders wanted to block the congress. I talked to them for two days explaining that their actions would be a distraction from the strike, that the congress would take place somewhere else anyway, that it was a democratic right. But they persisted in the idea of organizing pickets around the building where the congress was to be held.

Then socialist orators began speaking addressing the strikers on the square, and their words were well-received. People remembered the good things they had lost, that in retrospect it had not all been black. The leader of the Socialist Party, Aleksandr Moroz, a Supreme Soviet deputy, also came to Donetsk, and the crowd listened to him with great interest. He talked for an hour and a quarter about our anticrisis program and the situation in the Supreme Soviet, and was also very warmly received.

So the miners' leaders saw that the mood had changed and they decided against picketing the congress, though they still issued a statement condemning the congress.

So the crowd's favorable attitude to socialist orators is another new element in the labor scene?

Yes, the attitudes toward us definitely seem to be shifting.